MAKING HATE A CRIME

MAKING HATE A CRIME
FROM SOCIAL MOVEMENT
TO LAW ENFORCEMENT

VALERIE JENNESS AND RYKEN GRATTET

A Volume in the American Sociological Association's
Rose Series in Sociology

Russell Sage Foundation • New York

The Russell Sage Foundation

The Russell Sage Foundation, one of the oldest of America's general purpose foundations, was established in 1907 by Mrs. Margaret Olivia Sage for "the improvement of social and living conditions in the United States." The Foundation seeks to fulfill this mandate by fostering the development and dissemination of knowledge about the country's political, social, and economic problems. While the Foundation endeavors to assure the accuracy and objectivity of each book it publishes, the conclusions and interpretations in Russell Sage Foundation publications are those of the authors and not of the Foundation, its Trustees, or its staff. Publication by Russell Sage, therefore, does not imply Foundation endorsement.

Library of Congress Cataloging-in-Publication Data

Jenness, Valerie, 1963–
    Making hate a crime : from social movement to law enforcement / Valerie Jenness and Ryken Grattet.
        p. cm. — (American Sociological Association Rose series in sociology)
    Includes bibliographical references and index.
    ISBN 0-87154-409-1 (cloth)   ISBN 0-87154-410-5 (paper)
    1. Hate crimes. I. Grattet, Ryken. II. Title. III. Series.

    HV6773.5 .J46 2001
    364.1—dc21

                                                                        2001019332

Text design by Suzanne Nichols. Cover design by Lili Schwartz. Cover photography by David Frazier, Doug Menuez, Photodisc, and Duncan Smith.

RUSSELL SAGE FOUNDATION
112 East 64th Street, New York, New York 10021
10 9 8 7 6 5 4 3 2 1

In memory of James Byrd Jr., the young girls killed at Westside Middle School in Jonesboro, Arkansas, Matthew Shepard, and the many others who were murdered in 1998 because of who they are and what they represent.

Previous Volumes in the Series

Beyond College For All: Career Paths for the Forgotten Half
James E. Rosenbaum

Trust in Schools: A Core Resource for Improvement
Anthony S. Bryk and Barbara Schneider

America's Newcomers and the Dynamics of Diversity
Frank D. Bean and Gillian Stevens

Forthcoming Titles

Changing Rhythms of the American Family
Suzanne M. Bianchi, John Robinson, and Melissa Milkie

Good Jobs, Bad Jobs, No Jobs: Changing Work and Workers in America
Arne L. Kalleberg

Homeland Diversity and the Adaptation of Immigrants: Responses to Race, Ethnicity, and Discrimination Among Refugees in Small and Large American Cities
Jeremy Hein

Inequality and Poverty in Affluent Countries: Causes and Consequences
Lane Kenworthy

Is the Government Listening? Public Opinion and Public Policy
Paul Burstein

Morality by Choice: Politics, Personal Choice, and the Case of Covenant Marriage
Scott Feld and Katherine Rosier

Pension Puzzles: Questions of Principle and Principal
Melissa Hardy and Lawrence Hazelrigg

The Production of Demographic Knowledge: States, Societies, and Census Taking in Comparative and Historical Perspective
Rebecca Emigh, Dylan Riley, and Patricia Ahmed

Race, Place, and Crime: Structural Inequality, Criminal Inequality
Ruth D. Peterson and Lauren J. Krivo

Repressive Injustice: Political and Social Processes in the Massive Incarceration of African Americans
Pamela E. Oliver and James E. Yocum

Retrenching Welfare, Entrenching Inequality: Gender, Race, and Old Age in the United States
Madonna Harrington Meyer and Pamela Herd

Setting Out: Establishing Success in Early Adulthood Among Urban Youth
Frank Furstenberg Jr., Julie Kmec, and Mary Fischer

The Rose Series in Sociology

The American Sociological Association's Rose Series in Sociology publishes books that integrate knowledge and address controversies from a sociological perspective. Books in the Rose Series are at the forefront of sociological knowledge. They are lively and often involve timely and fundamental issues on significant social concerns. The series is intended for broad dissemination throughout sociology, across social science and other professional communities, and to policy audiences. The series was established in 1967 by a bequest to ASA from Arnold and Caroline Rose to support innovations in scholarly publishing.

DOUGLAS L. ANDERTON
DAN CLAWSON
NAOMI GERSTEL
JOYA MISRA
RANDALL STOKES
ROBERT ZUSSMAN

SERIES EDITORS

= Contents =

About the Authors

Valerie Jenness is professor and chair of the Department of Criminology, Law, and Society at the University of California, Irvine. She is also associate professor in the Department of Sociology at the University of California, Irvine.

Ryken Grattet is associate professor of sociology at the University of California, Davis.

═ Preface ═

S hortly after we sent the final version of *Making Hate a Crime* to
Russell Sage Foundation to be published, two important events
relevant to our book drew national attention. One of those events,
the first federal prosecution of a hate crime in the United States, provides further evidence for the central argument laid out in this book:
the concept of "hate crime" has become increasingly institutionalized
in American political discourse, criminal law, and law enforcement
practices. It is now a social fact, in the Durkheimian sense: ineluct-
able, taken for granted by citizens, activists, policymakers, and social
commentators alike. The other event, now commonly referenced simply as "9/11," increased awareness of the possible worst-case scenarios of intergroup hatreds of all sorts and our seeming inability to
manage them through government policy in an era when the world
has replaced the nation as the context within which we define social
problems and policy responses designed to ameliorate them. The social, political, and legal fallout of 9/11 raises serious and as yet unanswered questions about the future of "making hate a crime" in the
United States and, increasingly, abroad.

Less than one year after the publication of this book, an amazing
thing happened: the attorney general of the United States of America
filed the first federal hate crime charges. Nearly six years after two
women—Marie Williams and Laura Winnans—were bound and gagged
and had their throats slit while camping and hiking in the Shenan-
doah National Park, U.S. Attorney General John D. Ashcroft held a
historic and nationally televised press conference on April 11, 2002, to
announce that the U.S. Justice Department was invoking the federal
hate crimes statute for the first time to charge the alleged murderer—
Darrell David Rice, a computer programmer from Columbia, Maryland, who is, by his own account, a man who hates lesbians and
enjoys intimidating and assaulting women—with hate crime. In an-
nouncing the indictment, Ashcroft spoke at length about his meeting
with the parents of the victims and about the lives and character of

the young women: two midwesterners who migrated to New England, met and became lovers, and shared a love of science and the outdoors.

Justifying the invocation of federal hate crime law, which carries with it enhanced penalties, Ashcroft said, "Criminal acts of hate run counter to what is best in America, our belief in equality and freedom. The Department of Justice will aggressively investigate, prosecute, and punish criminal acts of violence and vigilantism motivated by hate and intolerance." Moreover, he said, "we will pursue, prosecute, and punish those who attack law-abiding Americans out of hatred for who they are." He added, "Hatred is the enemy of justice, regardless of its source" (U.S. Department of Justice 2001). Tellingly, the Department of Justice is pursuing charges against an alleged murderer not only for *what* he is accused of doing (murder), but for *who* he chose do it to (two lesbians) and *why* he chose to do it as well (because of his hatred of women and lesbians).

Quite apart from how this historic legal case concludes, this book provides an understanding of how we arrived at this point—the point at which the "top cop" in the United States, a conservative attorney general who originally opposed hate crime legislation and the use of the criminal justice system to curb bigotry, summoned the media to enable him to stand before a national audience and announce the morally and legally justified pursuit of enhanced penalties—in this case the death penalty—for a serious violent crime motivated by bigotry. Preceding this moment, the term "hate crime" had to be invented and circulated; moreover, its legal parameters had to be formulated, contested, and ultimately agreed upon before it became a fairly uncontested criminal category. It is only in the context of these precedents that Attorney General Ashcroft's historic decision makes sense.

Thus, in *Making Hate a Crime*, we describe the complicated and lengthy process whereby hate crime, in a legal and policy sense, is the product of the activities of a wide variety of participants and social forces within numerous institutional contexts. As the chapters of this book detail, from the introduction and politicization of the term in the late 1970s to the continued enforcement of hate crime law at the beginning of the twenty-first century, modern civil rights movements constructed the problem of bias-motivated violence in ways that distinguish it from other forms of violent crime; state and federal politicians passed legislation that defined the parameters of hate crime in ways that distinguish it from other types of violent crime; judicial decisionmakers elaborated and enriched the meaning of "hate crime" as they determined its constitutionality as a legal concept that distinguishes types of violence based on the motivation of the perpetrator;

and law enforcement officials began to report, investigate, and prosecute bias-motivated incidents as a special type of crime that warrants enhanced penalties. All these players have continued to engage in these activities in ways forecasted in the original publication of *Making Hate a Crime*.

In the immediate aftermath of the attacks on New York City and Washington on September 11, 2001, there was a predictable upsurge in reported anti-Muslim hate crimes, which was accompanied by an increase in media and policymaking attention to this type of violence. Twenty-eight such crimes had been reported nationally in the year prior to 9/11. The total for 2001 rose to 481, and most of these occurred in the last three months of the year (U.S. Department of Justice 2002). The rise in anti-Muslim hate crime has been accompanied by the emergence of legal and definitional confusion. Certain acts, like the shootings by Hesham Mohamed Hadayet at the El Al counter in the Los Angeles International Airport on Independence Day 2002, raise a controversy about which acts are properly defined as hate crime and which are terrorism (Boehler 2003). Moreover, linkages between terrorism and organized hate crimes are now routinely made by advocacy groups like the Anti-Defamation League as well as by law enforcement practitioners (Ronczkowski 2003). It is relevant to wonder whether the national preoccupation with terrorism now subsumes the territory where hate crime once reigned. Has the focus on hate crime been displaced by concerns about combating terrorism? Or could it be that the focus on terrorism has strengthened the national consensus and outrage about the socially destructive consequences of violent expressions of intergroup hatred? While it is too early to answer these questions, it should be acknowledged that the future currency of the concept of hate crime might very well hang in the balance. Despite these uncertainties in the U.S. context, the concept of hate crime appears to be flourishing elsewhere.

The concept of hate crime has diffused across international borders as various Western countries, especially those sharing a predominantly English-speaking culture, appropriate and deploy the concept to characterize bias-motivated conduct in their own legal and cultural contexts. Australia, for example, has outlawed at the federal, state, and territorial levels words and images that incite hatred toward particular groups of people. Relying on discrimination law, Australian legislators have outlawed conduct that constitutes "vilification" or "racial hatred." Britain and Canada have also each passed a series of laws designed to curb racial-ethnic violence. Finally, Germany has passed laws that forbid "public incitement" and "instigation of racial hatred," including the distribution of Nazi propaganda or literature liable to corrupt the youth. Unlike the United States, these countries have adopted a fairly limited view of hate crime, focusing primarily on racial, ethnic, and religious violence. Other countries—mostly in the non-Western world—have not yet adopted the term to describe racial, ethnic, religious, or other forms of intergroup conflict.

Still, the international diffusion of the term "hate crime" brings with it a variety of questions about the future of "making hate a crime." These questions are intimately connected to, and indeed arguably derivative of, larger processes of institutionalization, globalization, and modernization. Most interesting from our point of view, it remains to be seen how the continued development of what some have called a "world polity," complete with attendant international norms, system pressures, and shared governing bodies, interfaces with local (that is, national) contexts to "make hate a crime"—or not. Moving beyond U.S. borders, the empirical and theoretical picture associated with "making hate a crime" will no doubt get more interesting and more complicated as the concept continues to traverse time and space, including the international borders that demarcate nation-states, with their various orientations to the problem of terrorism.

Valerie Jenness and Ryken Grattet
February 12, 2004

Reference

Boehler, Eric. 2003. "Terrorism or Hate Crime?" Salon.com, April 17, 2003.

Ronczkowski, Michael. 2003. *Terrorism and Organized Hate Crime: Intelligence Gathering, Analysis, and Investigations*. Boca Raton, Fla.: CRC Press.

U.S. Department of Justice. 2001. "News Conference with USA John Brownlee: Indictment of Darrell David Rice." Washington: U.S. Department of Justice Conference Center (April 10).

———. 2002. "Hate Crime Statistics, 2001." Washington: U.S. Government Printing Office.

═ Acknowledgments ═

W e would like to acknowledge the many activists, policy makers, scholars, and students who provided us with the information and insight necessary to bring this work to fruition. First and foremost, we are grateful for assistance from the National Institute Against Prejudice and Violence, the Center for Democratic Renewal, the Southern Poverty Law Institute, the National Gay and Lesbian Task Force, and the Anti-Defamation League of B'nai B'rith. Their work makes our work possible.

We would also like to thank the many colleagues who offered helpful comments, including Don Barrett, Joel Best, William Bielby, Kitty Calavita, Larry Cohen, David Greenberg, Laura Grindstaff, James Jacobs, Richard Leo, Nancy Naples, Jodi O'Brien, Dawn Robinson, Richard Scotch, Jim Short, John Sutton, Verta Taylor, Charles Tittle, and especially Paul Burstein and George Farkas. In addition, the diligent research assistance provided by Julie Abril, Wida Ahmadi, Nicole Breznock, Sarah Knofel, Gary Lopez, Jason Cinq-Mars, Ursula Abels Castellano, Teresa Flores, Karen Kvashny, Wanjiru Muchiri, Don Ojoko-Adams, Scott Phillips, and Kim Richman contributed to the contents of this book. Finally, we gratefully acknowledge the cooperation of the University of California Press for allowing us to reprint portions of an article previously published in *Social Problems*.

In the final stages of putting this book together we found *Hate Crimes: Criminal Law & Identity Politics*, by James Jacobs and Kimberly Potter, and *Punishing Hate: Bias Crimes Under American Law*, by Frederick M. Lawrence, especially useful. These books and authors, like many other published works and scholars, have stimulated our thinking and offered a valuable backdrop against which this book emerges. We also thank Felice Levine, Michael Schwartz, Suzanne Nichols, and Katherine Kimball, who ensured that the work came to fruition. Finally, we thank each other—who else would work with either of us?

═ Chapter 1 ═

Introduction:
The Hate Crime Agenda

A s THE *National Law Journal* has noted, the 1990s may go down in history as the "decade of hate—or at least of hate crime" (Rovella 1994, A1). Although it remains an open question whether America is actually experiencing greater levels of hate-motivated conduct than it has in the past, it is clear that the ascendancy of hate crime as a concept in policy discourse has focused attention on the behavior in a new way. It is an age-old problem approached with a new conceptual lens and sense of urgency. During the 1980s and 1990s, multiple social movements began to identify and address the problem of discriminatory violence directed at minorities. Federal, state, and local governments instituted task forces and commissions to analyze the issue. Legislative campaigns sprang up at every level of government. New sentencing rules and categories of criminal behavior were established in law. Prosecutors and law enforcement officials developed special training policies and specialized enforcement units (Kelly 1993). Scholarly commentary and social science research on the topic exploded. The U.S. Supreme Court weighed in with its analysis of the laws in three highly controversial cases. In the process, criminal conduct that was once undistinguished from ordinary crime has been parsed out, redefined, and condemned more harshly than before.

These extraordinary developments attest to the growing concern with, visibility of, and public resources directed at violence motivated by bigotry, hatred, or bias. They reflect the increasing acceptance of the idea that criminal conduct is "different" when it involves an act of discrimination. Hate crime has clearly secured a place in the American public sphere and the "social problems marketplace" (Best 1990; Hilgartner and Bosk 1988). As this process unfolds, it is as timely as it is important to ask how we got here. Why did the reconceptualization

1

of intergroup violence as hate crime emerge at this particular historical moment? Why has it come to signify the range of biases and behaviors that it has? How has the way in which hate crime has been
conceptualized affected our ability to respond to violence in the
United States?

The Hate Crime Policy Domain

That the use of the term "hate crime" is now commonplace in settings
as diverse as prime-time television, the evening news, academic conferences, and presidential proclamations reflects the success of the
anti-hate-crime movement and subsequent policy making. In a short
period of time, hate crime has arrived as a political, media, and scholarly category. To those who have promoted and embraced it, the concept of hate crime evokes drama, passion, and righteousness, and it
signifies human tendencies toward tribalism and the historic challenges to freedom and equality faced by minority groups. It is a re-
minder of the shameful and vivid episodes of racism, anti-Semitism,
nativism, xenophobia, homophobia, misogyny, and other forms of
discrimination and brutality of our collective and recent past.

A seemingly simple pairing of words—"hate" and "crime"—
creates a signifier that conveys an enormous sense of threat and an
attendant demand for response. With regard to the former, advocates
have portrayed the problem as increasing, even reaching "epidemic"
proportions.[1] As for the latter, war metaphors are frequently used to
describe the desired response. For example, during the Persian Gulf
war, President George Bush drew a parallel between the actions of
Saddam Hussein and hate crimes: It is "a sad irony," he noted, "that
while our brave soldiers are fighting aggression overseas, a few hate
mongers here at home are perpetrating their own brand of cowardly
aggression. These hate crimes have no place in a free society and we
are not going to stand for them" (George Bush, "State of the Union
Address," *New York Times*, February 1, 1990, D22). More recently,
President William J. Clinton has called for an expansion of hate crime
laws as "what America needs in our battle against hate" (Sullivan
1999, 52).

From the beginning, however, discussions of what to do about bias
violence have been inextricably linked to considerations of law and
policy rather than military confrontation. Hate violence politics is,
first and foremost, a law-centered politics. As Representative Mario
Biaggi (D-N.Y.) argued during an early congressional debate on hate
crime, "The obvious point is that we are dealing with a national prob-

lem and we must look to our laws for remedies" (*Congressional Record* 1985, 19844). More than a decade later, New York governor Mario Cuomo argued that "as government, our single most effective weapon [against hate crime] is law" (cited in Jacobs 1998, 169). In the war on hate violence, criminal law, rather than domestic military intervention, educational programs, media campaigns, or community activism, has been the primary weapon of choice.

Centering the discussion of hate-motivated violence on law means that the key questions concern how to craft a legal definition of hate crime, focusing attention on which forms of law and policy are justifiable, likely to be effective, and constitutional. In the early 1980s, state lawmakers throughout the United States put forward a novel legal strategy: the reclassification and enhancement of penalties for criminal acts stemming from certain kinds of bias. These laws have since spread to nearly every state in the union. By the middle of the 1980s, federal lawmakers were considering legislation to add hate crime to federal crime data collection laws. Since then, several pieces of federal hate crime legislation have been passed, forming an increasingly elaborate system of federal laws on the subject. More appear likely to follow in the near future.

Ironically, throughout these legislative campaigns, the symbolic dimensions of both hate crimes and hate crime policies have been highlighted. According to proponents of hate crime law, hate-motivated violence is different from other crime because it is not only an act of brutality and violence against an individual victim, but it also transmits a terrorizing symbolic message to the victim's community. As John Conyers (D-Mich.), the congressional representative most responsible for initiating federal hearings on the issue, has explained, "Hate crimes, which can range from threats and vandalism to arson, assault, and murder, are intended to not just harm the victim, but to send a message of intimidation to an entire community of people" (*Congressional Record* 1988, 11393). In effect, hate crimes have two kinds of victims, individuals and their communities. This broadening of the parameters of victimization associated with hate crime serves to justify enhanced penalties and other governmental policy responses (Lawrence 1999).

Hate crime policies are also partly justified on symbolic grounds. They are designed to transmit the symbolic message to society that criminal acts based upon hatred will not be tolerated. As Conyers notes, "Enactment of such legislation will carry to offenders, to victims, and to society at large an important message, that the Nation is committed to battling the violent manifestations of bigotry" (Congress 1985a, 62). Thus, the symbolic spirit of hate crime policy is to affirm principles of tolerance and to reassure the actual and potential victims of bias-motivated violence that their safety will be protected.

Fueling these policy changes is a steady stream of incidents that have been easily incorporated into and analyzed under the rubric of hate crime in the popular media. Examples from the last decade are easy to come by: repeated attacks on African Americans who moved into a predominately white neighborhood in Philadelphia; attacks by neighborhood youths on families of Cambodian refugees who fled to Brooklyn; the beating death of a Chinese American because he was presumed to be Japanese; the harassment of Laotian fishermen in Texas; the brutal attack on two men in Manhattan by a group of knife- and bat-wielding teenage boys shouting "Homos!" and "Fags!"; the assault on three women in Portland, Maine, after their assailant yelled antilesbian epithets at them; the stalking of two lesbian women while they were camping in Pennsylvania, including the brutal murder of one of them; the gang rape, with bottles, lighted matches, and other implements, of a gay man who was repeatedly told that he was getting "what faggots deserve"; the stabbing to death of a heterosexual man in San Francisco because he was presumed to be gay; and the gang rapes of a female jogger in Central Park and a mentally handicapped teenager in Glen Ridge, New Jersey (Sheffield 1992).

In 1998—the year this book was in progress—three highly publicized cases of homicide occurred in which the victims appeared to have been chosen because of a social characteristic. Each of these cases provided a platform for renewed public discussion of the meaning of hate crime and the responsibility of law to recognize the difference between hate crime and "ordinary crime." The first was the murder of James Byrd Jr. in Jasper, Texas, in June 1998. This event, covered extensively in the national media, presented the murder as a hate crime after it was revealed that Byrd, a forty-nine-year-old black man, had been beaten, and then dragged behind a truck until he died, by three white men known to be affiliated with a white supremacist group. Despite this construction, which has been promoted by leading civil rights groups, the case was not prosecuted under the Texas hate crime law. Although publicly understood as a hate crime, in legal terms the incident was defined as aggravated homicide. The maximum penalty for the murder could not have been enhanced because aggravated homicide is a capital crime; however, in the eyes of many, Texas's decision not to charge the offenders with a hate crime signaled a failure of the legal system to correctly identify and therefore hold out for public condemnation the evil that had precipitated the crime. More recently, the murder of Matthew Shepard, a young gay man who was pistol-whipped, tied to a fence, and left to die, was treated as a hate crime by the national news media and immediately inspired federal hearings to pass yet another piece of hate crime legislation in the United States. However, like the Byrd case, it was not prosecuted as a hate crime because Wyoming is one of a handful states that currently has no hate crime law on the books. Thus, both cases have evoked the notion of hate crime and triggered demands that the coverage of hate crime law be extended and rendered more uniform.

In contrast with these two incidents, the murder of four young girls in a Jonesboro, Arkansas, school yard in March 1998 generally has not been viewed as a hate crime, despite the revelation that the young boys in custody for the killings sought to shoot girls because it was girls that angered them. That is, they selected their victims on the basis of gender. *Time* magazine referred to it as a "youth crime," and *Newsweek* called it "schoolyard crime" (Labi 1998; McCormick 1998). Because of this framing, the incident triggered a different set of legal and policy discussions, most often presented in terms of school violence and the debate over gun control (J. R. Moehringer, "Boys Sentenced for Arkansas School Murders," *Los Angeles Times,* August 12, 1998, A1).

The fact that the events in Jasper and Laramie were interpreted as hate crimes and that the event in Jonesboro was not reveals a key aspect of the contested terrain of hate crime: that who and what is included is a matter of interpretation, legal and otherwise. Yet how those interpretations are formed, how some persons and some behaviors become considered eligible for inclusion, and how law is shaped in light of diverse interpretations is a fundamentally political process. Whereas other research focuses on determining the causes, manifestations, and consequences of intergroup violence, hate-motivated violence, and hate crimes (see, for example, Baird and Rosenbaum 1992; Barnes and Ephross 1994; Green and Rich 1998; Green, Strolovitch, and Wong 1998; Pinderhughes 1993), we examine hate crime as a specific policy domain. Our view is that what we are witnessing is a broad phenomenon: the birth and formation of an entire domain of public policy. Accordingly, the way this policy domain has emerged— its key players, practices, and substantive focus—forms the backdrop against which the behavior and consequences of hate crime can be best understood. To understand what hate crime has come to mean we must understand the political processes that allowed it to become a meaningful category in the first place.

Throughout this study we frequently refer to hate crime as a policy domain. As Paul Burstein notes in a review of the literature on the formation and evolution of policy domains, "sociologists interested in politics have increasingly turned in recent years to the study of policy domains." The term policy domain denotes "components of the political system organized around substantive issues" (1991, 328, 327).[2] Policy domains are fundamentally rooted in definitional and classification schemes that are properly characterized as "social constructions." This means that the substantive focus and boundaries of policy domains are not based upon inherent qualities of "problems." Instead, the distinctions reflect evolving and prevailing dominant modes of conceptualizing issues. Such distinctions are routinely revealed as "constructed" by problems that stretch across boundaries. For example, education, employment training, and crime policies are usually seen as distinct policy domains with different core interest groups, policy theories, and state agencies at work to address these issues, despite the fact that education, employment, and criminality are empirically intertwined phenomena. Recognizing that policy domains are rooted in social constructions does not, however, mean that the social conditions they address are not real or, by extension, that the social facts and attendant suffering underlying a problem are only illusory. Rather, it merely acknowledges that the way problems are defined and the responses they elicit are contingent upon available frameworks of meaning that actors appropriate and deploy in key institutional settings.[3]

Our orientation to the dynamics of policy domains implies that the causes and consequences of a social problem cannot be fully comprehended apart from an understanding of the larger processes that identified, defined, and ultimately generated the problem. More specifically, the term policy domain refers to two things. First, it refers to the range of collective actors—for example, politicians, experts, agency officials, and interest groups—who have gained sufficient legitimacy to speak about or act upon a particular issue. Second, it refers to the cultural logics, theories, frameworks, and ideologies those actors bring to bear in constructing and narrating the problem and the appropriate policy responses.

The culture and structure of a policy domain is organized in four overlapping phases: issue creation, the point at which a problem is recognized, named, and deemed in need of a solution; the adoption of a particular policy solution from a range of alternatives; the rule-making phase, in which government officials and the courts "flesh out" the precise meaning of the policy; and, finally, the classification and application of the rules by enforcement agents to specific "real world" circumstances. Thus, policy making occurs not just at the moment of legislative enactment; it is renegotiated and redefined at multiple points. In the process, the problem is similarly renegotiated and redefined. Thus, the "problem" is as much a consequence of how the policy domain is organized as it is a cause of its construction.

Across these four phases of the policy-making process, hate crime is likely to be understood differently over time, across space, and across institutional locations that constitute the policy domain. Temporal, spatial, and institutional variation in the meaning of hate crime occurs because the formation of a policy domain is rooted in the social processes of innovation, diffusion, and institutionalization. That is, the social construction of hate crime and its official responses diffuse across jurisdictional and geographical space and across the "streams" of the policy-making process. This phenomenon is contingent upon institutionalization, the process by which the meanings and practices that constitute hate crime stabilize, become cognitively taken for granted by actors, and attain a high level of normative consensus (Meyer and Rowan 1977; Powell and DiMaggio 1991; Zucker 1987).

From this perspective, the appropriate target of analysis of an emergent social problem like hate crime is not the horrifying incidents that reach the public consciousness (though those are certainly worthy of examination); rather, it is the social processes that generated and sustained the problem as a framework for understanding such incidents. Accordingly, in the pages that follow we show how the concept of hate crime emerged, how its meaning has been transformed across multiple segments of the policy domain, and how it became institutionalized. Figure 1.1 summarizes this approach.

We show how social movements constructed the problem of hate-motivated violence, how politicians—at both federal and state levels—passed legislation defining the parameters of hate crime, how courts have elaborated the meaning of hate crime, and how law enforcement officials classify, investigate, and prosecute that behavior which is defined by statute as criminal. Throughout, we take a fundamentally sociological approach, one most heavily informed by the work of political scientists, criminologists, and sociolegal scholars. This approach allows us to examine how specific policy decisions relate to the broader social forces that surround them, which in turn allows us to reveal the social processes that have resulted in the production of hate crime and hate crime policy, both within and outside of the justice system.

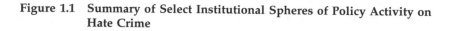

Figure 1.1   Summary of Select Institutional Spheres of Policy Activity on
Hate Crime

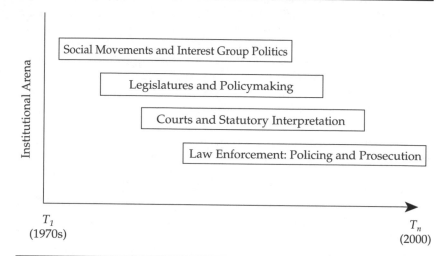

Source: Authors' compilation.

Theoretical Underpinnings

The broader theoretical context for this work derives from social constructionist, social movement, and institutionalist literatures on social
problems and policy solutions. Although each perspective is deployed throughout the book, here we offer a brief overview for
readers who are not familiar with these perspectives.

All policy domains emerge from the process of issue creation. For a
social condition to become a public issue, some group of persons
must first define it as a problem requiring an organized response
(Burstein 1991, 331). How public issues are created and defined is a
key question addressed by constructionist social problems scholars.
Over the past three decades the social constructionist approach to social problems has constituted the dominant paradigm for research
and theory in the area (Schneider 1985, 210; compare, Goode and Ben-
Yehuda 1994). It has generated an enormous body of empirical
studies on a wide range of social conditions, including alcohol and
driving (Gusfield 1963, 1967, 1975, 1976, 1981), hyperactivity (Conrad
1975), child abuse (Best 1987, 1990; Coltrane and Hickman 1992; Johnson 1989; Pfohl 1977), acquired immunodeficiency syndrome (AIDS)
(Albert 1986, 1989), alcoholism (Chauncey 1980), cigarette smoking
(Markle and Troyer 1979), crime (Fishman 1978), rape (Rose 1977),
homosexuality (Spector 1977), premenstrual syndrome (Rittenhouse

1992), chemical contamination (Aronoff and Gunter 1992), drug abuse (Orcutt and Turner 1993), satanism (Richardson, Best, and Bromley 1991), and prostitution (Jenness 1990, 1993, 1996). Rather than focusing on the causes and correlates of the behavior or condition, however, this work explores the claims-making activities and efforts of experts, the media, politicians, legal officials, activists, religious leaders, and other actors and organizations who define such conditions as problematic (that is, a social problem).

Consistent with constructionists' commitment to analyzing "the interpretive processes that constitute what comes to be seen as oppressive, intolerable, or unjust conditions" (Miller and Holstein 1993, 4), our examination of hate crime focuses on how the actors operating within the spheres summarized in figure 1.1 narrate specific acts of violence and specific types of people as victims of such conduct. As is the case with most social conditions that achieve the status of a social problem, the victims of hate crimes have been rendered apparent in this process. The construction of victims unfolds according to a well-established pattern. Persons who have been unjustly harmed or damaged by forces beyond their control are labeled victims and hence interpreted as deserving of support and protection (Holstein and Miller 1990; Weed 1995). In the case of hate crime, we can now point to racial minorities who are victimized by racially motivated violence, Jews who are victimized by anti-Semitism, gays and lesbians who are harmed by violence motivated by homophobia, and women who are harmed simply because they are female. In each case, individuals clearly suffer from psychological and physical harm born of exogenous conditions. However, it is only recently that these types of harms have been deemed sufficient to warrant specific legal protection against bias-motivated hatred; and who is deemed a victim worthy of policy response is time specific and institutionally qualified. In light of this, in this book we identify the processes by which such victim status has been and continues to be constructed as a function of a criminal act and institutionalized as a large-scale social problem with particular—and routinely changing—features.

Constructionists are particularly interested in understanding the definitional processes that result in the assignment of victim status to some individuals and groups but not to others. Such processes are critical to our understanding of social problems insofar as victim status, once designated, carries with it distinct understandings of the social relations that surround the individual as well as his or her relationship to a larger social problem. Among other things, the label of victim underscores the individual's status as an injured person who is harmed because of forces beyond his or her control; dramatizes the injured or harmed person's essential innocence; renders him or her worthy of others' concern and assistance; and often evokes calls for legal reform designed to address the attendant social problem (Holstein and Miller 1990; Weed 1995). John Leo (1989) recognizes the benefit of victim status in his *U.S. News and World Report* article entitled "The Politics of Hate." "More and more aggrieved groups," he writes, "want to magnify their victim status. This is one of the little intergroup truths nobody talks about: The more victimized you seem, the more political leverage you have. But you cannot win the victimization Olympics without lots of plain hard work" (Leo 1989, 24). This book documents that work as it relates to hate crime.

In light of the constructionist formulation of social problems as projections of collective sentiments rather than simple mirrors of objective conditions (Best 1999; Holstein and Miller 1989, 1990; Mauss 1975; Spector and Kitsuse 1977; Miller and Holstein 1993), understanding the construction of emergent and institutionalized victimization requires not so much a focus on objective harm as a focus on the categorization processes and institutional workings that bestow victim status upon select groups and individuals at particular points in time. Accordingly, in this work we do not devote analytic attention to assessing the factual characteristics of victims, nor are we concerned with determining which types of harm should or should not constitute a hate crime and qualify as bias-motivated victimization. Rather, our focus is on processes of recognition, categorization, and institutionalization through which some types of people get social recognition as victims and some types of events are deemed hate crimes. This approach to understanding victimization departs radically from conventional formulations of the victimization process insofar as it allows us to reconceptualize victimization in terms of interactional, discourse, and institutional practices.

One way (some would say the dominant way) in which social conditions come to be seen as social problems and injured people are, at least initially, recognized as victims is through the work of social movements (Gerhards and Rucht 1992; Mauss 1989; Troyer 1989; Goode and Ben-Yehuda 1994; Holstein and Miller 1989; Miller and Holstein 1993). As early as 1975, Armand Mauss (1975, 38) presented the case for considering "social problems as simply a special kind of movement." This case rests in large part on the proposition that the characteristics of social problems are typically also those of social movements, and social problems are always outcomes of social movements. Mauss (1989, 33) argues that "because claims-making activities are indistinguishable from social movements activities, social problems are indistinguishable from social movements." In this formulation, the study of social movements and the study of social problems are rendered compatible through an examination of the genesis of social movements, the organization, mobilization, and natural history of a social movement, and the decline and legacy of the social problem it seeks to redress.

More recently, in *Social Problems & Social Movements*, Harry Bash (1995, xiii–xiv) argues that "what is addressed as the Social Movement, in the one instance, and what is targeted as a host of social problems, in the other, may not reflect distinctive sociohistorical phenomena at all." Although we recognize that not all agree with this position, we nonetheless find it useful to employ this conceptualization in this work.[4] This allows us to focus on social movement organizations as a key source of claims-making activity that has proved consequential for the development of the policy domain under study. Indeed, no fewer than five major social movements (examined later in this chapter) are implicated in the study of hate crime.

Finally, this work draws on and elaborates institutional analysis. Walter Powell and Paul DiMaggio (1991, 3) recognize that "there are in fact many new institutionalisms—in economics, organization theory, political science and public choice, history, and sociology." However, we draw on the sociological variant of institutional analysis.[5] Sociological institutionalism rejects the reductionist impulse of much social science theory, which is based on the idea that the organization of social, economic, and political activities is ultimately attributable to the aggregation of individual interests and choices, the level of technological or economic development, or the social and demographic composition of society (Powell and DiMaggio 1991; Schneiberg and Clemens 1999). From an institutionalist perspective, the way activities within these spheres are organized is highly contingent upon broadly held cultural theories and rules, which generate templates, schemas, and models of organization—that is, institutions.

Institutions have cognitive, normative, and regulatory mechanisms that affect the organization of social practices. Cognitively, institutions create patterned social action by supplying actors with basic constructions of reality so that the way a particular activity is organized seems obvious, natural, and appropriate. Normatively, institutions operate by attaching positive or negative informal social sanctioning to conformity and violation of the underlying cultural rule—that is, penalties for transgressing an institution are paid in the currency of legitimacy. Finally, regulatory mechanisms operate through formal sanctioning procedures—usually carried out by superior organizations like the state or a professional association—that enforce institutionalized rules by restricting specific organizations' access to social goods.

Thus, central research questions in institutionalism concern how and why economic, social, and political organizations assume particular forms. From an institutional perspective, organizational design results more from a process of conforming to supraorganizational models than from the internal characteristics of an organization or efficiency, the needs of the organization's service population, or a rational calculation of the costs and benefits of one form or another. Institutionalism has been primarily concerned with the analysis of the diffusion of organizational forms (that is, the spread of particular organizational practices across fields of organizations). In the aggregate, institutionalism notes that one by-product of diffusion is a striking homogenization of organizational forms both within and across sectors of society (Grattet, Jenness, and Curry 1998; Powell and DiMaggio 1991; Strang and Meyer 1993).

Applied to the design of governmental and political organizations, institutionalism has several implications. First, it suggests that policy formation is substantially determined by intergovernmental processes and developments, such as the endorsement of a particular policy model by a powerful interstate organization, galvanizing period-specific events that dramatize the need for a policy response, and the formation of interstate social networks that channel the communication of models across social space. Second, policy domains are characterized by temporal homogenization. That is, over time units come to adopt similar organizational models. Institutionalism points to specific variables—such as "cultural linkages" (Strang and Meyer 1993), number of prior adopters, and interorganizational networks—that affect the rate of diffusion and thus help to account for why some units adopt policies early and others not until later. Third, increasingly, the taken-for-grantedness of a particular policy approach is reflected in the discourse of official actors (Dobbin 1994); debate and discussion diminish as actors converge around a set of policy practices and definitions of problems. Fourth, over time the role of collective action in sustaining policy definitions diminishes; a policy formula takes on a life of its own and no longer requires active promotion by particular collective actors. Finally, moments in the policy-making process, from formulation, agenda setting, and adoption to enforcement, are "decoupled." That is, practices, definitions, and categories are used differently across phases of the policy-making process (Meyer and Rowan 1977).

We invoke these theoretical resources for the purpose of understanding hate crime as a policy domain with three audiences in mind. First, we hope to speak to social scientists interested in the development and organization of policy domains, processes of institutionalization, and the creation and content of law. As social scientists, we situate the work that follows in a sociohistorical perspective and build a general framework for understanding hate crime as a political, legal, and policy concept. Second, consistent with the spirit of the Rose Series, of which this volume is a part, we have policy concerns in mind. Drawing from the sociological insight provided in the pages that follow, it is our aim to reflect on the nature of hate crime as a particular type of criminal activity, as well as the range of state responses to this particular type of conduct. As Burstein (1991, 330) has noted, "To explain policy outcomes, it is necessary to focus on policy domains." Third, and most important, we have tried to write this book in such a way that it speaks to the general public, or at least those interested in seeking to be informed about hate crime and to think critically about the topic as they participate in the multitude of responses to bias crime.

Overview of the Book

Chapter 2 considers the question, "Why now?" Why did the hate crime policy domain emerge in the mid-1980s and 1990s in the United States, despite the fact that the conduct at issue has been around for centuries? By pointing to the historical precursors and the political developments that coincided with the formation of hate crime policies, we first discuss the social movements and discursive themes that animated the discovery of "hate crime" as a particular type of social problem and the development of policy responses to this problem. The modern civil rights movement, the contemporary feminist movement, the gay and lesbian movement, and the crime victim movement provided key organizational and ideational resources that facilitated the growth of an anti-hate-crime movement in the United States. Accordingly, we identify the key watchdog organizations that accompany and sustain the anti-hate-crime movement and, in so doing, bring newfound policy attention to select forms of violence. These historical sources fed into the early conceptualization of hate crime as a kind of violence and intimidation that victimized blacks, Jews, and immigrants. Later, gays and lesbians, women, and persons with disabilities were incorporated into the concept. Chapter 2 demonstrates how both liberal and conservative social movements and the public discussions they inspired provided the crucible for subsequent policy making that transformed hate-motivated violence into hate *crime*.

Chapter 3 addresses the question of how the social movement mobilization interfaced with the policy-making process to shape the official definition of hate crime in such a way that some forms of violence are recognized and some are not. As with other kinds of policy reforms, the legislative conceptualization of hate crime emerged from the process by which proposals are introduced, managed, and accepted or rejected in legislative arenas as legislative debates occur, constituency interests are negotiated, and political wills are enacted. The emergence and evolution of three federal hate crime laws (the Hate Crime Statistics Act, the Violence Against Women Act, and the Hate Crimes Sentencing Enhancement Act) reveal that one of the most important elements of the substantive character of hate crime law—the adoption of select status provisions, such as race, religion, ethnicity, sexual orientation, gender, and disabilities—unfolded in such a way that some victims of discriminatory violence have been recognized as hate crime victims whereas others have gone unnoticed. In particular, people of color, Jews, gays and lesbians, women, and those with disabilities increasingly have been recognized as victims of hate crime, whereas union members, the elderly, children, and police officers, for example, have not. The difference between categories of victims that are included and those that are not reveals the crucial role social movements play in the early formulation of policy: those constituencies unconnected to a social movement that has effectively called attention to violence related to the category are not initially included. However, later in the process, social movement involvement in the formulation of the laws, through drafting, testifying, and campaigning for the legislation, is no longer critical.

The issue of what types of people and what types of conduct occupy center stage in the battle against bigotry is further developed in chapter 4. Here we explain the diffusion of hate crime laws across the United States. As with federal hate crime law, the central issue faced by state legislators was what exactly the laws should cover, in terms of both conduct and constituencies. Ultimately, conduct and constituency coverage is highly sensitive to the timing of adoption. Early on, there was little agreement about how the laws should be drafted and what they should cover. Later, in a pattern that is well know in policy diffusion research, states began to converge around a dominant basic approach to lawmaking that reflects an expanded conception of the types of activities that qualify as hate crime and the types of people who are vulnerable to hate crime. However, once that happened, successive adopters actually began to expand the coverage from the basic template, thereby embracing increasingly robust versions of the law. In concrete terms, as time went on, states adopted laws that covered more status categories and a wider array of conduct. As a result, laggard states, those who passed the laws later, ironically tended to employ a more expansive and progressive definition of hate crime.

Once a social movement concept is expressed in statute form, courts intervene to sharpen the meaning of the statutes. Accordingly, chapter 5 is devoted to understanding the evolution of the hate crime concept within judicial discourse. Across all appellate case law, including two U.S. Supreme Court cases, judicial opinions reflect the increasing "settledness" of hate crime laws. In the process, the judicial interpretations have rejected some meanings of the statutes and embraced others. As the concept of hate crime has become more settled, its meaning has become more nuanced and complex and its range of coverage more expansive. In particular, judges have created a foundation for hate crime laws that situates them within a broader body of antidiscrimination principles. This has helped resolve the highly controversial constitutional question of whether hate crime statutes punish motives by specifying, instead, that they punish acts of discrimination. The development of the case law mimics the dynamics uncovered in chapter 4 with respect to legislation. Thus, the institutionalization of the laws within judicial discourse is reflected in the convergence in the behavioral and motivational characteristics judges associate with hate crime. In other words, the case law suggests that judges increasingly agree about what hate crime is and how the law should be framed to respond to it and to pass constitutional challenges.

After legislatures and courts have spoken, legal concepts must be put into use in concrete day-to-day circumstances by officials on the front lines of the criminal justice system. As much research on law enforcement suggests, law enforcement officials—especially police and prosecutors—possess a considerable amount of discretion in their work. Chapter 6 addresses the way law enforcers wield this discretion in the policing and prosecution of hate crimes. With respect to policing, the consensus among researchers is that the awareness and enforcement of hate crime laws varies considerably from one jurisdiction to another. Not surprisingly, then, the general orders of California police and sheriff's departments reveal substantial variation in the working definition of hate crime across policing units. Of course, discretion results in variation in enforcement behavior in all kinds of crime. Perhaps more important than the observation that there is variation in hate crime policing is the question of whether it is increasing or decreasing over time. Recent evidence suggests that variation in hate crime policing is decreasing and will likely continue to do so. Similar patterns are reflected in the prosecution of hate crime. Although some have suggested that hate crime laws are unenforceable, we show that prosecutors in California are not encountering any significant and consequential difficulties. Once cases are filed as hate crimes, prosecutors obtain convictions at rates that are comparable to those for other kinds of crimes; moreover, hate crime conviction rates have shown a general increase in recent years. Thus, like legislators and judges, prosecutors appear to be converging in their understandings and practices of dealing with hate crime as ambiguity about what the concept is and how it should be applied are diminishing.

Based on the empirical analyses put forth in separate chapters throughout this book, our concluding chapter is devoted to teasing out theoretical and policy implications. With regard to the former, we highlight a series of interrelated and temporally bound processes through which the concept of hate crime—and indeed, the entire policy domain of hate crime—has emerged and been transformed in the United States. We argue that through these processes, cultural forms, especially policy and legal forms, are both affirmed and reconstituted over time. As for policy implications, we address a debate provoked by the publication of *Hate Crimes: Criminal Law and Identity Politics*, by James Jacobs and Kimberly Potter (1998) and, more recently, *Punishing Hate: Bias Crimes Under American Law*, by Frederick Lawrence (1999). Jacobs and Potter argue that policy makers would be ill advised to use criminal law to address the problem of intergroup violence manifest as discrimination, whereas Lawrence suggests otherwise. We respond to these positions with an alternative view that recognizes the symbolic and instrumental importance of law and, at the same time, concedes that the law alone will not solve the problem of discriminatory violence in the United States.

═ Chapter 2 ═

The Emergence of an Anti-Hate-Crime Movement and the Construction of an Epidemic of Violence

V IOLENCE organized around select social characteristics and statuses, what is currently referred to as bias- or hate-motivated violence, is not a new phenomenon. Rather, it is an identifiable feature of human societies across the globe, both historically and at present. So why is it only in the latter part of the twentieth century that hate crime has come to the fore as a major social problem worthy of public attention, legislative action, judicial review, and punitive response? Why and how has "hate crime" become a part of our social and legal lexicon? How did such an issue come into being?

Referencing the recent explosion of attention devoted to hate crimes in the United States, Terry Maroney (1998, 568) argues that "if, indeed, 'times have changed,' such change is attributable to the rise and societal impact of a social movement dedicated to hate crime victims." Energized by several previous social movements, an anti-hate-crime movement emerged in the late 1970s to bring public attention to violence directed at certain minorities. Surprisingly, this movement united groups on both the Right and the Left to redefine violence perpetrated because of bigotry as "bias-motivated violence." Advocates argued that such violence has consequences beyond the pain and suffering of the individual victim because it terrorizes entire communities. Moreover, bigoted violence was primarily described as a problem affecting a select group of minorities—Jews, immigrants, blacks, gays and lesbians, women, and persons with disabilities. Advocates presented the condition as an urgent social problem in need of public remedy. As a result, this movement is responsible for inciting policy makers to rethink the causes, scope, and consequences of violence motivated by bigotry.

Thus, the hate crime policy domain was built upon a foundation laid by the anti-hate-crime movement, which, in turn, was made possible by a handful of earlier social movements that provided its central discursive themes and strategies. To understand the initial issue creation phase of the formation of the hate crime policy domain, then, it is important to examine how the anti-hate-crime movement successfully engaged in an organizational and ideological struggle to place discriminatory violence on the public agenda.

A History of Bias-Motivated Violence

From the vivid and well-documented atrocities of the Holocaust to the lynching of African Americans in the United States in the post–Civil War era to the more recent ethnic cleansing in the former Yugoslavia, violence organized around real or imagined social characteristics and group membership punctuates human history. Social scientists from many disciplines have noted that the history of human societies is a history of intergroup conflict. This type of violence has taken a variety of forms, from symbolic to fatal assaults on both individuals and entire groups of people. It also has involved a range of perpetrators, from intimates to strangers and from individuals to groups to institutions such as the state. As Carole Sheffield (1992, 388) observes with reference to the United States, "Our history reveals a pattern of violence, brutality, and bigotry against those defined as 'other.' State violence was committed against Native Americans, captured and enslaved Africans, African Americans, workers, and citizens who protested domestic and foreign policies." In a similar vein, James Jacobs and Kimberly Potter (1998, 391) note that "it is hardly necessary to point out our nation's history of bias: Native Americans were brutally murdered as the West was conquered; the blood and sweat of Chinese and other immigrant workers stain the expanses of railroad tracks across the Midwest; lynchings of blacks were once common; violence against various European immigrants and Jews was a fact of life. Clearly, violence motivated by racism, xenophobia, anti-Semitism and other biases is not new." Similarly, using only recently invented, and thus historically specific, terms like "hate crime," "bias crime," and "hate-motivated crime" interchangeably, Maroney (1998, 564–65) observes that

> hate crime, far from being an anomaly, has been the means of maintaining dominant power relationships throughout United States history.

Hate crime may be defined as acts of violence motivated by animus against persons and groups because of race, ethnicity, religion, national origin or immigration status, gender, sexual orientation, disability (including, for example, HIV status), and age. Thus defined, the category encompasses a wide range of historical practices, such as the many individual acts of violence against African Americans used strategically to cement slavery's power base. Historically, such crimes have been actively encouraged, passively condoned, or simply ignored by systems of governance, especially the criminal justice system. Acts such as these authors describe have been well documented, especially with reference to violence based on race, religion, ethnicity, sexual orientation, and gender.

In *Racial and Religious Violence in America: A Chronology*, Michael and Judy Ann Newton (1991, ix) document "a time line of atrocity, acts of mayhem, murder, and intimidation perpetrated on the grounds of racial or religious prejudice, from the discovery of North America to modern times." They conclude that "bloodshed based on race or creed is interwoven with the fabric of our culture from the first arrival of explorers to the present day. Our modern spate of ethnic mayhem is by no means new, unprecedented, or unique." Focusing on this century in particular, and moving beyond U.S. borders, Neil Kressel (1996, 1) observes that "the twentieth century has been a century of hostility, an epoch in which the brutality of humankind has erupted and flowed more expansively than ever before. During the past eight decades, mass hatred has reached genocidal proportions in Turkey, Germany, Indonesia, Nigeria, Bangladesh, Burundi, Cambodia, Bosnia, Rwanda, and elsewhere. Blood has gushed so freely, and with such frequency, that one might consider the urge to kill one's neighbor an inborn characteristic of our species." "Killing one's neighbor" does not only occur as a result of racial, ethnic, and nationalistic conflicts; sexual orientation and gender are routinely implicated in bias-motivated assaults and murders.

Violence against homosexuals and people presumed to be homosexual has occurred for as long as the lives of gay men and lesbians have been documented. In *Gay American History*, which covers a period of more than four hundred years, Jack Katz (1976) documents a history of violence directed at individuals because of their same-sex orientation, sexual identity, or sexual behavior. Historically, such violence has often represented official state policies and has been perpetrated by representatives of the state as well as private citizens. More recently, the National Gay and Lesbian Task Force (1991) has cited literally thousands of incidents of violence against gay men and lesbian women in the United States throughout the latter part of the twentieth century. These data led President Ronald Reagan's Department of Justice to commission a report on bias violence in 1987, which concludes that "the most frequent victims of hate violence today are blacks, Hispanics, Southeast Asians, Jews, and gays and lesbians. Homosexuals are probably the most frequent victims" (NGLTF 1987, 10; see also Vaid 1995, 11).

Finally, over the past few decades, feminist historians, activists, and scholars have documented thousands of cases of violence against individuals because of their gender (see, for example, Caputi 1992 and Davies 1994). This violence, which includes everything from rape to wife burning, spans history and is not bound by culture or region (Davies 1994; Radford and Russell 1992; Sheffield 1987, 1992). Indeed, in the preface to Miranda Davies's *Violence and Women* (1994, vii) refers to violence against women as simply a "universal problem."

Although violence based on race, religion, ethnicity, sexual orientation, gender, and the like is a historical given, it is only recently that it has been viewed as hate crime by members of the morally concerned citizenry as well as policy makers, legislative bodies, judges, and the criminal justice system. The beginnings of this redefinition can be found in the development of an anti-hate-crime movement that draws on the organizational and ideational resources of preexisting liberal and conservative movements that initiated and sustained a new narrative surrounding the causes, manifestations, and consequences of violence directed toward minorities. The anti-hate-crime movement can be traced to the social changes connected to two larger movements: the civil rights and the victim's rights movement (Jacobs and Potter 1998; Jenness and Broad 1997; Levin and McDevitt 1993; Maroney 1998).

The Anti-Hate-Crime Movement

It is not surprising that the issue of hate-motivated violence and hate-crime legislation came to the fore in the late twentieth century. Multiple civil rights movements emerging in the 1960s, coupled with the more recent crime victim's rights movement, created the conditions conducive to the development of an anti-hate-crime movement in the United States. As others have demonstrated, the so-called rights movements of the 1960s and 1970s provided the structural basis and discursive themes necessary to set the stage for the reconceptualization of violent conduct and hateful expressions directed toward minorities as hate crime (Bensinger 1992; Jacobs and Potter 1998; Jenness and Broad 1997; Levin and McDevitt 1993; Maroney 1998).

In *Hate Crimes: New Social Movements and the Politics of Violence,*

Valerie Jenness and Kendal Broad (1997, 22–23) demonstrate that "'new social movements' have inspired and sponsored organizations whose *raison d'être* is to monitor and publicize the evolving contours and consequences of violence born of racism, nationalism, anti-Semitism, sexism, and heterosexism." In particular, the civil rights movement (Bloom 1987; Morris 1984), the contemporary women's movement (Buechler 1990; Ferree and Hess 1985), the gay and lesbian movement (Adam 1987; Vaid 1995), and the crime victim's movement (Weed 1995) have fundamentally reshaped the politics of violence in the United States and abroad. The discursive themes emanating from the rights movements of the 1960s and 1970s formed the sociopolitical terrain that made the anti-hate-crime movement possible during the final decades of the twentieth century (Jenness and Broad 1997 and Maroney 1998).

Without preexisting civil rights movements and the identity politics that are incited by them, the issue of hate crimes simply would not have emerged, marshaled significant media and legislative attention, and become institutionalized as a modern social problem. The discursive themes emanating from the rights movements of the 1960s and 1970s, coupled with a well-established tradition of targeting the state and public policy to remedy social inequalities, formed the sociopolitical terrain that inspired and continues to fuel the contemporary anti-hate-crime movement to recognize, respond to, and criminalize violence motivated by bigotry. Accordingly, to situate the development of an anti-hate-crime movement historically, an anti-hate-crime movement sector, and current policies that define the parameters of discriminatory violence and specify punishment for hate crime, an overview of these historical precursors is instructive.

Strange Bedfellows: Civil Rights Movements and the Crime Victim Movement

The emergence, organization, evolution, and success of what Aldon Morris (1984, ix) calls "the modern civil rights movement" has been well documented and analyzed (Bloom 1987; McAdam 1982; Morris 1984; Piven and Cloward 1977). Jack Bloom (1987) has shown that the modern civil rights movement was the culmination of a political struggle that began in the Reconstruction period of the 1860s. Emerging in the mid-1950s (Morris 1984), the modern civil rights movement has remained committed to enhancing the legal, social, and economic status and welfare of blacks in particular and racial and ethnic minorities in general in the United States. Early on, the modern civil rights movement focused on contesting legal prohibitions based on skin color in public accommodations and voting and injustices rooted in economic disparities. Bias-motivated violence committed against blacks and other racial minorities in the 1950s and 1960s increased the civil rights movement's willingness to challenge racism in all its forms, including race-based violence.

As the movement grew, the "realities of Southern power dictated that organizers had to do more than promote salience and efficacy at the grassroots" (Goldberg 1991, 142). The need for regionwide and nationwide coordination among activists and organizations became clear. A proliferation of coordinated civil rights organizations characterizes the history and structure of the modern civil rights movement (Minkoff 1995), and increasing numbers of networked organizations have emerged during the second half of the twentieth century (Bloom 1987) to sustain the movement. For example, the National Association for the Advancement of Colored People (NAACP), the "dominant black protest organization" (Morris 1984, 12), was founded in 1910 by a group of black and white intellectuals "vehemently opposed to racism that confronted the black community" (Morris 1984, 12). With branches in many southern communities, "the NAACP had already built a substantial organizational base by 1950" (Goldberg 1991, 145). Since the establishment of the NAACP, well before the ascendancy of the modern civil rights movement, and consistent with the growth of the NAACP since then, there has been a steady growth in the number of organizations, associations, and task forces committed to combating a diverse array of manifestations of racism at the local, state, regional, and national level.

From the mid-1970s onward, one issue in particular—physical and symbolic violence directed toward blacks, as well as other racial, religious, and ethnic minorities—has received increasing attention from organizations identifying themselves as civil rights organizations. This component of the "the racial justice movement" (Vaid 1995, 207) focuses on police brutality and other forms of violence against people of color and other minorities. Nonprofit organizations such as the Anti-Defamation League of B'nai B'rith, the National Institute Against Prejudice and Violence, the Center for Democratic Renewal, and the Southern Poverty Law Center have emerged to document instances of violence against racial and ethnic minorities. These organizations, as well as others, have drafted and sponsored legislation to protect minority constituencies vulnerable to victimization stemming from racial, religious, and nationalistic beliefs. Clearly, these organizations are among the many organizational and cultural products of the modern civil rights movement. Contemporary civil rights organizations such as these continue to battle discrimination on a variety of fronts as we enter the twenty-first century.

History has already revealed that "the aspirations and demands of blacks fed back into the minds of members of other disadvantaged groups and legitimized their rejection of socially prescribed places and roles" (Goldberg 1991, 198). Early advances by the modern civil rights movement spurred more than awareness, however. They also defined for other constituencies the potential of mobilization. As a model and groundbreaker, the black struggle facilitated the mobilization of future movements in the United States (see Morris 1984; McAdam 1982) by sensitizing opinion makers, polity members, authorities, and the wider public to the challenges, promises, and consequences of protest. As Debra Minkoff (1995) and others have demonstrated, the modern civil rights movement has had a precedent-setting effect on subsequent civil-rights-minded movements and social movement organization, especially the contemporary women's movement and the gay and lesbian movement—each of which is also centrally concerned with violence against minorities, in this case women and gays and lesbians, respectively.

Like other causes of the 1960s, activism for the rights of women in the middle part of the twentieth century evolved in an environment conditioned by the civil rights movement and culminated in the amalgam of groups collectively labeled the women's movement.[1] Although the contemporary women's movement addresses a broad set of concerns, the social control of sex and sexuality has certainly dominated its agenda (D'Emilio and Freedman 1988; Ferree and Hess 1985; Snitow, Stansell, and Thompson 1983; Weeks 1985). For example, feminists' fight for reproductive rights, especially access to legal abortions, historically has been packaged as a struggle for women's absolute right to control and use their bodies as they see fit. This right, in turn, has been viewed as a necessary prerequisite for women's sexual freedom and self-determination and has encompassed everything from the right to refuse sex to the right to a freely chosen sexuality to the right to be free from violence while doing either one.

Feminist activists' sustained emphasis on the importance of sexual freedom and self-determination has served to focus the contemporary women's movement on institutionalized violence against girls and women. Feminist scholars and activists have worked over the past three decades to bring attention to the scope and consequences of violence against girls and women in this country and globally (Caputi 1992). In *Violence and Women*, Miranda Davies (1994, vii) notes that "women's groups and individual activists across the world have campaigned vigorously against abuses such as rape, wife-beating, sexual slavery, and sexual harassment. Countries as far apart as Zimbabwe, France, Brazil, and the Philippines have seen the problem raised onto the political agenda, both at the local level and the national level." As a result, an array of other manifestations of violence against girls and women have been increasingly recognized as social problems that need to be remedied if the status and welfare of girls and women is to be enhanced.

Identifying various forms of violence against women as a manifestation and consequence of patriarchal oppression has been one of the lasting contributions of the contemporary women's movement. The women's movement has accomplished this by documenting instances of violence against girls and women, bringing attention to the range of manifestations of such violence, developing crisis intervention and assistance programs, founding and sustaining shelters and networks of safe houses, establishing and maintaining telephone hotlines, sponsoring public education campaigns and public protests, challenging law enforcement practices that fail to intervene effectively to assist injured women, and drafting new legislation to protect women from violence (Caputi 1992; Dobash and Dobash 1981). Combined, these activities have ensured that battery, rape, sexual harassment, forced prostitution, and other forms of violence directed at girls and women are no longer seen as a personal problem to be resolved within the private sphere of family and home (Caufield and Wonders 1993). Instead, such conduct is now recognized as a societal problem; as such, it has secured a home in public discourse in the United States and is an identifiable feature of society that produces recognizable victims. This shift in meaning is primarily attributable to the contemporary women's movement's ability to bring attention to violence against women as a form of institutionalized discrimination and to effect legislative reform aimed at redress.

Like the contemporary women's movement, the gay and lesbian movement addresses a broad set of concerns. Although the founding of the Mattachine Society in 1950 and the Daughters of Bilitis in 1955 are often cited as the first signs of a gay and lesbian movement in the United States, it was not until the late 1960s that gay men and lesbian women became politically mobilized to fight discrimination (Adam 1987; Altman 1971, 1982; D'Emilio and Freedman 1988; Stivison 1982; Weeks 1985). The struggle against homophobic discrimination has been fought on many levels. The initial intent of the early gay and lesbian movement was to disrupt stereotypical perceptions of homosexuality as a peculiar condition (Adam 1987; Katz 1976; Weeks 1985).

Since then, the movement has continually sought to establish homo-sexuality as a nonstigmatized public alternative to heterosexual standards, equally worthy of public respect and legal protection.

Consistent with the modern civil rights movement and the contemporary women's movement, legal redress has been at the core of the gay and lesbian movement's political activities (Adam 1987; Stivison 1982; Vaid 1995). Many proposals to alter state- and national-level legislation on behalf of homosexuals have been put forth since the 1960s (Leonard 1992). For example, gay and lesbian advocates proposed to amend the 1964 Civil Rights Act by adding "affectional or sexual preference" to the list of protected categories. However, in 1976 and again in 1986 the Supreme Court upheld the constitutionality of state antihomosexuality laws. In the 1990s, lesbian and gay advocates lobbied for the removal of military regulations that consider homosexual acts grounds for dishonorable discharge, denial of military benefits, or court-martial (Scott and Stanley 1994; Vaid 1995), resulting in the current "Don't ask, don't tell" policy. Finally, more recently, gays and lesbians have pursued legal recognition of domestic partnerships approximating marriage.

Regardless of the particular issue at hand, representatives of the gay and lesbian movement have continually admonished the law's interference with what is construed as an activity of choice, without a victim, that is mutually agreed upon by the involved parties. At the same time, the movement has pursued the expansion of sexual civil liberties and legal protection for gays and lesbians (Adam 1987; Altman 1971, 1982; D'Emilio 1983; Katz 1976; Marotta 1981; Vaid 1995). As a result, some states have liberalized laws concerning homosexuality, primarily by eliminating penalties against private sexual relationships—both homosexual and heterosexual—between consenting adults. These and other changes have led some analysts to argue that there has been an increased tolerance toward gays and lesbians, in large part because of the gay and lesbian movement and the general liberalization of the past few decades (Adam 1987; Altman 1971; Goode and Troiden 1974; Jones, Gallagher and McFalls 1988; Katz 1976; Rubin 1984; Weeks 1985). Others, however, fear that the conservative backlash of the 1980s and 1990s threatens to reverse the many gains won by the movement (Brownworth 1993; Vaid 1995).

The gay and lesbian liberation movement has served to fundamentally shape the discourse of contemporary sexual politics in general and the politics of violence more particularly. One of the ways in which the movement has played a key role in shaping contemporary politics of violence is by establishing and institutionalizing gay- and lesbian-sponsored antiviolence projects throughout the United States (Jenness and Broad 1997). To this end, it has followed in the footsteps of the modern civil rights movement and the contemporary women's movement. In *Virtual Equality: The Mainstreaming of Gay and Lesbian Liberation*, Urvashi Vaid (1995, 2), the former director of the National Gay and Lesbian Task Force, notes the similarities between the civil rights, women's, and gay and lesbian movements in the United States:

> Like the civil rights movement that preceded us and on which we model our goals and strategies, we have reached the moment of partial fulfillment. The system has adapted to our existence, but it has not changed in fundamental ways. We are freer than we were in the 1940s and 1960s, but we have failed to realize full equality or win full acceptance as moral human beings. The modern civil rights movement began to face this dilemma in the 1960s, soon after the passage of major federal civil rights legislation, like the Civil Rights Act of 1964 and the Voting Rights Act. Laws were changed, people's lives improved, but the economic condition of a large number of African Americans remained the same or, indeed, deteriorated over the next thirty years. Racial prejudice stayed in place even as its age-old legal operation was dismantled. The women's movement faced this moment in the late 1970s, as its national leadership targeted the Equal Rights Amendment (ERA). By the mid-1980s, the effort to pass the ERA had failed, the radical and grassroots women's movement was splintered into warring, single-issue factions, and the term *postfeminism* was more popular than *feminist*. Gender-based discrimination, sexism, and violence persisted, even as women's participation in all aspects of cultural life increased. Today, the gay and lesbian movement is at a similar decisive moment.

Clearly, then, the modern civil rights movement, the women's movement, and the gay and lesbian movement share a historical backdrop, are connected by shared commitments to the expansion of civil rights, and maintain a joint commitment to reducing violence directed at minority constituencies. The incorporation of concerns about violence into a larger antidiscrimination agenda established the terms of the anti-hate-crime movement, which relies heavily on the image of hate crime as an expression of discrimination.

Consistent with the themes emanating from the antiviolence projects established and sustained by these rights movements, President Richard Nixon declared in 1968 that freedom from violent crime is "the first civil right of every American" ("Transcripts of Acceptance Speeches by Nixon and Agnew to the GOP Convention," *New York Times*, August 9, 1968, A20). This marks an important moment in what is now commonly referred to as the crime victim movement, typically recognized as a conservative social movement (Maroney 1998; Weed 1995). Surprisingly, however, this movement found allegiances with various, more liberal-minded rights movements. Although it makes for strange bedfellows, this allegiance has proved crucial to the formation of an anti-hate-crime movement.

Three kinds of anti-hate-crime movements currently operate in the United States: the citizen action model of communities mobilizing to mount patrols, run neighborhood watch programs, and try to make the streets and neighborhood safe (or, at least, safer); the victim services movement, which staffs hotlines, centers, and support groups; and the racial justice movement that has organized against police brutality, state-sanctioned violence, and social violence against people of color and other minority constituencies. As Vaid (1995, 207) has noted, "Each of these anti-violence movements organizes around the framework of civil rights; each argues that we have the right to be safe in our person and property, regardless of who, where, or what we are." Moreover, Vaid continues, "each pursues legal reforms through legislative activity [and] each engages in education aimed at more understanding, awareness, prevention, and support for victims of violence."

A central component of these antiviolence efforts—the support for victims of violence—has been recognized as a key element in a larger "crime victim movement" (Best 1999; Weed 1995). According to Frank Weed (1995) and Maroney (1998), the "discovery" of crime victims in the late 1960s can be most directly connected to two things: First, the Warren Court's expansion of defendant's rights led to the countermovement that is associated with victim's rights. Second, by drawing attention to the criminal justice system's treatment of victims of rape and domestic violence, women's rights groups in the early 1970s highlighted the problem of secondary victimization—the psychological trauma experienced by survivors of violence as a result of maneuvering through the criminal justice system. Specifically, secondary victimization most commonly refers to abuse suffered by victims at the hands of police, prosecutors, social and medical service providers, and judges.

Emerging in the face of rising fear of victimization, penal reforms perceived to benefit criminals, and diminished confidence in the legal system, the crime victim movement is a national reform movement that promotes the rights of crime victims. In *Certainty of Justice: Reform in the Crime Victim Movement*, the only book on the history, organization, and agenda of the crime victim movement in the United States, Weed (1995, 1) describes the movement as a "coalescence of ideas, events, and organizations that has produced a set of grievances against the legal machinery of the government." The basic grievance put forth by the crime victim movement is simple: victims of crime, especially violent crime, not only need but are also entitled to special assistance, support, and rights. Because "the criminal justice system was not perceived as providing certainty of justice for the criminal or the victim" (Weed 1995, 21), legal and extralegal mechanisms needed to be put into place to recognize and serve those injured by crime; in simple terms, this is done by expanding the rights of crime victims.

The rights of crime victims were raised to formal legal stature in 1980 when the first Basic Bill of Rights for Crime Victims and Witnesses passed in Wisconsin, followed by the passage of similar legislation in four more states in 1981 and in forty-two states by 1989 (Weed 1995, 22). By 1999 almost every state had adopted a legislative package consisting of a variety of prerogatives for crime victims and thirty-one states had also ratified state constitutional amendments designed to enhance the rights of crime victims (see figure 2.1), and in 2000 Senator Dianne Feinstein (D-Calif.) introduced a federal constitutional amendment to extend the rights of crime victims. In general, these amendments provide constitutional protection of the rights of crime victims in the same way that defendants' rights are protected. Crime victims' rights are now a permanent part of the criminal justice system, and courts are able to punish violations of a victim's rights.

Combined, these legislative changes culminated in the recognition of crime victims as bearers of rights under American law and of their legitimate claim on the criminal justice system (Best 1999). In general, a "victim's bill of rights" articulates the proper response of government agencies to victims of crime and their needs, including a legal definition of "crime victim"; a statement that victims are to be treated with dignity, respect, sensitivity, compassion, and fairness throughout the criminal justice process; a guarantee that victims of crime will be allowed to be heard at various stages of the criminal justice process; protection from intimidation, harassment, or abuse from the defendant or any person acting on behalf of the defendant; and allowance for some elements of tort law, which allows for payment by the offender of compensation and restitution for harm done to the victim (Weed 1995). Together, these types of provisions have brought newfound attention to victims of crime and, in effect, have brought into the public consciousness an understanding of what it means to be a victim of crime (Best 1999).

This notion is informed by a well-documented "rights revolution" in the United States as well as the emergence of a victim ideology and corresponding victim industry. With regard to the former, Weed (1995,

Figure 2.1   Year of Ratification of Victim Bill of Rights, 1982 to 1999

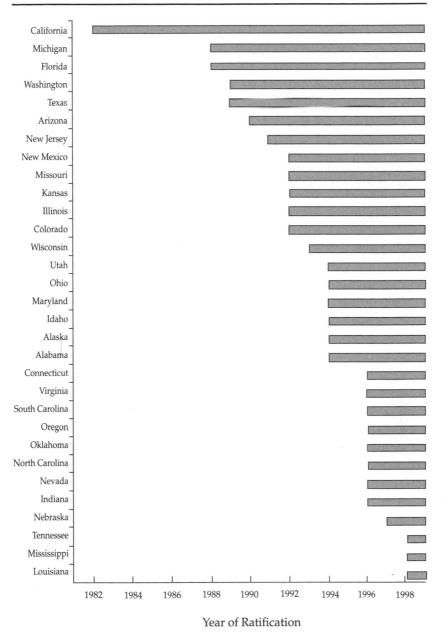

Year of Ratification

Source: Authors' compilation.

21) borrows from Lawrence Friedman's (1985) work to explain that the crime victim movement, and the rights it seeks to institutionalize, can best be seen as a function of increased "rights consciousness":

> Legal scholars talk about the "rights revolution," where legal protections are extended to groups in society on the basis of expanded concepts of "due process" and "equal protection under the law." The development of this "rights consciousness," to use Lawrence Friedman's term, is clearly a phenomenon that has developed starting with civil rights for minority groups, and spreading to claims of special rights made by prisoners, students, mental patients, the elderly, children, homosexuals, the handicapped, and women, just to name a few. The rights revolution is based on the claims of real people to an evolving concept of "fair treatment."

Just as the major social movements of the latter part of the twentieth century—the civil rights movement, the women's movement, the gay and lesbian movement, the victim's rights movement—have successfully portrayed particular groups as systematically victimized by a society organized around inequality, ideas promulgated by the modern self-help movement contributed to the development of a "contemporary ideology of victimization" (Best 1999). As Joel Best describes in his book, *Random Violence: How We Talk About New Crimes and New Victims* (1999, 102), "Gradually, a coherent, albeit implicit, ideology evolved" as "a broad range of authorities—including social movement activists, political conservatives and liberals, therapists, scientists, and lawyers—became more likely to talk about victimization in society."[2] The contemporary ideology of victimization offers a formula—a familiar set of claims—that can be adapted by would-be advocates of new forms of victimization (Sykes 1992).

With the help of the rights revolution and the victim industry, the crime victim movement has enhanced the status of victims of crime, especially victims of violent crime. It has done so primarily by seeking to establish, articulate, and expand the rights of those harmed by crime. By 1983, "the so-called victims' rights movement seemed to be making faster progress than any previous civil rights thrust in United States history" (Curtis J. Sitomer, "New Civil Rights Thrust: Aid for Victims," *Christian Science Monitor*, April 5, 1983, 1). As a result, "the entire issue of victims' rights was elevated to its proper place in the criminal justice system" (Maroney 1998, 576).

The civil rights movement, the women's movement, the gay and lesbian movement, and the crime victim movement have converged to put into question, and make publicly debatable, issues of rights and harm as they relate to a variety of constituencies (see figure 2.2).

Figure 2.2   The Convergence of Rights Movements and the Emergence of an Anti-Hate-Crime Movement in the Late Twentieth Century

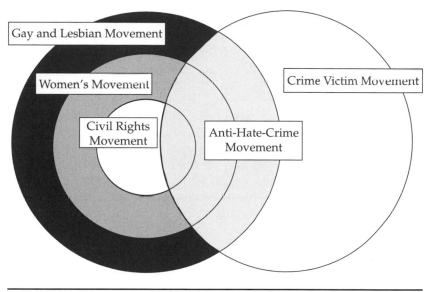

Gay and Lesbian Movement

Women's Movement

Crime Victim Movement

Civil Rights Movement

Anti-Hate-Crime Movement

Source: Authors' compilation.

They have "called attention to the personal costs of minority groups' political victimization," just as "the victims' rights movement called attention to the political context of personal victimization" (Maroney 1998, 579). Combined, these movements have instigated public discussions about violence that manifests as discrimination. Hate crime victims represent the overlap between the subjects of these movements, and the anti-hate-crime movement represents the movement devoted to bringing attention to the existence and consequences of hate crime.

However, the modern civil rights movement, the gay and lesbian movement, and the women's movement do not completely overlap with the crime victim movement. Maroney (1998, 578) has described the anti-hate-crime movement as a social movement made up of strange bedfellows:

The victim's rights and civil rights movements would have little common ground from which an anti-hate movement could emerge. The victim's rights movement was in many respects a reaction against civil rights activity.[3] Accordingly, hate crime victims and their communities—a core constituency of civil rights movements—never have been a focus of the crime victim movement. That an anti-hate-crime movement did emerge from such seemingly opposing forces is a testament to the unintended consequences that often flow from social movements. Each movement had impressed its distinct story on the culture, preparing that culture to understand a combined narrative of criminal victimization motivated by bias. The civil and victim's rights movements created the cultural conditions under which hate crime could be named as a specific form of victimization.

Thus, the naming of hate-motivated behavior or expression as a particular type of civil-rights-related crime begins with previously established new social movements but does not end with those movements. The infrastructure put into place by these movements, coupled with the flexibility of rights discourse (Grattet 1998; McCann 1991), facilitated the development of a social movement sector now known as the anti-hate-crime movement. The organizations at the core of the anti-hate-crime movement do the work of making an issue out of hate- or bias-motivated violence directed toward minorities.

The Anti-Hate-Crime Movement Sector

Beginning in the late 1960s and continuing into the present era, a plethora of organizations have come to constitute the anti-hate-crime movement in the United States. Emerging at the national, regional, state, and local levels, these organizations have played a key role in documenting instances of violence that target minority members of the community, identifying and publicizing harm associated with bias-motivated violence, submitting proposals for reform, calling on the law to intervene on behalf of select injured constituencies, and providing social services to victims of bias-motivated violence. In large part because of their efforts, attention to hate crime served as both a catalyst and the central focus of rights movements. As a result, "the image of the victimized individual and the correspondingly victimized community was well established as a symbol of the consequences of intolerance and bigotry" (Maroney 1998, 571).

The larger, more established, and influential antiviolence organizations compose the core of the modern anti-hate-crime movement. These organizations operate to monitor and publicize the evolving contours and consequences of bias violence connected to racism, nationalism, anti-Semitism, sexism, and heterosexism. At the same time, they promote the interests of select constituencies by demanding changes in public policy, including the law. Accordingly, the description that follows is not meant to provide a comprehensive overview;[4]

rather, it is presented to illustrate the way in which various organizations emerged and responded to what they perceived to be an escalation of racial, ethnic, religious, and other forms of intergroup conflict and how, in so doing, they have brought newfound attention to age-old conduct, redefining it in the process.

The most established antiviolence organization in the United States, the Anti-Defamation League of B'nai B'rith (ADL) was founded in 1913 to combat the racial discrimination against Jewish people.[5] The ADL is concerned with many types of bias crimes, but its primary focus is anti-Semitic violence. Since 1979 the ADL has tracked anti-Semitic violence and published an annual "Audit of Anti-Semitic Incidents." Based on data reported to ADL regional offices around the nation, these reports describe various "acts of harassment, threat and assault against individuals, their property and their institutions" (ADL 1990, 1). These reports reveal changes in anti-Semitic vandalism and violence from year to year (see figure 2.3). In addition to the audit, the ADL produces and disseminates other publications on bias-motivated violence in an effort to bring attention and redress to reported anti-Semitic violence.

In response to the findings documented in these publications, the ADL's counteraction program has sought to increase media exposure, establish and sustain education programs, demand more effective law enforcement, and actively support new legislation designed to combat a reported rise in anti-Semitic and racist violence. In 1981 the ADL's Legal Affairs Department drafted a model hate crimes bill to be introduced in state legislatures.[6] Like other lesser known organizations, including many civil rights groups, the ADL's work has underscored the victim status of those harmed by violence because of their race or religion. In recent times the ADL has broadened its concerns to include more types of hate-motivated conduct—most notably, adding gender to its model hate crimes legislation in 1996, based on its conclusion that gender-based crimes could not be easily distinguished from other forms of hate-motivated violence.[7]

Like the ADL, the National Institute Against Prejudice & Violence (NIAPV), centered in Baltimore, Maryland, has broadly focused on what is now termed "ethnoviolence." In an article by the NIAPV's Howard J. Ehrlich (1989, 71), ethnoviolence is defined as "an act in which the 'other' is an ethnic group, an ethnic member, or a person perceived to be an ethnic group representative or identified with an ethnic group. Ethnoviolence is a subset of group violence." Comprising acts that are motivated by racial, religious, or ethnic prejudice, ethnoviolence includes physical assaults, verbal harassment, attacks on people's homes, and various forms of vandalism. The NIAPV acts

Figure 2.3   Incidence of Anti-Semitic Violence, National Totals, from 1980 to 1998

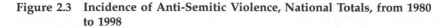

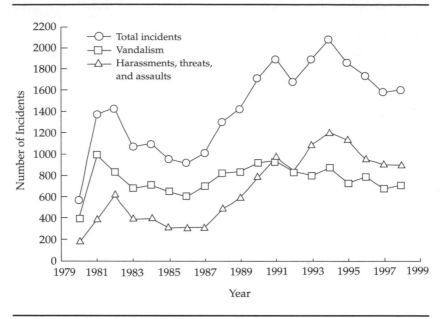

Source: Anti-Defamation League, 1999.

as a clearinghouse of information on reported incidents of intergroup conflict, studies the effects of victimization, tracks the quantity and quality of news media activity, publishes reports and educational materials, works with lawmakers on appropriate state and federal legislative remedies, and provides training, education, and counseling within communities.

Since its founding in 1984, the NIAPV has published a series of documents, including *Striking Back at Bigotry: Remedies Under Federal and State Law for Violence Motivated by Racial, Religious, or Ethnic Prejudice* (NIAPV 1991). This document inventories the criminal and civil remedies available under federal and state law for violence motivated by racial, religious, and ethnic hatred. It is intended primarily to inform victims of these crimes and their attorneys of the various avenues of legal recourse against offenders of bias crime. The goal is to enable attorneys and their clients to arrive at the most effective combination of legal remedies to fully vindicate the victims' rights. As a NIAPV membership letter declares, "Central to all of our work is our own motivation to help people break free of the norms of denial and the culture of silence that has characterized intergroup relations in the U.S. through[out] its history." For this reason, the NIAPV is recognizable as a central player in the anti-hate-crime movement.

Founded in 1979, the Center for Democratic Renewal (CDR), formerly known as the National Anti-Klan Network, is an Atlanta-based antiracist organization with offices in Kansas City and Seattle. According to their bimonthly newsletter, the *Monitor* ("Hate Crimes Laws" 1991, 23), the CDR is "leading the fight against bigoted violence and hate group activity in America today. The CDR is a multiracial, multi-ethnic, interfaith, non-profit organization dedicated to promoting constructive, non-violent responses to hate violence and the white supremacist movement." Like the ADL and the NIAPV, the CDR acts as a national clearinghouse for efforts to counter hate group activity and bigoted violence through public education, community response, leadership training, and research. The CDR has been primarily concerned with monitoring and making public racist and "far right" violence, especially that which is associated with the Ku Klux Klan (KKK) and related organizations. To this end, for example, the CDR publishes books and periodicals that bring attention to the issue of discriminatory violence, including *They Don't All Wear Sheets: A Chronology of Racist and Far Right Violence, Peddling Racist Violence for a New Generation: A Profile of Tom Metzger and the White Aryan Resistance,* and *Ballot Box Bigotry: David Duke and the Populist Party.*

In addition to tracking the organization and activities of organizations associated with the far right, the CDR collects data on bias-motivated violence and seeks legal and extralegal redress in light of their discoveries. Although the CDR's original focus was on racist violence, over the years it has developed a much broader agenda. Like the ADL and the NIAPV, the CDR has increasingly devoted attention to violence against women as well as gays and lesbians. One of their recent publications, *When Hate Groups Come to Town: A Handbook of Effective Community Responses* (CDR 1992), for example, contains sections on anti-gay bias and homophobic violence, violence against women, and hate violence.

Similar to the CDR, the Southern Poverty Law Center (SPLC) is a nonprofit foundation supported by private donations. Located in Montgomery, Alabama, the SPLC's Klanwatch Project was established in 1980 to address racist violence through litigation, education, and monitoring. Since then, the Klanwatch Project has operated as a private intelligence agency, collecting data on the KKK, white supremacist organizations, and other hate groups (see figure 2.4). It also maintains one of the most complete lists of leaders in the white supremacist movement in the United States, compiles perpetration

Figure 2.4   Distribution of Hate Groups in the United States, 1999

Christian Identity
Neo-Nazi
Ku Klux Klan
Racist Skinheads

Source: Southern Poverty Law Center, 1999.

and victimization data based on police and news sources, and pursues legal redress by bringing lawsuits against such organizations as the Klan's "Invisible Empire" in Alabama, Texas, North Carolina, and Georgia and the White Aryan Resistance in Oregon.

Although the Klanwatch Project primarily focuses on racist violence (the traditional targets of Klan violence), it nonetheless acknowledges the importance of devoting attention to antigay and antilesbian violence, as well. Indeed, the Klanwatch Project uses the term "hate violence" to refer to "crimes committed by whites against minorities, Jews, and gays where there is evidence of bias motivation" ("Hate Violence and White Supremacy" 1989, 28).

The National Gay and Lesbian Task Force (NGLTF) was founded in Washington, D.C., in 1973. As a civil rights organization representing the interests of gays and lesbians in the United States, the NGLTF houses various projects, including a privacy and civil rights project, a lesbian and gay families project, a campus organizing project, and an antiviolence project (Vaid 1995). The Anti-Violence Project was established in 1982 to contribute to the overall goals of the NGLTF, including the specific civil rights and social change goals articulated by other divisions within the organization. In particular, the project devotes attention to promoting an appropriate official response to antigay violence, improving the treatment of lesbians and gay men by the criminal justice system, and assisting local communities in organizing against prejudice and violence. By using a combination of incident reports and survey research, the NGLTF's Anti-Violence Project has been collecting data since 1984. Presented as both individual narratives and quantitative summaries, these data are reported in publications like *Anti-Gay/Lesbian Violence, Victimization, and Defamation in 1987* and *Anti-Gay/Lesbian Violence, Victimization, and Defamation in 1990* (NGLTF 1987, 1991).

Shortly after the publication of these reports, the NGLTF began to rely upon the National Coalition of Anti-Violence Projects, an umbrella organization comprising many antiviolence projects, to produce and disseminate annual reports on violence directed at gays, lesbians, bisexuals, and transgender people. These reports summarize known incidents of heterosexist violence. For example, a recent report, "Anti-Lesbian, Gay, Bisexual, and Transgender Violence in 1998," released in 1999, summarizes known incidents of violence that occurred throughout 1998 against lesbian, gay, bisexual, or transgender individuals in sixteen cities, states, and regions across the United States. This report highlights the following trends: the number of actual or suspected antigay murders in the reporting cities, states, and regions increased 136 percent; the number of serious assaults (those in which the victims sustained major injuries) grew 12 percent, despite an 11 percent decline in the number of assaults generally; and the number of weapons reportedly used in conjunction with assaults against gay, lesbian, bisexual, and transgendered individuals grew at an unprecedented rate, with the use of firearms increasing 71 percent, the use of bats, clubs, and blunt objects increasing 46 percent, the use of vehicles increasing 150 percent, the use of ropes and restraints increasing 133 percent, and the use of knives and sharp objects increasing 13 percent. In addition, the report documented a 242 percent increase in the number of incidents committed by hate groups; a 103 percent increase in the number of incidents occurring at or near lesbian, gay, bisexual, or transgender community public events, such as parades and rallies; and a deterioration in police response to antigay and antilesbian violence, which was indicated by a 155 percent increase in reported incidents of verbal harassment and abuse of victims by police officers and a 866 percent increase in reports of physical abuse by police officers (National Coalition of Anti-Violence Projects 1999).

In addition to sustaining data collection efforts that result in publications such as these, the NGLTF also continues to pursue legal and extralegal redress for violence directed at gays and lesbians. Indeed, by 1990, "within lesbian and gay communities across the United

States there was an unprecedented level of organizing against violence" (NGLTF 1991, 22). Literally hundreds of gay and lesbian resource and community centers and antiviolence projects have emerged to respond to the multitude of threats that violence poses to gays and lesbians.[8] The former director of the NGLTF, Urvashi Vaid, acknowledged the successful work of these organizations when she proclaimed that

> the gay and lesbian anti-violence movement has made stunning advances in a very short period. From 1982 to today, the movement has won near universal condemnation of gay-bashing from governmental, religious, and civil bodies. We got gay bashing classified as a hate crime motivated by prejudice as hate, secured passage of bias-penalty bills, produced studies into the causes and solutions to homophobic violence, and secured funding for a range of service programs. (Vaid 1995, 207–8)

These advances were supported by the other organizations in the anti-hate crime sector.

Finally, the work of the National Victim Center must be acknowledged. According to Weed (1995, 57), "The founding of NOVA [National Organization of Victim Assistance] in 1975 is an outgrowth of a perceived need by people working within crime victim programs who attended two conferences sponsored by the Department of Justice's Law Enforcement Assistance Agency (LEAA)." The need was twofold: to provide coordination and communication between smaller regional and local programs without threatening their autonomy, and to provide leadership at the national level, especially in terms of pursuing agreed-upon legislation. NOVA and the National Victim Center (NVC) "helped provide a larger focus to the efforts of thousands of grassroots crime victims' groups that address the specialized concerns of particular crime victims" (ibidem). To accomplish this, the National Center for Victims (NCV)[9] serves as a national resource for more than eight thousand organizations and many thousands of individuals each year (National Victim Center 1993).

As a nonprofit organization, the NCV engages in a number of activities designed to reduce the consequences of crime on victims. Most notably, it compiles statistics and produces a national report, which is then made available to libraries, governmental agencies, and political organizations across the United States; publishes and distributes the journal *Victimology*; engages in legal advocacy at the state and national level to protect and restore the rights of crime victims; raises funds to support programs and efforts across the country; and sponsors educational efforts designed to make citizens, law enforcement officials, crime victims, and offenders aware of the rights of victims. As one *Annual Report* of the National Victim Center (1993, 1) summarizes, "Our goal is to raise the consciousness of the entire nation with a powerful message: Victims are not to blame for the crimes committed against them. They deserve rights in the criminal justice system and services and programs to aid in their painful recovery." This message is embraced and promoted by all the organizations and social movements described in this chapter. It is also, of course, a central message of the anti-hate-crime movement in the United States.

Movement Strategies: Discovering and Publicizing an "Epidemic" of Violence

The organizations and attendant activities detailed in this chapter reveal the crucial role social movements play in establishing a policy domain. In this case, the anti-hate-crime movement sector has, almost single-handedly, "discovered" and publicized the existence and extent of hate-motivated violence in the United States. Although the movements described earlier in this chapter differ in various ways, a composite view of the problem can be gleaned. From the standpoint of these movements, a shocking lack of physical safety provided to minorities was at the heart of the problem. Hate violence was depicted as widespread and invisible, an almost normal feature of a society built around and sustaining inequalities based on race, religion, ancestry, national origin, gender, sexual orientation, and disability. Individual victims of hate crime were faultless, as all victims are, and were attacked because they were understood to be members of minority or subordinate groups in societies (Jews, blacks, immigrants, and later gays and lesbians, women, and persons with disabilities). Hateful behavior terrorizes particular groups of persons; in so doing, it communicates a message of intolerance that plays itself out as discrimination.

The organizations that make up the anti-hate-crime movement in the United States have brought newfound attention to hate-motivated violence as a form of discrimination by gathering, compiling, and publicizing statistical information. Jacobs and Potter (1998) have detailed the way in which advocacy groups that collect and report hate crime statistics use those statistics to further their claims, especially the claim that violence motivated by bigotry is growing at an alarming rate. Moreover, "by calling attention to the criminal victimization of their members, these advocates may hope to mobilize law enforcement resources on behalf of their members, and, more broadly, to make out a moral and political claim in furtherance of their groups' agenda and social and political goals" (Jacobs and Henry 1996, 368).

The anti-hate-crime movement's efforts to document the incidence and prevalence of hate-motivated violence in the United States are generally undertaken to establish the existence of such violence—to direct newfound attention to old conduct—and to challenge official reports produced by law enforcement agencies and legislative bodies. To mount this challenge, statistical portraits generated by the anti-hate-crime movement are distributed to law enforcement agencies, government officials, members of minority communities, the general population, and, as we discuss in the next chapter, lawmakers. This information highlights both undetected and unreported hate-motivated violence and hateful expressions. The result is a well-documented and well-publicized rise in violence motivated by bias.

More to the point, the anti-hate-crime movement has played a key role in narrating an epidemic of violence born of bigotry (Jacobs and Potter 1998; Jenness and Broad 1997). Although from a social science point of view it remains debatable whether violence directed toward minorities is on the rise, it nonetheless is now common to hear that hate crimes have reached "epidemic" proportions. For example, Steven Spielberg, the movie producer, told the U.S. Senate Judiciary Committee that "hate crimes are an epidemic curable only through education"; Leo McCarthy, lieutenant governor of California, has declared that "there is an epidemic of hate crimes and hate violence rising in California"; Mississippi state senator Bill Minor warned that "this is the type of crime that easily spreads like an epidemic"; and a journalist from the *San Francisco Chronicle* declared that "hate-motivated violence is spreading across the United States in epidemic proportions" (cited in Jacobs and Henry 1996, 367–68). As others have pointed out, this rise is attributable, at least in part, to revised documentation methods and increased reporting by the victims (Herek and Berrill 1990, 1992). This, in turn, is attributable to the political work of anti-hate crime organizations (Jacobs and Potter 1998; Jenness and Broad 1997).

The discovery and documentation of newly recognized forms of violence, coupled with reports of a rise in all or select forms of violence, has provided the social problem of hate crime with empirical credibility.[10] Claims are considered empirically credible "to the extent that there are events and occurrences that can be pointed to as documentary evidence" (Snow and Benford 1992, 140). As William Gamson (1992a, 69) notes, however, the term "contains a subtle hedge": empirical credibility arises not because the claims have been proved true but because they have the appearance of truth. In the case of hate crime, some challenge the validity of reports that indicate an increase in hate-motivated conduct in the United States. For example, the editor of *Bias Crime: American Law Enforcement and Legal Responses* cites

New York City data to suggest that "bias incidents were down some 14 percent in 1991" (Kelly 1993, 6). More recently, Jacobs and Potter (1998, 64) have offered a critical assessment of the data on bias-motivated violence. "In contemporary American society," they conclude, "there is less prejudice-motivated violence against minority groups than in many earlier periods of American history. Clearly, violence motivated by racism, xenophobia, anti-Semitism, and other biases is not new and is not 'on the rise.' Professor Abramovsky asserts that 'no one is seriously questioning the severity of the problem.' We are." Despite research that questions the prevalence of the phenomenon, the portrayal of the hate crime problem as an "epidemic" has been deemed empirically credible and is generally assumed to indicate the need for legislators to draft new policies.

Lending empirical credibility to the problem of hate-motivated violence is a first step in issue creation and a necessary precursor to making demands on the larger political system. Once what Peter Ibarra and John Kitsuse (1993) refer to as a "condition category"—in this case, hate crime—is discovered, documented, and rendered "epidemic" in proportion, the stage is set for policy makers to craft a treatment. Although it is not our objective to evaluate the legitimacy of the statistical claims emanating from the anti-hate crime sector, we recognize that calling a phenomenon "epidemic" implies the existence of a crisis. As Jacobs and Jessica Henry (1996, 367) note, it is "a calamity that demands immediate political and social action." This is the key outcome of collective action: it represents a second phase of social movement activity in which the newly constructed social problem must be met with a policy solution. Throughout the 1980s and continuing into the 1990s, legislation that criminalizes violence and intimidation motivated by bigotry and targeting minority constituencies has been introduced, adopted, institutionalized, and invoked for both symbolic and prosecutorial purposes at both the federal and state levels. To understand this phase in the creation of the policy domain under study requires an investigation of how social movement work gets translated into public policy, especially law. How this occurs is especially interesting when legal mobilization is informed by the politics of new social movements (Jacobs and Potter 1998; Jenness and Broad 1994, 1997; Merry 1995) and centered around "justice and the politics of difference" (Young 1990). This is certainly the case with the anti-hate-crime movement's campaign to bring bigotry into the legal realm, which is the focus of the next chapter.

Chapter 3

Social Movement Mobilization, Categorization Processes, and Meaning Making in Federal Hate Crime Law

I F, AS Terry Maroney (1998, 579) suggests, the "first task of the anti-hate-crime movement was to create a societal perception that hate crime was a specific evil requiring a specific response," the second task was to seek legal redress. Recognizing the movement's orientation toward legal redress, Jacobs and Potter (1998, 63) argue that "advocacy groups for gays and lesbians, Jews, blacks, women, Asian Americans, and disabled persons have all claimed that recent unprecedented violence against their members requires special hate crimes legislation. These groups have sought to call attention to their members' victimization, subordinate status, and need for special governmental assistance." Special governmental assistance has taken many forms, most notably, the enactment of hate crime law at both the state and federal levels. Thus, since early on, hate-motivated violence has been conceived as a social problem requiring a legal response, especially by those at the forefront of activism around the issue.

In response to the social movement activity described in the previous chapter, U.S. state and federal lawmakers began to devote attention and resources to the development of hate crime policies. In 1988, Representative John Conyers Jr. proclaimed that "hate crimes motivated by intolerance need to be distinguished from other crimes motivated by other factors" (Congress 1988c, 8). Which types of distinctions would be written into law, however, was an open-ended question. The anti-hate-crime movement highlighted some types of victims, but as the hate crime concept entered the legislative arena, its limits remained unclear. Who else should be included? As Laurence Tribe, professor of constitutional law at Harvard University, told federal lawmakers, "Nothing in the U.S. Constitution prevents the Government from penalizing with added severity those crimes directed against people or their property because of their race, color, religion, national origin, ethnicity, gender or sexual orientation, and nothing in the Constitution requires that this list be infinitely expanded" (Congress 1992c, 7).

If, as Tribe suggests, legislators had considerable latitude, why did they select some categories and not others? This was the key question in the congressional proceedings about hate crime, and it is the core issue we address in this chapter. How was the anti-hate-crime movement's constructions of hate crime translated into law as it entered the legislative arena and was subjected to the work of lawmakers? With some exceptions, the literature on legislative reform and policy making is relatively silent regarding how proposals for legal reform are introduced, managed, and accepted or rejected in legislative arenas as legislative debates occur, constituency interests are negotiated, and political wills are enacted.[1] In his review of the literature on policy domains, for example, Burstein (1991) concludes that although there is a sizable literature on how policy proposals develop over time, little systematic research has been conducted about how policy makers sift through alternative proposals (see also Kingdon 1995). We need to know more about how law is made in legislative bodies, the institutional arena most proximate to lawmaking, as key players— most notably, social movement representatives and lawmakers—negotiate about the parameters of particular policies (Burstein 1991, 327).

We need to know how hate crime law was constructed in discrete moments and over time such that some forms of discriminatory violence became identified as hate crime. We need to know how social movement communities organized around the pursuit of legal reform interacted with policy makers' interpretive and discursive practices to give meaning to hate crime statutes as they developed and stabilized over time. After all, it is hate crime law that defines the parameters of the hate crime problem in the United States.

Federal Hate Crime Law

Throughout the 1980s and the 1990s most state legislatures passed at least one piece of legislation designed to deal with violence born of bigotry. Following the states' lead, the U.S. Congress passed three laws specifically designed to address bias-motivated violence.[2]

In 1990, President George Bush signed into law the Hate Crimes Statistics Act (HCSA), which requires the U.S. attorney general to collect statistical data on hate crime. This was the first federal law to use the term "hate crime," defining it as a complex of "crimes that manifest evidence of prejudice based on race, religion, sexual orientation, or ethnicity, including where appropriate the crimes of murder; nonnegligent manslaughter; forcible rape; aggravated assault; simple assault; intimidation; arson; and destruction, damage or vandalism of property" (Public Law 101-275). The HCSA does not stipulate new penalties for bias-motivated crimes, nor does it provide legal recourse for victims of bias-motivated crime. It merely requires the collection of empirical data necessary to develop effective policy, which has been done since 1991 (table 3.1 provides a summary of some of these data). Those supporting the statute argue that involving police in identifying and counting hate crimes could help law enforcement officials measure trends, fashion effective responses, design prevention strategies, and develop sensitivity to the particular needs of victims of hate crimes.

In 1994, the Congress passed the Violence Against Women Act (Public Law 103-322).[3] Although declared unconstitutional in 1999, Title III of the act specifies that "all persons within the United States shall have the right to be free from crimes of violence motivated by gender" (*Brzonkala v. Morrison* 529 U.S. 598; 120 S. Ct. 1740, 2000). To ensure protection of this right, the act creates a new civil remedy for victims of crimes of violence motivated by gender, defining the term hate crime as "a crime of violence committed because of gender or on the basis of gender, and due, at least in part, to animus based on the victim's gender" (ibidem). Although this law creates civil remedies, it is predicated upon and promotes the inclusion of gender in the concept of a hate crime.

Also in 1994, Congress passed the Hate Crimes Sentencing Enhancement Act (HCSEA), which identifies eight predicate crimes—murder; nonnegligent manslaughter; forcible rape; aggravated assault; simple assault; intimidation; arson; and destruction, damage, or vandalism of property—for which judges are allowed to impose penalties of "not less than three offense levels [above the penalty for the parallel crime] for offenses that a finder of fact at trial determines beyond a reasonable doubt are hate crimes" (Public Law 103-322). For the purposes of this law, hate crime is defined as criminal conduct wherein "the defendant intentionally selected any victim or property as the object of the offense because of the actual or perceived race, color, religion, national origin, ethnicity, gender, disability, or sexual orientation of any person" (Public Law 103-322). Although broad in form, this law is somewhat narrow in its coverage: it addresses only those hate crimes that take place on federal lands and properties. Despite this limitation, the law prompted a third round of discussions on the meaning of hate crime in federal criminal law.

These federal laws define hate crime in strikingly different ways. Despite similarities—each involves a policy action, focuses on bias, and articulates status provisions to be considered relevant—they nonetheless vary in terms of the kind of conduct at issue, the type of people recognized, and the desired policy action. The question of which categories would be protected was at the center of discussions, both in the social movement and policy arenas, and was nowhere more hotly debated than in congressional hearings on hate crime.

Hearings on Federal Hate Crime Laws

The emergence and institutionalization of federal hate crime law provides an opportunity to examine empirically the dynamics that underlie policy making in general as well as hate crime lawmaking more specifically. The official records of the Congress provide the empirical basis for investigating how this was accomplished. We examined transcripts of the hearings, reports, debates, and committee prints addressing the three bills that ultimately became law: the Hate Crimes Statistics Act, the Violence Against Women Act, and the Hate Crimes Sentencing Enhancement Act.[4] Table 3.2 provides a summary of these documents, which reflect the work of six Congresses grappling with three bills designed to recognize and address hate-motivated violence. The official record of this lawmaking consists of forty-three documents (twenty-two congressional hearings, twelve congressional reports, seven congressional debates, and two committee prints) and totals 4,140 pages.

Combined, these materials reveal the legislative workings of lawmakers and other government officials, activists, victims, representatives from social movement and watchdog organizations, and survivors of bias-motivated crime. For the purposes of our study, these documents represent "critical discourse moments" (Gamson 1992b, 26; Chilton 1987). Critical discourse moments are symbolically revealing discrete historical events that stimulate discourse on a particular topic, make an issue especially visible, and facilitate the specific definition of a social problem.[5] James Abourezk, chair of the Arab American Anti-Discrimination Committee in Washington, D.C., underscored the significance of congressional attention to the problem during hearings on ethnically motivated violence against Arab Americans. "Until today," Abourezk observed, ". . . no . . . official body or . . .

Table 3.1 Bias-Motivated Offenses Reported by the Uniform Crime Reports, 1991 to 1998

Type of Bias-Motivation	1991	1992	1993	1994	1995	1996	1997	1998
Race	2,963	5,050	5,085	4,387	6,170	6,767	5,898	5,360
Anti-white	888	1,664	1,600	1,253	1,511	1,384	1,267	989
Anti-black	1,689	2,884	2,985	2,668	3,805	4,469	3,838	3,573
Anti-Native American or Alaskan native	11	31	36	26	59	69	44	66
Anti-Asian or Pacific Islander	287	275	274	267	484	527	437	359
Anti-multiracial group	88	198	190	173	311	318	312	373
Ethnicity or national origin	450	841	701	745	1,022	1,163	1,083	919
Anti-Hispanic	242	498	414	407	680	710	636	595
Anti-other ethnicity or nationality	208	343	287	338	342	453	447	324
Religion	917	1,240	1,245	1,232	1,414	1,500	1,483	1,475
Anti-Jewish	792	1,084	1,104	1,080	1,145	1,182	1,159	1,145
Anti-Catholic	23	18	31	17	35	37	32	62
Anti-Protestant	26	29	25	30	47	80	59	61
Anti-Islamic	10	17	13	16	39	33	31	22
Anti-other religious group	5	77	58	72	122	139	173	138

Anti-multireligious group	11	14	11	14	25	27	26	45
Anti-atheist, agnostic, and so on	4	1	3	3	1	2	3	2
Sexual orientation	425	944	938	780	1,266	1,256	1,375	1,439
Anti-male homosexual	—	—	665	561	915	927	912	972
Anti-female homosexual	—	—	113	119	189	185	229	265
Anti-homosexual	421	928	111	77	125	94	210	170
Anti-heterosexual	3	13	28	16	19	38	14	13
Anti-bisexual	1	3	1	7	18	12	10	19
Disability	—	—	—	—	—	—	12	27
Anti-physical	—	—	—	—	—	—	9	14
Anti-mental	—	—	—	—	—	—	3	13
Multiple bias	—	—	—	—	23	20	10	15
Total	4,755	8,075	7,969	7,144	9,895	10,706	9,861	9,235
Number of participating agencies	2,771	6,181	6,551	7,356	9,584	11,354	11,211	10,461
Number of states, including District of Columbia	32	42	47	44	46	50	49	46
Percentage of U.S. population represented	—	51	58	58	75	84	87	79

Source: U.S. Department of Justice, 1992 to 1999.

group of opinion leaders . . . have raised their voice against this kind of thing; . . . what you have done is more important than you realize" (Congress 1986b, 34). Representative Conyers agreed with Abourezk's observation: "These hearings have been seminal, extraordinarily important, they have been far more revealing than I had hoped. Our first task is to communicate the thrust of these hearings to as many people as possible" (Congress 1986b, 157).

The significance of these hearings is best revealed through a consideration of how the substantive character of hate crime was defined and institutionalized in federal law. From the beginning, federal legislators have generally agreed that the conduct of hate crime can range from threats to vandalism to arson to murder. In sharp contrast, however, there has been little agreement on which "target groups" (Soule and Earl 1999) should be protected by hate crime legislation, and the issue was still unresolved by the time federal legislators turned their attention to the issue of legal remedies to hate-motivated violence.

The Establishment of Race, Religion, and Ethnicity as Core Status Provisions

Even before the first congressional hearings on hate crime in 1985, many rights organizations in the United States had already mobilized around bias-motivated violence. Having achieved some measure of success at the state level, they now turned their attention to federal law. Although the term "hate crime" was commonly used to denote a range of bias-motivated behaviors, the term was more narrowly defined than it is today, its application restricted to criminal acts directed at a victim's race, religion, or ethnicity.

This conceptual restriction reflected the dominant constructions of social movement actors in the mid-1980s. The issue of hate crime had been brought to national attention primarily through the efforts of watchdog agencies focused on racial and religious discrimination, most notably, the Anti-Defamation League of B'nai B'rith (ADL). An innovator in the collection, documentation, and publication of incidents of hate-motivated violence, the ADL increasingly became a central player in national efforts to enhance the monitoring of bias crimes and the dissemination of hate crime data. The definition of the problem, its extent, and whether it was worsening or improving were largely a result of their efforts.

The ADL's data collection work did not go unnoticed in federal hearings on hate crime. Senator Paul Simon (D-Ill.) acknowledged that "the group that has kept the best statistics in this whole field is

(Text continues on p. 53.)

Table 3.2 Federal Legislation Regarding Hate Crime, from 1985 to 1997 (Excluding Pending Legislation)

Bill or Law	Title	Document	Legislative Body or Audience	Congress	Date	Number of Pages
HCSA	Hate Crimes Statistics Act	Hearing	Subcommittee on Criminal Justice, House Judiciary Committee	99th	3/21/85	148
HCSA	Crimes Against Religious Practices and Property	Hearing	Subcommittee on Criminal Justice, House Judiciary Committee	99th	5/16/85	52
HCSA	Crimes Against Religious Practices and Property	Hearing	Subcommittee on Criminal Justice, House Judiciary Committee	99th	6/19/85	39
HCSA	Hate Crimes Statistics Act	Report	Committee on the Judiciary	99th	7/18/85	4
HCSA	Hate Crimes Statistics Act	Debate	*Congressional Record*	99th	7/22/85	7
HCSA	Ethnically Motivated Violence Against Arab-Americans	Hearing	Subcommittee on Criminal Justice, House Judiciary Committee	99th	7/16/86	205
HCSA	Anti-Gay Violence	Hearing	Subcommittee on Criminal Justice, House Judiciary Committee	99th	10/9/86	223
HCSA	Anti-Asian Violence	Hearing	Subcommittee on Civil and Constitutional Rights, House Judiciary Committee	100th	11/10/87	459
HCSA	Hate Crimes Statistics Act	Report	Committee on the Judiciary	100th	4/20/88	13

(Table continues on p. 50.)

Table 3.2 *Continued*

Bill or Law	Title	Document	Legislative Body or Audience	Congress	Date	Number of Pages
HCSA	Racially Motivated Violence	Hearing	Subcommittee on Criminal Justice, House Judiciary Committee	100th	5/11/88	111
HCSA	Hate Crimes Statistics Act	Debate	*Congressional Record*	100th	5/18/88	19
HCSA	Hate Crimes Statistics Act	Hearing	Subcommittee on the Constitution, House Judiciary Committee	100th	6/21/88	287
HCSA	Racially Motivated Violence	Hearing	Subcommittee on Criminal Justice, House Judiciary Committee	100th	7/12/88	73
HCSA	Hate Crimes Statistics Act	Report	Committee on the Judiciary	100th	9/15/88	8
HCSA	Hate Crimes Statistics Act	Report	Committee on the Judiciary	101st	5/1/89	13
HCSA	Hate Crimes Statistics Act	Report	Committee on the Judiciary	101st	6/23/89	10
HCSA	Hate Crimes Statistics Act	Debate	*Congressional Record*	101st	6/27/89	11
HCSA	Hate Crimes Statistics Act	Debate	*Congressional Record*	101st	2/8/90	26
HCSA	Hate Crimes Statistics Act	Debate	*Congressional Record*	101st	4/3/90	4
HCSA	Hate Crimes Statistics Act	Debate	*Congressional Record*	101st	4/4/90	1
VAWA	Women and Violence	Hearing	Committee on the Judiciary	101st	6/20/90	112
VAWA	Women and Violence	Hearing	Committee on the Judiciary	101st	8/29/90	82
VAWA	Violence Against Women Act	Report	Committee on the Judiciary	101st	10/19/90	88
VAWA	Women and Violence	Hearing	Committee on the Judiciary	101st	12/11/90	223

	Title	Type	Committee	Congress	Date	Page
VAWA	Violence Against Women: The Increase of Rape in America	Print	Committee on the Judiciary	102d	3/21/91	37
VAWA	Violence Against Women: Victims of the System	Hearing	Committee on the Judiciary	102d	4/9/91	442
VAWA	Violence Against Women Act	Report	Committee on the Judiciary	102d	10/29/91	111
VAWA	Violence Against Women Act	Hearing	Subcommittee on Crime and Criminal Justice, House Judiciary Committee	102d	2/6/92	120
HCSEA	Bias Crime	Hearing	Subcommittee on Crime and Criminal Justice, House Judiciary Committee	102d	5/11/92	184
HCSEA	Hate Crimes Sentencing Enhancement Act	Hearing	Subcommittee on Crime and Criminal Justice, House Judiciary Committee	102d	7/29/92	214
HCSA	Hate Crimes Statistics Act	Hearing	Subcommittee on the Constitution, House Judiciary Committee	102d	8/5/92	139
VAWA	Violence Against Women: A Week in the Life of America	Print	Committee on the Judiciary	102d	10/1/92	38
HCSEA	Hate Crimes Sentencing Enhancement Act	Report	Committee on the Judiciary	102d	10/2/92	7
VAWA	Violent Crimes Against Women	Hearing	Committee on the Judiciary	103d	4/13/93	84
VAWA	Violence Against Women Act	Report	Committee on the Judiciary	103d	9/10/93	111
HCSEA	Hate Crimes Sentencing Enhancement Act	Report	Committee on the Judiciary	103d	9/21/93	7

(Table continues on p. 52.)

Table 3.2 *Continued*

Bill or Law	Title	Document	Legislative Body or Audience	Congress	Date	Number of Pages
VAWA	Violence Against Women: Fighting the Fear	Hearing	Committee on the Judiciary	103d	11/12/93	57
VAWA	Crimes of Violence Motivated by Gender	Hearing	Subcommittee on Constitutional and Civil Rights, House Judiciary Committee	103d	11/16/93	129
VAWA	Violence Against Women Act	Report	Committee on the Judiciary	103d	11/20/93	66
HCSA	Hate Crimes Statistics Act	Hearing	Subcommittee on the Constitution, House Judiciary Committee	103d	6/28/94	58
HCSA	Reauthorization of the Hate Crimes Statistics Act	Hearing	Committee on the Judiciary	104th	3/19/96	110
HCSA	To Reauthorize the Hate Crimes Statistics Act	Report	Committee on the Judiciary	104th	5/13/96	6
HCSA	Hate Crimes Statistics Act	Debate	*Congressional Record*	104th	6/21/96	2

Source: Authors' compilation.

the Anti-Defamation League of B'nai B'rith. They report a rising tide of antisemitic activity. It is the only solid statistical evidence we have in the Nation." (*Congressional Record* 1990a, 1072).[6] The ADL's efforts were frequently noted as pathbreaking, useful, and unique. For example, when law enforcement representatives, especially those from the Bureau of Justice Statistics, opposed the legislation on the grounds that hate crime data simply could not be collected, Senator Simon responded that "if Mr. Schwartz over here with the ADL can collect data on this kind of problem, we ought to be able to do it in the Department of Justice. I think it is an important service that is needed in the nation" (Congress 1988a, 122). Because data from the ADL was the primary source of information on hate crime, however, the concept tended to favor race and religion over other statuses, and early legislation reflected that bias. Introduced in 1985, with the support of the Coalition on Hate Crimes,[7] the Hate Crimes Statistics Act was the first piece of federal legislation to bring national attention to the problem of hate-motivated violence, and though the "race, religion, and ethnicity" restriction remained in place, the foundation was laid for later expansion. Testifying at the first federal hearings on the proposed bill, Arthur Green, the director of the Connecticut Commission on Human Rights and Opportunities, remarked,

> This bill . . . represents more than merely collecting data about incidents of racial, religious, and ethnically motivated violence. It also will constitute a statement to the general public of our country that this Congress and this administration and, indeed, the State and local governments, will not tolerate further acts of violence. (Congress 1985b, 76)

In the same hearing, Representative Norman Mineta (D-Calif.) testified that the passage of the HCSA "is important because it is a piece of legislation that will help protect Americans from the most insidious types of crimes, those that are motivated by a hatred of a person merely because of their race, their religious or their ethnic background" (Congress 1985b, 27). Shortly thereafter, in a congressional debate, Representative Biaggi argued that "the effect of hate crimes, whether directed against racial, religious, or ethnic groups—eats away at the very core of society. It is a form of poison spreading through our land. It affects people physically and psychologically" (*Congressional Record* 1985, 19844).

After hearings on "crimes against religious practices and property" in July 1985, the House Judiciary Committee submitted a report to the Committee of the Whole House that urged passage of the HCSA in order to "collect and publish statistics on crimes motivated by racial,

ethnic, and religious prejudice" (Congress 1985b, 1). Although representatives from the Federal Bureau of Investigation (FBI) raised objections to the bill on the grounds that it was unenforceable, no testimony contested the legitimacy of race, religion, and ethnicity as core
provisions in hate crime legislation. Moreover, no additional status
provisions were mentioned, much less formally introduced as amendments to the bill.[8]

Adding Sexual Orientation to the List of Status Provisions

Race, religion, and ethnicity did not remain the sole provisions in hate
crime legislation. Early on in the history of federal hate crime lawmaking, the domain of hate crime law began to expand as new target
groups were identified. Domain expansion occurs when claims-
makers offer new definitions for and thus extend the boundaries of
the phenomenon under discussion.[9] Thus, the substantive territory
covered in federal hate crime legislation—most notably, in terms of
the inclusion of new status provisions—grew as new target groups
were identified. After the Hate Crimes Statistics bill was introduced
in 1985 but before it passed the Congress in 1990, a "sexual orientation" clause was added to its list of status provisions. This addition
expanded the domain of protected groups recognized. It also gave
new meaning to the concept hate crime.

Similar to the role the ADL played in the initial hearings on hate
crime, the voice of the National Gay and Lesbian Task Force and
other gay and lesbian civil rights groups proved crucial in evoking
and sustaining the expansion of the law. Joan Weiss, executive director of the National Institute Against Prejudice and Violence, has acknowledged the importance of the NGLTF's work: "We have the
Anti-Defamation League data; we have the National Gay and Lesbian
Task Force data; we have data from a variety of sources and, in fact,
as far as we're concerned, the evidence of the existence of the problem is irrefutable" (Congress 1988c, 18).

On October 9, 1986, the Subcommittee on Criminal Justice of the
House Judiciary Committee conducted an oversight hearing on antigay violence at which the NGLTF and other gay and lesbian organizations played a central role. Kevin Berrill, the director of the NGLTF's
Anti-Violence Project, was the first to testify. His chief concern was to
"recommend official monitoring of antigay incidents and other hate
crimes" (Congress 1986a, 4). "Presently," he reported, "there is a bill,
H.R. 2455, which has passed the House and is pending in the Senate,
that would mandate the collection of statistics on hate crimes moti-

vated by racial and religious prejudice. We [the NGLTF] urge its passage and ask Congress to enact legislation that would require the collection of data on antigay crimes" (Congress 1986a, 4). Diana Christianson, the executive director of San Francisco's Community United Against Violence (CUAV), was in agreement: "I want to make several recommendations, given the severity of the problem. One is that we need to recognize antigay violence as a crime. It is as basic as that" (Congress 1986a, 8).[10] To support this recommendation, representatives from many gay- and lesbian-sponsored civil rights organizations offered testimony on the causes, manifestations, and consequences of antigay and lesbian violence, as well as the public invisibility and epidemic scope of the problem.

Throughout the testimony, frequent comparisons between violence against gays and lesbians and violence based on race, religion, or ethnicity were made. Berrill concluded his testimony with the following statement: "I would like to point out that many of the witnesses at this hearing will be wearing a pink triangle, which was the badge that identified homosexual inmates of Nazi concentration camps. Although it is an often overlooked fact, tens of thousands of gay persons were herded into the camps, and, along with Jews, gypsies, and others, were gassed and incinerated. We wear the triangle to remember them and to remind people of the terrible cost" (Congress 1986a, 5).

On behalf of the American Psychological Association, Gregory Herek, coeditor of *Hate Crimes: Confronting Violence Against Lesbians and Gay Men*, put forth a similar comparison:

All of the measures we've been talking about are very important. We can't pass a law and say to people "you can't be bigoted." But we know from a mass of social psychological research that when people change their behavior, often not too long after they start to change their attitudes. If we simply make it illegal to discriminate and illegal to be openly hostile, to be openly prejudiced against gay people in the same way we have tried to address prejudice against racial minorities, ethnic minorities, and religious minorities, then that is going to help to achieve that climate in which violence is unacceptable. (Congress 1986a, 18–19)

A report prepared by the NGLTF and included as part of the official record of the hearing on antigay violence succinctly articulated the objective of the gay and lesbian movement:

We urge Congress to pass legislation that would clarify the scope of federal statutes 18 U.S.C. 241 and 42 U.S.C. so that they clearly protect the full range of groups in this country that are subjected to acts of violence because of their status or identity. [By] failing to include provisions for gay and lesbian people in hate crime legislation, lawmakers send a message to the public and to criminals that anti-gay violence is considered less serious than crimes against other minorities. (Congress 1986a, 55–56)

Recommendations such as these, as well as the testimony offered in support of them, render violence motivated by homophobia or heterosexism equivalent to violence motivated by race, religion, or ethnicity. At the same time, similarities between racial, religious, ethnic, and sexual minorities are underscored. Indeed, in a 1988 congressional debate dominated by discussions of the appropriateness of the sexual orientation provision, Representative Howard Berman (D-Calif.) argued that "sexual orientation should not be separated from other forms of violence because the perpetrators of racial, religious, and anti-gay crimes are frequently the same" (*Congressional Record* 1988, 11397).

The importance of these claims, along with the groups that presented them, were continually referenced by lawmakers. Representative Conyers, for example, observed that "the proliferation of these groups, along with existing civil rights organizations, is very helpful in formulating remedies" (Congress 1988c, 25). Later, when questioned about the addition of the sexual orientation provision in the bill, Conyers explained why provisions are made for some groups and not for others: "We did not include octogenarians who are assaulted . . . because there was no testimony that suggested that they ought to be, as awful as the crimes visited upon them are, and the reason we did not account for policemen killed in the line of duty, although police organizations do, is that there was no request that they be separated out from the uniform crime statistics" (*Congressional Record* 1988, 11395).

Further underscoring the importance of social movement mobilization to the formation of hate crime law, Representative George Gekas (R-Pa.) immediately responded to Conyers' admission that social movements provide the crucial impetus for legal reform:

The chairman of the subcommittee . . . took pains to explain that [the inclusion of sexual orientation] was . . . the subject of a request made presumably by the gay and lesbian rights groups. . . . I would submit to you that groups of the elderly, our elderly citizens, groups who are interested in the victimization of children under the vicious child abuse cases that come to our attention daily in the newspaper, daily on the screen, in law enforcement groups like the police, who are banded together to ask for continued protection for their rights would request the same, I am sure, that the gentleman [from Michigan] would feel the same kind of compassion for these groups as he did for the gay rights or lesbian rights groups that implored the inclusion of their particular interest in this bill.

Therefore, according to Representative Gekas,

If the only criterion is to have the gay rights organization have its request acceded to by inclusion in that, I say to the Members that the gentleman should join with me now in a motion to recommit, to put this bill back into committee and allow the inclusion in this bill of statistics to be gathered on the incidence of child abuse, of attacks on the elderly, attacks on policemen, and attacks on other groups which might for one reason or another be victims of such type of crime. (*Congressional Record* 1988, 11403)

Twelve years after this statement was made, federal hearings have yet to be held on hate crimes devoted exclusively to the problem of violence directed at children, the elderly, or police officers.

Increasingly widespread acceptance of comparisons between gays and lesbians and racial, religious, and ethnic minorities followed the hearings on antigay violence as sexual orientation was routinely acknowledged as a basis for hate crime. In the first subsequent hearing—a July 10, 1987, hearing devoted to anti-Asian violence—reference is continually made to race, religion, ethnicity, and sexual orientation. In the first testimony presented, Representative Mineta noted that the hearing's focus on violence against Asian Americans "is not to minimize attacks upon other individuals who become victims of violence merely because of their heritage or beliefs. All such attacks are appalling and destructive. Worse still, acts of racial, religious, ethnic or sexual intolerance appear to be on the upswing" (Congress 1987, 3).

Six months after the hearing on violence against gays and lesbians the House Judiciary Committee submitted a report to the Committee of the Whole House that reflected an acceptance of sexual orientation as a necessary provision in the revised bill. Citing evidence presented in the previous hearings, especially the testimony and reports presented at the hearing on antigay violence, the report justified this revision in the bill, as well as the bill more generally, by noting that "only a few jurisdictions have, thus far, enacted laws mandating the collection of data on hate crimes. They also found that blacks, Hispanics, Southeast Asians, Jews, and gays and lesbians are the most frequent victims of hate crime" (Congress 1988b, 3). From this point on in the history of federal hate crime legislation, sexual orientation routinely appears in the list of provisions to be considered for inclusion in law.[11]

This revision in the language of hate crime law—the inclusion of sexual orientation in the bill—did not go uncontested; it prompted an assault on the part of conservatives in both houses of Congress (Fernandez 1991, 272). In subsequent hearings and reports, opposition to the inclusion of the sexual orientation provision was vehemently expressed. Some objected on the grounds that including sexual orientation along with race, religion, and ethnicity would make the data collection effort too broad and expensive. However, the primary objection to the inclusion of sexual orientation in the HCSA was that the federal government should not provide gays and lesbians with "special rights" and that to do so would render violence against gays and lesbians equivalent to violence against racial, ethnic, and religious minorities. The first official report submitted to the Committee of the Whole House that included a recommendation for the passage of the HCSA with the sexual orientation provision included was greeted with formally submitted dissenting views by Representatives George Gekas, Bill McCollum (R-Fla.), Howard Coble (R-N.C.), and William Dannemeyer (R-Calif.).

Legislation somewhat similar to this bill had passed the House without controversy during the 99th Congress after evidence of a rise in racial and religious hate crime was presented at hearings of the Judiciary Committee. Unfortunately, some felt that the proposed legislation had been merely a tempting vehicle with which to dramatize the claim of an increase in crime against homosexuals. Proponents had succeeded in expanding the definition of hate crimes in the 1988 bill to include crimes based upon something described as the "sexual orientation" of the victim, and opponents felt that this expansion should be reversed by amendment (Congress 1988a, 12).

Their rationale for removing sexual orientation from the Hate Crime Statistics Act was justified on multiple grounds:

> Normally a Federal nexus is essential to justify a Federal response. Absent such a nexus, one must be able at the very least to base Federal involvement in state matters on the goal of either supporting the common good or promoting State law enforcement. It must be emphasized that crime against any class of persons is obviously reprehensible. However, there is no reason to believe that crime against homosexuals transcends the ability of individual States to respond. There is no evidence of an interstate organization such as the Ku Klux Klan or the Aryan Nation focused on homosexuals. There is no mention of homosexual rights in the Constitution. In fact, there appears no convincing evidence that homosexuals are more targeted for crime than groups such as

women, the elderly, members of the police or passengers on urban mass transit. Thus, gathering at considerable cost Federal statistics on crime against homosexuals is not only unjustified in itself but also unfair vis-à-vis other affinity groups. (Congress 1988a, 12)

"It is a Federal responsibility," opponents concluded, "to ensure the equal protection of all citizens regardless of their race, religion, or ethnic origin. It is not a Federal obligation to protect citizens in their sexual orientation" (Congress 1988a, 13).

These protests continued in subsequent congressional debates. Representative Dannemeyer and Senator Jesse Helms (R-N.C.) in particular voiced dissent in congressional hearings immediately leading up to the passage of the HCSA (*Congressional Record* 1989, 1990). Senator Helms claimed that the Congress was being "hoodwinked" into passing the "flagship of the homosexual, lesbian legislative agenda" (*Congressional Record* 1989, 1076). In the second to last congressional debate on the HCSA, Helms argued:

Where do you think the idea of legislation to require the collection of statistics on so-called hate crimes originated? If this is such a wonderful crime fighting tool, it surely must have originated with a group known for its tough stance on crime, right? Wrong. This idea was dreamed up by the National Gay and Lesbian Task Force. That is a matter of record. It is clear that the militant homosexuals have been building up the numbers of complaints—not, let me emphasize, of criminal offenses or charges. They have been building up numbers of complaints to bolster their case that this type of legislation is necessary. The evidence is clear, Mr. President. Studying hate crimes against homosexuals is a crucial first step toward achieving homosexual rights and legitimacy in American society. This Senator cannot, and will not, be party to any legislation which fuels the homosexual movement. (*Congressional Record* 1989, 1076)

In response to similar protests, Representative Gene Green (D-Tex.) asserted that "the removal of sexual orientation from H.R. 3193 would reinforce the widespread perception that victimization of homosexuals is acceptable" and that "sexual orientation should not be separated from other forms of hate violence because perpetrators of racial, religious, and antigay crimes are frequently the same" (*Congressional Record* 1988, 11397).

After much heated debate, but before the vote on inclusion of sexual orientation in the HCSA, the term sexual orientation was replaced with the phrase "homosexuality or heterosexuality" as a way of appeasing dissenting opinion concerned about "special rights" for gays and lesbians. Representative John R. Miller (R-Wash.) proposed to amend the bill in such a way that "whether we agree or disagree, whether we support or do not support such antidiscrimination rights, no such rights are created by this bill. I believe with this perfecting amendment, Mr. Chairman, that we have a chance to put this issue to rest and pass what is basically a good bill" (*Congressional Record* 1988, 11404). This amendment was supported by many of those who had previously opposed the inclusion of sexual orientation in the bill. Representative Patrick Swindall (R-Ga.), for example, proclaimed,

> I opposed the bill in the full committee because . . . I thought the term "sexual orientation" is on its face an ambiguity. It could very easily, I believe, be construed to include child molestation. It could be inclusive of a great many things far beyond the scope of what I believe the evidence in the full committee focused on. For that reason, I for one support the change in the wording "sexual orientation" to the more specific language of homosexuality or heterosexuality. I further support the language that states that in no way is this to be construed as to give rights that do not currently exist; specifically, the right to complain of discrimination based on homosexuality. (*Congressional Record* 1988, 11405)

In light of comments of this sort, the committee chair, Representative Conyers, agreed to a change in wording of the bill as well as the addition of a provision to the legislation: "I think that the gentleman advances our description in 3193 immeasurably by removing sexual orientation and replacing it with homosexuality or heterosexuality and also a provision that carefully explains that H.R. 3193 does not create an additional cause of action" (*Congressional Record* 1988, 11404).[12] Conyers' estimation was correct, insofar as the HCSA became law in 1990 and the sexual orientation provision was not debated in subsequent oversight hearings on the HCSA (Congress 1992a, 1994), a hearing on reauthorization of the HCSA (Congress 1996a), and an attendant report (Congress 1996b).[13]

Although the status of gays and lesbians as victims of hate-motivated violence was contested to a greater degree than was the status of racial, ethnic, and religious minorities, ultimately it was recognized and later institutionalized as a key element of the character of hate crime law.[14] This is important to note as an illustration that domain expansion efforts are not always successful. According to Best (1990, 85), "Claimants usually begin their campaigns by typifying problems in especially compelling ways. Domain expansion extends the claims into more controversial territory, often challenging existing arrangements." In this case, discursive tactics by social movements rendered seemingly disparate and dissimilar phenomena comparable. Sexual orientation was the first social status rendered similar to race, religion, and ethnicity, and violence against gays and lesbians was thereby rendered equivalent to violence based on a victim's race, religion, or ethnicity.

The grounds for framing these categories as comparable varied but were generally articulated in one of two ways. First, it was argued that these categories reflect the usual targets of hate- or bias-motivated violence. Representative Gerry Studds (D-Mass.) observed that race, religion, ethnicity, and sexual orientation were included in the bill because "so far as we know, . . . these are the principal categories of such acts of hate. That is what the testimony before the committee revealed" (*Congressional Record* 1988, 11406). Furthermore, as Kevin Berrill, director of the NGLTF, argued, "any effort to combat hate crimes that excludes antigay violence sends a dangerous message. And the message is that antigay violence is somehow qualitatively different from, or less reprehensible than, other crimes of bias. . . . That . . . is an immoral message to be sending" (Congress 1988b, 112).

Similarly, other proponents of domain expansion argued that various status characteristics—race, religion, ethnicity, and sexual orientation—were comparable because all constitute ascribed, rather than achieved, social statuses. In an early debate Representative John W. Bryant (D-Tex.) justified his support for the passage of the HCSA by pointing to the importance of this distinction: "In the committee hearings that preceded the presentation of this bill to the House there was an adequate amount or an abundant amount of testimony . . . of prejudice and hate-motivated crimes which were motivated by prejudice toward individuals for being what they innately are" (*Congressional Record* 1988, 11405). The construction of sexuality, like race, religion, and ethnicity, as an ascribed rather than an achieved status, then, became the grounds for equivalence. In contrast, those contesting the inclusion of the sexual orientation provision did so on the grounds that "homosexual" is not equivalent to "black," "Jew," "Arab American," and the like. Most notably, homosexuality was positioned as an achieved status, an "affinity group" according to Representative Dannemeyer (1988, 12) and a "lifestyle choice" according to Senators Helms and Orrin Hatch (R-Utah) (*Congressional Record* 1990). Race, religion, and national origin, in contrast, were construed as innate and apoliticized individual characteristics, beyond an individual's realm of choice or volition.

Comparability is also achieved or contested by referencing the spirit of previously established law, especially civil rights law, and framing certain status characteristics as commensurate with it. In one of the initial hearings on hate crime a report from Victoria Toensing, the deputy assistant attorney general of the Criminal Division, recommended the passage of the HCSA, stating that "it is important to note that the conduct prohibited by this legislation is covered, in part, by existing federal law" (Congress 1985a, 50). In contrast, in one of the final congressional debates on the HCSA, Representative Dannemeyer objected to the inclusion of crimes motivated by prejudice on the basis of sexual orientation on the grounds that doing so "will adopt as a matter of public policy sexual orientation on a par with what we have traditionally brought within the protected classes of the 1964 Civil Rights Act, namely, race, religion, and ethnicity" (*Congressional Record* 1990b, 1425). From his point of view, such a move would "change the basic definition of the 1964 Civil Rights Act to include a new status that would have the dignity of being within the proscription[s] of the Act" (quoted in Fernandez 1991, 276). Representative Gekas, a fellow detractor, claimed that "we were wading into dangerous waters when we were attempting to raise the homosexuals to a constitutionally guaranteed or protected class which was not in accord with race, creed, and color, as already articulated in the Civil Rights Act of 1964" (*Congressional Record* 1989, 13542). Representative Barney Frank (D-Mass.) contested this commonly expressed justification for the exclusion of sexual orientation in the HCSA:

> I would [argue against] the suggestion that this bill somehow puts homosexuality on the same basis as religion, ethnicity, et cetera. As a factual matter, [the 1964 Civil Rights Act] never did, and does not [protect homosexuals], because under our law you may bring an antidiscrimination suit in housing or in employment or in other areas with a Federal contractor if you are discriminated against based on religion, ethnicity, or race. You may not under existing law do that on the basis of homosexuality. (*Congressional Record* 1988, 11406)

In the end, discursive moves that expand the domain of the law in ways that are fundamentally consistent with the qualities and characteristics of previously recognized legal subjects or previously legitimated and institutionalized legal terrain proved successful, in both the immediate and subsequent legislative efforts.[15]

Legitimating Gender as a Status Provision

Once race, religion, ethnicity, and sexual orientation were inscribed into hate crime law, gender followed suit, albeit by a different route. Gender was first mentioned as a legitimate provision in 1986 by Representative Mary Rose Oakar (D-Ohio) during a hearing on ethnically motivated violence against Arab Americans.[16] Oakar observed that, "regrettably, in each generation it seems that some members of our society are singled out for discrimination and harassment solely on the basis of their race, national origin, religion, or gender" (Congress 1986b, 24). Two years later, in 1988, the National Organization for Women (NOW) submitted a written report, without accompanying verbal testimony, to be included in the official record of a hearing on the HCSA. The report includes the following statement:

> While NOW fully supports S. 2000, we believe it is imperative that this nation through this Congress take the crucial step of recognizing the scope and level of hate crimes directed at women and begin dealing with the reality of this common tragic problem. Therefore H.R. 3193/ S.2000 should be amended to include women so that illegal acts that "manifest prejudice" based on gender, including terrorist threats against abortion clinics or provider, are categorized appropriately, as well as those that reveal prejudice "based on race, religion, sexual orientation, or ethnicity." Defining this statistical information in this way would send a clear message that the federal government takes the commission of misogynistic crimes seriously. (Congress 1988b, 263)

Despite these pleas, it was not until two years later that the Congress began to seriously consider gender as a status provision in hate crime legislation, and only recently did it place gender under the protection of federal hate crime law. It did so through a separate bill, the Violence Against Women Act (VAWA), which ultimately was passed into law as part of President Clinton's Violent Crime Control and Enforcement Act of 1994 (Public Law 103-322).

In the early 1990s the VAWA, itemized in table 3.4, represented an innovative idea. One reporter described it as a "novel approach" to violence against women that would have been "virtually unthinkable by mainstream politicians just a few years ago" (Roni Rabin, "Anti-Crime Bill Gives Women New Weapon Against Gender Offenses," *Detroit News,* August 5, 1994, 8A). In the first congressional hearing on legislation "to reduce the growing problem of violence against women" (Congress 1990b), Senator Joseph Biden Jr. (D-Del.), the chief sponsor of the bill, devoted his opening statements to the goals of the VAWA. "The bill has three goals," he stated. "The first goal is to try to make streets a little bit safer for women; the second goal is to make their homes a little bit safer; and the third goal is to protect their civil rights" (Congress 1990c, 2, 3, 4). To meet the first and second goals, the VAWA allocated more than $1.6 billion for education, rape crisis hotlines, training of justice personnel, victim services (especially shelters for victims of battery), and special units of police and prosecutors

Table 3.3   Summary of the Violence Against Women Act of 1994

Title I: Safe Streets for Women
  Chapter 1: Federal Penalties for Sex Crimes
  Chapter 2: Law Enforcement and Prosecution Grants to Reduce Violent Crime
  Chapter 3: Safety for Women in Public Transit and Public Parks
  Chapter 4: New Evidentiary Rules

Title II: Safe Homes for Women
  Chapter 1: National Domestic Violence Hotline
  Chapter 2: Interstate Enforcement
  Chapter 3: Arrest Policies in Domestic Violence Cases
  Chapter 4: Shelter Grants
  Chapter 5: Youth Education
  Chapter 6: Community Programs on Domestic Violence
  Chapter 7: Family Violence Prevention and Services Act Amendments
  Chapter 8: Confidentiality for Abused Persons
  Chapter 9: Data and Research
  Chapter 10: Rural Domestic Violence and Child Abuse Enforcement

Title III: Civil Rights for Women[1]

Title IV: Equal Justice for Women in the Courts
  Chapter 1: Education and Training for Judges and Court Personnel in State Courts
  Chapter 2: Education and Training for Judges and Court Personnel in Federal Courts

Title V: Violence Against Women Act Improvements

Title VI: National Stalker and Domestic Violence Reduction

Title VII: Protections for Battered Immigrant Women and Children

Source: Public Law 103–322.
1. Includes a provision for a cause of action for crimes committed because of gender.

to deal with crimes against women. To meet the third goal, Title III of the VAWA provides a civil remedy for "gender crimes":

> The Congress finds that (1) crimes motivated by the victim's gender constitute bias crimes in violation of the victim's right to be free from discrimination on the basis of gender; (2) current law provides a civil remedy for crimes committed in the workplace, but not for gender crimes committed on the street and in the home; and (3) State and Federal laws do not adequately protect against the bias element of gender

crimes, which separates these crimes from acts of random violence, nor do they adequately provide victims the opportunity to vindicate their interests. (Congress 1990a, 23)

To accomplish this, the VAWA entitles victims to compensatory and punitive damages through the federal courts for a crime of violence if it is motivated, at least in part, by animus toward the victim's gender.[17] This allowance implicitly acknowledges that at least some violence against women is motivated by gender animus and is therefore a proper subject for civil rights action.

Title III of the VAWA positions select crimes against women as equivalent to acts of violence based on race, ethnicity, national origin, religion, and sexual orientation. As the *New Republic* reported before the passage of the VAWA, "Title 3, called Civil Rights for Women, would make sexual violence a violation of federal civil rights law. 'This is the beginning, middle and end of the legislation,' says Biden. In reclassifying rape, wife-beating, and other gender-based felonies as bias crimes, the provision would write into law the view of rape as a socially embedded institution" ("Caught in the Act" 1993, 14). From the point of view of the VAWA and its supporters, rape, domestic violence, and other forms of violence against women are akin to civil rights violations and, thus, comparable to other forms of hate crime based on race, religion, ethnicity, and sexual orientation. Before the passage of the VAWA, an article in the *Texas Journal of Women and the Law* concluded that "the purpose of Title III is to put gender-motivated crimes against women on the same footing as other bias crimes" (Kelly and Long 1992, 287).

Testimony presented at multiple hearings on the VAWA (Congress 1990b, 1990c, 1991b, 1992a, 1993a, 1993b, 1993d) and reflected in the associated congressional reports (Congress 1990a, 1991a, 1993c) reveal that support for Title III was based on the logic previously used to justify the status provisions included in the HCSA. Hate crimes were viewed as acts of discrimination that victimize not only specific individuals but also the broader social groups the victims represent; this notion was easily extended to women's victimization. Supporters maintained that acts of violence against women—particularly rape and domestic violence—are not merely private injuries to unfortunate individuals but essentially hate crimes—violent sexism—that warrant federal civil rights protection. As Biden explained, "One of the things we're trying to do in the Violence Against Women Act is to make it a policy of the country that rapes are hate crimes committed against women, crimes of violence directed disproportionately at one group based on their gender. That is why it makes a civil rights violation"

(Congress 1990b, 36). Similarly, Helen Neuborne, the executive director of the NOW Legal Defense and Education Fund, observed that "just as a democratic society cannot tolerate crimes motivated by the victim's membership in a minority racial group and must pass special laws to combat such oppression, so too we must put into place effective laws to prevent and redress violent crime motivated by the victim's sex" (Congress 1990b, 57).

Thus, in the end, the rationale underlying Title III was that harassment, intimidation, and assault directed at individual women assumes a particularly offensive, dangerous, and socially disruptive character when motivated by animus based on gender—just as harassment, intimidation, and assault directed at individual people of color, members of ethnic minorities, and gays and lesbians assume a particularly disruptive character when motivated by animus based on race, ethnicity, and sexual orientation, respectively. That advocates employed this argument and that it was largely uncontested suggests that the logic of the argument had already achieved legitimacy. In other words, criminal conduct that targets an individual in order to discriminate against or express bias toward a larger community of persons was increasingly understood as a core component of a hate crime.

Interestingly, the redefinition of gender violence required to convert acts such as rape into hate crimes did not evoke much debate, especially compared with the contestation that had ensued when gender and sexual orientation were considered for inclusion in the HCSA.[18] Indeed, some hearings on the VAWA (Congress 1993b, 1993d), contain no oppositional testimony. The documents related to the VAWA manifest little evidence of contestation over the status of gender in contemporary society and with regard to violent conduct in particular. Biden acknowledged that this lack of explicit opposition might reflect the political risks involved: "I am in the unusual position here of trying to build a case against my own bill because . . . I want it to be an honest record. I think some people may be reluctant to come forward and criticize my legislation because they would view it as putting them in the position of being anti-woman" (Congress 1990b, 107).

The minimal resistance to the civil rights remedy—and the incorporation of gender into the legal definition of hate crime that it reflected—was expressed in a handful of ways. Some suggested that the inclusion of gender in hate crime legislation would open the door to demands for provisions based on age, disability, position in a labor dispute, party affiliation, and membership in the armed forces. Biden revealed these concerns early on in hearings devoted to the VAWA:

There may be some legitimate criticisms here. One of them . . . [is] the following: "If you are going to make women able to qualify under the Civil Rights Act, why not the elderly? The elderly are victims. They are preyed upon by pursesnatchers [and] . . . junkies, they are . . . in many cases . . . abused by their children. Why not do that?" And if you do that, Joe, then what you have essentially done is made criminal violation in America a civil rights violation. You have essentially taken everything out of the control of the States and you have diluted the major and primary impact and rationale for the civil rights laws in the first place. (Congress 1990b, 107)

Others argued that although it is appropriate to include gender under hate crime law, it is nonetheless unfeasible to do so. In particular, some believed that including gender would make the concept of hate crime too cumbersome, if not entirely impossible, given the pervasiveness of violent crimes against women. Still others argued that not all acts of violence against women fit the definition of a hate crime for at least one or two reasons: because women are frequently acquainted with their attackers, whereas other victims of bias-motivated violence are not, and because, statistically speaking, violence against men is as common, if not more common, than violence against women. In light of a report submitted by the U.S. Supreme Court, there were suggestions that the bill might burden the Federal courts unnecessarily. Finally, concerns about the constitutionality of Title III were expressed, discussed, and eventually dismissed (see, for example, Congress 1992b).

Objections to the incorporation of gender were not anchored in the types of concerns and expressed with the same logic that had dominated testimony and debate about sexual orientation in the HCSA hearings. For example, there was no debate about the legitimacy of gender as a status in need of protection and legal consideration, in large part because the legitimacy of gender as a line of stratification resulting in discrimination had long since gained legal and extralegal currency. Neither were objections incessantly expressed or hotly debated. In fact, the testimony and debates concerning the VAWA reveal tacit agreement about the importance of the act.[19] Finally, those objections that were posed were dispelled by advocates' willingness to consider more status provisions in future legislative efforts to address bias-motivated violence, by their demonstrations of the feasibility of collecting data on bias-motivated violence against women, through their identification of the commonalities between gender-based violence and other forms of recognized hate crime, by their creation of a constitutional justification for the civil rights remedy, and by their acceptance of a slight modification of the wording of the bill before it became law.[20]

The social movement factors were also quite different. In the campaign for the HCSA, civil rights organizations, Jewish groups, and later gay and lesbian organizations played a significant role in shaping the laws. By contrast, comparable groups were much less visible, if not entirely absent, in the VAWA hearings. The most influential group, the National Victim Center (NVC), is more a professional broad-based public interest organization than a direct channel for aggrieved groups. Thus, unlike the HCSA, the VAWA was formulated within an organization that was largely removed from the civil rights movements discussed in the previous chapter. This "top-down" approach to lawmaking, coupled with the fact that a template for the development of hate crime law had already been constructed, resulted in minimal resistance by detractors.

Neither is there evidence to suggest that feminist antiviolence projects were central in the initiation and early formulation of the VAWA (Jenness and Broad 1997; Broad and Jenness 1996). It was not until 1993, well after the VAWA had been conceived and a just a year before it was enacted into law, that representatives from NOW and the Feminist Majority offered testimony in a federal hearing on hate crime. Responding to testimony from Elizabeth Symonds, the legislative counsel for the American Civil Liberties Union, who had expressed concern that VAWA's Title III raises a plethora of civil rights issues involved in enforcement (Congress 1993a), NOW president Patricia Ireland told the House Judiciary's Subcommittee on Civil and Constitutional Rights,

> It is critical that . . . what is so often seen as a personal problem . . . is identified [in this bill] as indeed a political or systematic problem. It's very clear to all of us who see the bombings of the NAACP offices, the vandalizing of synagogues, that these are more clearly political and public violence. But, because so much of the violence against women is behind closed doors, is a private violence, . . . [and] the political aspect of it has often been ignored. It's not just a problem that an individual woman faces when she is beaten, because she crashes her husband's car, as the ACLU put as one example in their brief, . . . but rather a systematic problem that all women face. If one out of three women, according to the Senate Judiciary Committee's report, will face violent crime in her life, I can tell you that three out of three of us fear it. We fear every crime that men fear, and on top of that, the violence and contempt that is heaped upon us just because we are women. I find the ACLU's failure to support the civil rights provisions unfathomable. [I] think it's very clear that the current civil rights laws do not work for

women. Some types of bias that are identified under those laws that apply in race cases apply equally to crimes against women. (Congress 1993a, 113)

In the same hearing Sally Goldfarb, the senior staff attorney for the NOW's Legal Defense and Education Fund, along with Eleanor Smeal, the president of the Feminist Majority, also offered supporting testimony to the Subcommittee on Civil and Constitutional Rights.

Although the support of these groups comes as no surprise, given the historical commitment of the women's movement to combating violence against women, the fact that it emerged fairly late in the history of federal lawmaking around hate crime is telling. Both state- and national-level feminist civil rights organizations were notably absent from discussions of the VAWA (Broad and Jenness 1996; Jenness and Broad 1997). With the exception of a few state coalitions that initiated and sponsored letter-writing and consciousness-raising campaigns, feminist organizations devoted surprisingly few resources and attendant mobilization to the VAWA until after the act had received enough support to marshal predictions of its imminent passage (Broad and Jenness 1996; Jenness and Broad 1997). "The VAWA and all that it represents has become an important element in the institutional environment of [antiviolence projects sponsored and sustained by feminists], *one that has been externally generated and presented to the organizational field, rather than internally developed and imposed on the larger socio-political environment*" (Jenness and Broad 1997, 162).[21]

In the end, the passage of the VAWA, as well as the public discussions surrounding it, represented a step toward placing violence against women in the context of previously debated and ultimately legitimated definitions of and templates for bias-motivated crimes. In so doing, it further expanded the domain of hate crime. Occurring relatively late in the history of the institutionalization of federal hate crime law, this domain expansion was not driven by the same processes that determined earlier domain expansion to cover sexual orientation. With respect to the inclusion of gender, domain expansion was less a function of direct and sustained social movement mobilization than of increased agreement on the parameters of hate crime law within a particular institutional arena (the U.S. Congress). Much like the course of the cross-national acquisition of women's suffrage rights (Ramirez, Soysal, and Shanahan 1997), the legislative history of the VAWA suggests that once hate crime law became institutionalized, the importance of social movement mobilization declined as general agreement was reached as to what constitutes a hate crime.[22]

Social Movement Mobilization and the Institutionalization of Law

Through the inclusion of key provisions in hate crime law, the substantive character of federal law has been shaped in ways that are racialized, sexualized, and gendered. Early in the history of federal lawmaking around hate crime, the empirical credibility of the scope and consequences of violence based on race, religion, and ethnicity was imported from social movement activity concerned with anti-Semitic and anti-black violence. Shortly thereafter, a growing awareness of this type of violence was cited as grounds for the development of federal hate crime legislation by a limited number of collective actors and their representatives. During this incipient stage in the history of hate crime lawmaking, a trio of core provisions for hate crime law, "race, religion, and ethnicity," emerged. These provisions were cemented as the anchoring provisions of all hate crime law, without contestation over their legitimacy.

The character of hate crime law was reshaped when the domain of the law expanded to include additional provisions. Shortly after federal hate crime law was envisioned, domain expansion occurred through the addition of sexual orientation to the list of provisions. This was accomplished primarily through the work of specific social movements and their allies, who were able to bestow empirical credibility upon antigay violence. Furthermore, they succeeded in rendering the meaning of the sexual orientation status provision as similar to previously legitimated and institutionalized status provisions (race, religion, and ethnicity). In so doing, they remained consistent with the logic of previously established hate crime law and thus contributed to the institutionalization of the legal construct.

At the same time, several other status provisions that had been recommended for inclusion were not written into the final bill. The key distinction between those that were included and those that were not concerns the level of social movement involvement in the hearings. For example, before the passage of the HCSA, some legislators expressed support for the bill "as an effective means of establishing the level of hate motivated violence against segments of our society" but went on to argue that "the measure does not go far enough and [should] include violence by and against union members" (Congress 1989, 7). Because hearings were not held on this type of bias-motivated violence, there was never a structural opportunity for representatives from relevant union organizations to establish the empirical credibility of the problem and to engage in the categorization work required to legitimate this provision. Accordingly, union affiliation is not included as a provision in any federal hate crime law.

In contrast, an examination of the legislative history of gender as a provision in federal hate crime law suggests that the importance of social movement activism declines over time. Once a corpus of hate crime law had been established and select provisions cemented in law, new provisions—in this case, gender—were adopted without direct pressure from sustained mobilization of relevant social movements and their representatives. Although many federal hearings on violence against women have been held, they were neither initiated nor sustained by feminist organizations and their spokespeople. Instead, as lawmakers coalesced around the meaning of hate crime law in previous hearings, established policy pedigrees were institutionalized. This in turn facilitated subsequent domain expansion—in this case, the inclusion of gender—without much fanfare, without direct and sustained pressure on legislators on the part of movement organizations, and in a context in which gender as a legal subject has paralleled race for more than a quarter of a century.

This pattern is also evident in the history of the disability provision in hate crime law. In 1996, disability was included in both the reauthorization of the HCSA (Congress 1996a, 1996b) and in the HCSEA (Public Law 103-222). The changing character of the law along these lines occurred despite the fact that federal lawmakers have never held a hearing on violence directed at persons with disabilities. Moreover, the official records of federal-level hate crime lawmaking reveals that representatives from the disabilities movement have yet to make an appearance before the Congress to offer testimony related to federal hate crime legislation. Nevertheless, disability has found a home in hate crime legislation, albeit rather late in the institutionalization process. This occurred in a context in which disability—like race, religion, and gender—was already a standard subject of federal discrimination law, in large part because of the passage of the Americans with Disabilities Act in 1990.

Summarized in table 3.4, these findings reveal how organizational processes connected to social movement mobilization interface with microlevel processes of categorization work to determine the content of law in the arena most proximate to lawmaking: the legislature. This work confirms an insight consistent with the legal mobilization approach to understanding modern collective action. As Sally Merry (1995, 14) explained in her recent presidential address to the Law & Society Association, "Categories of law are often mobilized by social movements." However, this work also suggests a refinement of this

Table 3.4   Relationship Between Social Movement Organization (SMO) Mobilization and the Proposal and Adoption of Select Status Provisions in Federal Hate-Crime Legislation

	Provisions Proposed for Inclusion in Legislation	Provisions Adopted in Legislation
Legislation prior to 1990		
SMO mobilization around		
Race	X	X
Religion	X	X
Ethnicity	X	X
Sexual Orientation	X	X
No SMO mobilization around		
Octogenarians	X	
Union Members	X	
Children	X	
Elderly	X	
Legislation after 1990		
SMO mobilization around (No Groups)		
No SMO mobilization around		
Gender	X	X
Disabilities	X	X

Source: Authors' compilation.

insight by pointing to a temporal dimension in the process. Namely, at some point in the institutionalization of law, the development of policy pedigrees is more consequential than the presence of social movement forces. In this case, as agreement on what constitutes a hate crime from the point of view of the federal government increased, subsequent hate crime law was homogenized in accordance with previously established policy pedigrees, often quite independent of the strength of social movements. This theme is further developed in the next chapter, as we turn our attention to state-level hate crime law.

═ Chapter 4 ═

Diffusion Processes and the Evolution of State Hate Crime Law

CONTINUING with the empirical and theoretical themes developed in the previous chapter, in this chapter we direct attention to the content of state level hate crime and the way this body of law has diffused throughout the United States in a short period of time. As Maroney (1998, 567–68) has recently observed, "In seemingly no time at all, a 'hate crimes jurisprudence' had sprung up." In the past two decades most of the state legislatures have adopted at least one hate crime statute that recognizes, defines, and responds to discriminatory violence (see figure 4.1).

As a recent innovative approach to lawmaking around bias-motivated activity, state-level hate crime law has taken many forms, including statutes proscribing criminal penalties for civil rights violations, specific "ethnic intimidation" and "malicious harassment" statutes, and provisions for enhanced penalties. These laws cover crimes committed because of race, religion, color, ethnicity, ancestry, national origin, sexual orientation, gender, age, disability, creed, marital status, political affiliation, involvement in civil or human rights movements, and service in the armed forces. In addition, a few states have adopted statutes that require authorities to collect data on hate- or bias-motivated crimes, mandate law enforcement training, prohibit the undertaking of paramilitary training, specify parental liability, and provide for victim compensation. Finally, many states have statutes that prohibit institutional vandalism and the desecration or the defacement of religious objects, the interference with or disturbance of religious worship, cross burning, the wearing of hoods or masks, the formation of secret societies, and the distribution of publications and advertisements designed to harass select groups of individuals. This

Figure 4.1   Year of First Adoption of Hate Crime Statute by State, 1981 to 1999

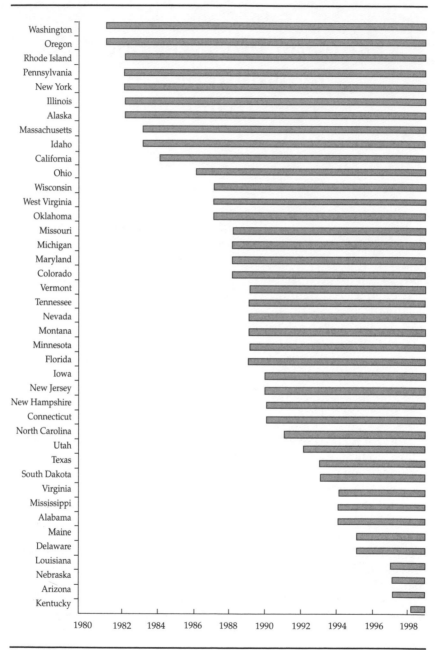

Source: Authors' compilation.

last group of laws reflects a previous generation of what, in retrospect, could be termed "hate crime" law (Jenness 1995a).[1] The diversity of approaches used by states reflects their struggles to respond to hate-motivated violence while also attending to civil-liberties-related concerns and remaining sensitive to the sociopolitical particularities of each state.

The evolution of state hate crime laws—as opposed to that of federal and civil lawmaking on data collection, police training, educational policy changes, and the like—is important to understand not only because the storm of controversy about the issue has centered specifically on state laws, but also because in the American justice system criminal law is principally a state-level function. Thus, the bulk of the legislative rule making and enforcement occurs at the state level. As with federal law, the central issue in the development of state law has been what to include and what to exclude from the concept of hate crime. The question of which intergroup conflicts are recognized and which are not, as well as how the recognized and unrecognized axes around which bias-motivated acts and expressions vary across time and space, is a compelling sociological and sociolegal question that must be addressed to reach an understanding of policy domain formation. Such variation reflects the changing legal and social meanings of the concept of a hate crime as well as the social and political influences that shape the construction of this particular policy domain.

A Focus on Criminalization as Diffusion

An accumulating body of work has examined the factors and dynamics that inspire and sustain legal reform, especially those that result in the criminalization of conduct or sets of activities (for reviews of the literature, see Galliher and Cross 1983; Hagan 1980; Hollinger and Lanza-Kaduce 1988; Rafter 1990). As a result, it is now beyond dispute that law—especially criminal law—emerges as a societal reaction to an assumed or real increase in some type of undesirable behavior (Ben-Yehuda 1992; Rafter 1990).[2] Moving beyond this simplistic single-variable explanation, however, the literature points to important exogenous factors that first provide the impetus for criminalization and then sustain the criminalization process over time. These factors include a diverse array of social actors (Coltrane and Hickman 1992; Farr 1995; Galliher and Basilick 1979; Hagan 1980; Hollinger and Lanza-Kaduce 1988; Neuman 1998), interest groups (Grattet, Jenness, and Curry 1998; Jenness 1995a; Jenness and Grattet 1996; Miller and Canak 1988; Savelsberg 1987), social movements (Broad and Jenness 1996; Berger, Searles, and Neuman 1988; DiChiara and Galliher 1994; Jenness 1995a; Jenness 1995b; Jenness and Broad 1997), political opportunities (Call, Nice, and Talarico 1991; DiChiara and Galliher 1994; Miller and Canak 1988), and structural conditions (Chambliss and Seidman 1982; Chambliss and Zatz 1993; Galliher and Basilick 1979; Gunnlaugsson and Galliher 1986; Humphries and Greenberg 1981; Jenness and Grattet 1996; Miller and Canak 1988).

Nonetheless, older (Hagan 1980; Galliher and Cross 1983; Humphries and Greenberg 1981) and more recent assessments of the field (see, for example, McGarrell and Castellano 1993; Steury 1991) agree that the criminalization literature remains theoretically under-developed and "mired in a sterile debate between conflict and consensus perspectives" (McGarrell and Castellano 1993, 347). In response to these criticisms, several authors (McGarrell and Castellano 1991, 1993; Chambliss and Seidman 1982; Chambliss and Zatz 1993; Galliher and Basilick 1979; Galliher and Cross 1983) have proposed a new generation of models that seek to move beyond conflict and consensus approaches and integrate structural and agency explanations for crime control policy in the process. Despite these important advances, however, "the criminalization literature reveals no consensus on what criminalization itself entails or means" (Steury 1991, 335).

Existing conceptualizations of criminalization tend to neglect the temporal and spatial aspects of criminalization, in particular. At least in part, this is because the literature is dominated by historically specific qualitative studies that identify key factors that affect criminalization in select cases (for example, rape shield laws, drug laws, computer laws, and sexual psychopathy laws) and focus on only one level of analysis (Hagan 1980; McGarrell and Castellano 1991). As a result, research attention has been diverted from intergovernmental dynamics associated with legislative policy formation in particular and diffusion processes more generally (Knoke 1982; Tolbert and Zucker 1983).

Diffusion, "the process by which an innovation spreads throughout a social system over time" (Gray 1973, 1175), has been a core social scientific concept since at least the 1940s, when rural sociologists began to analyze the spread of agricultural technology across time and space. Since that time, researchers have examined the spatial and temporal aspects of the spread of innovations in a remarkable variety of contexts: medical techniques, public policy, and organizational structures, among others. Borrowing from the institutionalist perspective, David Strang and John Meyer (1993, 487) note the importance of understanding how a particular cultural form comes into being and diffuses over time:

Much social scientific inquiry seeks to specify the conditions and mechanisms underpinning the flow of social practices among actors within some larger system. Sociology, rural sociology, anthropology, economics, and communication studies all have rich traditions in diffusion research. Virtually everything seems to diffuse: rumors, prescription practices, boiled drinking water, totems, hybrid corn, job classifications systems, organizational structures, church attendance, and national sovereignty. Diffusion seems critical to social analysis.

Although diffusion is, indeed, critical to social analysis, relevant theoretical and empirical literatures leave unanswered questions about the spatial and temporal diffusion of criminalization as a particular type of policy formation. It involves interorganizational units (states) and is consequential for the emergence and content of legal categories and the social problems they address, highlight, and affirm.

Defining and Examining
State Hate Crime Law

The empirical analyses undertaken in this chapter require that state hate crime legislation be demarcated from other types of legislation designed to control undesirable activities. To identify and document hate crime legislation across the United States, we relied upon inventories from six sources: the National Institute Against Prejudice and Violence, the Center for Democratic Renewal, the Southern Poverty Law Center, the National Gay and Lesbian Task Force, the Anti-Defamation League of B'nai B'rith, and state attorney general's offices.[3] We also used Lexis-Nexis and Westlaw to locate relevant statutes and identify dates of adoption. Combining these sources produced a comprehensive inventory of hate crime legislation in the United States and ensured accuracy in documentation. Thus, our analysis relies not on a sample of states or legislation but, rather, on all hate crime legislation in all fifty states as of 1999.

To qualify as a hate crime law, a state statute must criminalize, enhance penalties for, or amend existing statutes regarding crimes motivated by bias toward individuals or groups based on particular status characteristics such as race, religion, ancestry, sexual orientation, or gender. This definition consists of three elements. First, the law must propose a state policy action. That is, it must create a new criminal category, alter an existing law, or enhance penalties for select crimes. Second, it must contain an "intent standard." That is, it must explicitly refer to the subjective intention of the perpetrator. The implementation, measurement, and constitutionality of intent standards continue to be debated among legal scholars (Gellman 1991; Lawrence 1993; Mueller 1993), social scientists (Jacobs and Potter 1998), and policy makers ("Hate Crimes" 1993) while also remaining problematic for law enforcement officials (Martin 1995; Boyd, Berk, and Hamner 1996). However, for our purposes here a state law must simply contain something—anything—recognizable as an intent standard. We include only laws that specify criminal punishment for selecting a victim on the basis of their race, religion, or other group axis (or some facsimile of this kind of "intentional" wording). This use of the term "hate crime law" excludes institutional vandalism laws, laws prohibiting the wearing of masks and hoods, laws specifying civil penalties for hate crimes, laws defining the conditions of parental liability for youthful hate crime perpetrators, laws mandating the development of hate crime training programs for police officers, and laws mandating data collection. Finally, for a state law to qualify as a hate crime law it must specify a list of protected social statuses, such as religious affiliation, race, ethnicity, or sexual orientation. As Richard Berk, Elizabeth Boyd, and Karl Hamner (1992, 127) explain,

> Perhaps the best place to begin is with the broad observation . . . by Grimshaw (1969b), Sterba (1969), and Nieburg (1972) that one key ingredient in hate-motivated violence is the "symbolic status" of the victim. Thus Grimshaw (1969b, 254) speaks of violence as "social" when "it is directed against an individual or his property solely or primarily because of his membership in a social category." A social category is defined by one or more attributes that a set of individuals share, which have implications for how the individuals are perceived or treated.

Clearly, then, hate crime legislation demarcates select social characteristics and lines of stratification as worthy of legal recognition, what we refer to as "status provisions" and others have referred to as "target groups" (Soule and Earl 1999). This three-pronged operational definition captures the spirit of the hate crime legislation designed to prohibit bias-motivated *conduct*. It also focuses attention on the newest and most controversial of the network of laws discussed in the introduction to this chapter while at the same time capturing what is generally meant within the public discourse about the subject.

Once all state hate crime laws were collected, we coded each statute along multiple dimensions. First, we recorded each statute's "year of enactment" rather than the year the law went into effect. This allowed us to identify at what point the state legislature officially endorsed the idea of using law to combat hate-motivated violence, rather than depending upon the vagaries of state legislative procedures. Second, we coded the specific status provisions (race, religion, color, ethnicity, ancestry, national origin, sexual orientation, gender, age, disability, creed, marital status, political affiliation, involvement in civil or human rights, and membership in the armed services) included in each piece of legislation and the year in which each element was written into the law. In several cases, statuses were added through amendments in subsequent years. We tracked these amendments to obtain a comprehensive picture of the sequential unfolding of the law. Third, we coded previously referenced criminal conduct (assault, bodily injury, vandalism, property damage, arson, harassment, threat, trespass, for example) included in each piece of legislation and the year in which each element was written into the law. Fourth, we coded the legal strategy reflected in each statute. By "legal strategy" we refer to substantively distinct approaches or methods of invoking and deploying the law in response to hate- or bias-motivated conduct. Finally, we referenced an "intent standard" in the law by coding the way in which the "motivational phrasing" was accomplished.

Commensurate with these coding categories, there are two general dimensions along which state hate crime laws can be classified: method and content. Method refers to the way in which the criminal code was altered to add a hate crime law and the precise way criminal intent is worded and conceptualized in the statute. The method of hate crime law can be studied by examining the legal strategies and the motivational phrasing that characterize the law. Content, on the other hand, refers to the kinds of intergroup conflict referenced in the law and the types of conduct that qualify as hate crime. The content of hate crime law can be studied by examining the conduct and status provisions contained in the law. In the sections that follow, then, we examine hate crime law with reference to these dimensions, each of which reflects the most important constitutive features of law.

Variation in Method: Legal Strategies and Motivational Phrasing

Differences in the methods might, on the surface, appear to be inconsequential or merely a product of the vagaries of state criminal code organization. However, such distinctions are important insofar as they set the stage for important differences in the way courts and law enforcement agents, especially prosecutors, interpret the laws and, by extension, make sense of the concept "hate crime." In addition, different methods of constructing the law reflect the capacity and orientation of legislators to take strong versus weak, or risky versus conservative, action. Our discussion of the methodological differences in hate crime statutes is divided into two parts. The first addresses the variation in the basic legal strategies employed by legislators to insert a hate crime law into their criminal code. The second focuses on differences in the phrasing of the motive requirement in the statute and the introduction of "perception standards" in the law.

Legal Strategies

Five identifiable legal strategies—substantively distinct approaches or methods of invoking and deploying the law in response to hate- or bias-motivated conduct—are contained in hate crime legislation. Each legal strategy can contain varying combinations of conduct and status provisions.

Criminalization of Interference with Civil Rights   Statutes that criminalize interference with civil rights are characterized by two elements. They criminalize actions that, by force or threat of force, interfere with or intimidate others in the exercise of their civil rights, and they specify a list of protected statuses. For example, the Interference with the Exercise of Civil Rights statute, adopted by the state of California in 1987, states that "no person, whether or not acting under color of law, shall by force or threat of force, willfully injure, intimidate, interfere with, oppress, or threaten any other person in the free exercise or enjoyment of any right or privilege secured to him or her by the constitution or laws of this state or by the Constitution or the laws of the United States because of the other person's race, color, religion, ancestry, national origin, or sexual orientation" (California, *Penal Code,* sec. 422.6).

This type of law equates with a civil rights violation any hate- or bias-motivated conduct directed at individuals because of their real or imagined membership in selected social groups. It criminalizes acts of bias in the name of preserving previously recognized civil rights. Thus, in many ways it is consistent with a history of legal reform designed to install and protect civil rights.

"Freestanding" Statutes   Some statutes create a new and freestanding category of crime, commonly referred to as "ethnic intimidation" or "malicious harassment." Such legislation has two essential components. First, the statute specifies conduct and activities that qualify as harassment and intimidation (for example, bodily injury, property damage, trespass, threats). Second, it stipulates that the defendant

acted to intimidate or harass the victim because of the victim's real or imagined membership in a legally protected status. For example, Idaho's Malicious Harassment law, adopted in 1983, declares,

> It shall be unlawful for any person, maliciously and with the specific intent to intimidate or harass another person because of that person's race, color, religion, ancestry, or national origin to: (a) Cause physical injury to another person; or (b) Damage, destroy, or deface any real or personal property of another person; or (c) Threaten, by word or act, to do the acts prohibited if there is reasonable cause to believe that any of the acts described in subsections (a) and (b) of this section will occur. For purposes of this section, "deface" shall include, but not be limited to, cross-burnings, or the placing of any word or symbol commonly associated with racial, religious, or ethnic terrorism on the property of another person without his or her permission. (Idaho, *Code*, sec. 18-7902)

Statutes of this sort often specify that it is unlawful to intimidate, harass, or behave in a malicious manner and that intimidation, harassment, and maliciousness can include physical injury, property damage, and threats. The defining feature of statutes in this category, however, is that they directly distinguish hate- or bias-motivated violence from other forms of violent crime.

"Coattailing" Statutes   "Coattailing" statutes create crimes of ethnic intimidation or malicious harassment by embedding them within previously established criminal codes. That is, they create a separate crime (a hate crime) by referencing a previously enumerated crime. These statutes recognize as a hate crime any act in which the defendant engages in conduct that is already recognized as illegal and does so "by reason of" (or "because of") the victim's status characteristics (which are specified by the statute). The statute may either describe the recognized criminal activity by reference to other sections of the penal code or it may describe various crimes by title, element, or both. For example, a law adopted by Illinois in 1983 states that

> a person commits hate crime when, by reason of the race, color, creed, religion, ancestry, gender, sexual orientation, physical or mental disability, or national origin of another individual or group of individuals, he commits assault, battery, aggravated assault, misdemeanor theft, criminal trespass to residence, misdemeanor criminal damage to property, criminal trespass to vehicle, criminal trespass to real property or mob action as these crimes are defined in Sections 12-1, 12-2, 12-3, 16-1, 19-4, 21-1, 21-2, 21-3 and 25-1 of this Code, respectively. (Illinois, *Statutes*, 720, sec. 5/12-7.1)

The defining feature of such statutes is that they rely on previously established criminal codes to render the concept of "hate crime" meaningful.

Modification of a Preexisting Statute   These statutes modify a preexisting statute by adding a clause that reclassifies the crime if it was committed because of the victim's race, religion, or other group status characteristic. In such cases a separate crime is not created. Virginia's assault and battery statute, for example, was amended in 1994 to include a phrase about the selection of particular victims: "Any person who shall commit a simple assault or assault and battery shall be guilty of a Class 1 misdemeanor. However, if a person intentionally selects the person against whom the offense is committed because of his race, religious conviction, color or national origin, the penalty upon conviction shall include a mandatory minimum term of confinement of at least six months, thirty days of which shall not be suspended, in whole or in part" (Virginia, *Code*, sec. 18.2-57).

Penalty Enhancement Statutes   Penalty enhancement statutes increase the penalty for committing an enumerated crime when the crime was motivated by hate or bias. Enhanced-penalty statutes differ from statutes that create separate crimes because they rest on the separate conviction of an underlying crime wherein the defendant committed a criminal act that "evidences" or "demonstrates" prejudice or bigotry based on the victim's real or imagined membership in a legally recognized protected status. Penalties are increased in one of two ways. First, the law assigns a higher sentencing range for the offense. For example, in 1989 Montana adopted a sentence enhancement law declaring that

> a person who has been found guilty of any offense, except malicious intimidation or harassment, that was committed because of the victim's race, creed, religion, color, national origin, or involvement in civil rights or human rights activities or that involved damage, destruction, or attempted destruction of a building regularly used for religious worship, in addition to the punishment provided for the commission of the offense, may be sentenced to a term of imprisonment of not less than 2 years or more than 10 years, except as provided in 46-18-22. (Montana, *Code*, sec. 45-5-222)

Second, penalty enhancement may be achieved by "upgrading" the offense. For example, the Penalty If Offense Committed Because of Bias or Prejudice law adopted in Texas in 1993 states that "if the court makes an affirmative finding under Article 42.014, Code of Criminal

Procedure, in the punishment phase of the trial of an offense other than a first-degree felony, the punishment for the offense is increased to the punishment prescribed for the next highest category of offense" (Texas, *Penal Code,* sec. 12.47). Both penalty enhancement statutes increase penalties when the defendant "intentionally selects" the victim "because of" a given characteristic (Wisconsin, *Statutes,* sec. 939.645).

These five legal strategies reflect important differences in the degree to which legislators were willing to be innovative when creating laws in response to bias-motivated violence. Modifying an existing statute is the least ambitious approach insofar as it merely involves adding a clause to an established statute. Of the two "ethnic intimidation" forms, the "coattailing" strategy is somewhat less risky, insofar as it requires that each of the conduct elements of the law be linked with other parts of the criminal code, unlike the "freestanding" approach, which creates an entirely new self-contained category of crime, using descriptive terms to identify the behavioral attributes of hate crime. This means that the freestanding statute might cover the broader nonlegal definitions of terms like bodily injury, property damage, and harassment rather than the more narrow definitions drawn in the criminal code (Grannis 1993, 183). The "freestanding" strategy is also more innovative than the penalty enhancement law, which, rather than creating an entirely new category of crime, simply relies upon the logic of all kinds of other penalty enhancements—for such things as having a knife or a gun during the commission of a crime, killing a law enforcement agent, and so on. Thus, penalty enhancement, as a strategy, can be envisioned as a fairly established route to changing the criminal code. Finally, the "interference with civil rights" strategy is a somewhat more conservative legal strategy than both ethnic intimidation forms by relying on phrasing meant to connect the statute with established civil rights laws.

In general, what determines the riskiness of these strategies is the extent to which they are "embedded" in preexisting crime categories and strategies of changing law. Strategies that are less embedded signal that lawmakers were willing to depart to a greater degree from preexisting legal frameworks and scripts. These strategies can be arrayed on a continuum in terms of their reliance on preexisting law (see figure 4.2). The modification of a preexisting category is clearly the most embedded; penalty enhancement, criminalization of interference with civil rights, and "coattailing" ethnic intimidation laws occupy the middle of the continuum; and "freestanding" laws anchor the least-embedded end of the continuum.

The timing of the introduction of the various legal strategies is also

Figure 4.2 Relative Embeddedness of Legal Strategies in States' Hate Crime Legislation

Most "Embedded" ➤ ————————————————————————————————— ➤ Least "Embedded"

Modification of Preexisting State	Interference with Civil Rights	Penalty Enhancement	"Coattailing" Ethnic Intimidation Statute	"Freestanding" Ethnic Intimidation Statute
Minnesota (1989)	California (1987)	Arizona (1997)	Delaware (1995)	Colorado (1988)
New Jersey (1990)	New York (1982)	Alabama (1994)	Illinois (1982)	Idaho (1983)
New York (1982)	Tennessee (1989)	Alaska (1982)	Iowa (1990)	Louisiana (1997)
Virginia (1994)	West Virginia (1987)	California (1984)	Kentucky (1998)	Maryland (1988)
		Connecticut (1990)	Missouri (1988)	Massachusetts (1983)
		Florida (1989)	New York (1982)	Michigan (1988)
		Illinois (1988)	Ohio (1986)	Montana (1989)
		Maine (1995)	Pennsylvania (1982)	Nebraska (1997)
		Mississippi (1994)	Utah (1992)	North Carolina (1991)
		Montana (1989)	Vermont (1989)	Oklahoma (1987)
		Nevada (1989)		Oregon (1981)
		New Hampshire (1990)		Rhode Island (1982)
		New Jersey (1990)		South Dakota (1993)
		North Carolina (1991)		Washington (1981)
		Rhode Island (1998)		
		Texas (1993)		
		Wisconsin (1987)		

Source: Authors' compilation.

significant. Figure 4.3 shows the cumulative frequency of these five strategies. All five approaches were introduced in the initial phase of lawmaking, between 1981 and 1983, and there is little evidence of widespread agreement among lawmakers about exactly what constitutes the "preferred strategy." The subsequent history consisted entirely of replication of earlier strategies. That is, states considering the adoption of legislation after 1986 emulated one of the initial successes rather than introducing an entirely new legal strategy. However, they did not emulate all options equally. For example, after about 1990 three strategies began to emerge as the most popular: penalty enhancement, coattailing ethnic intimidation, and freestanding ethnic intimidation statutes. The use of the two remaining strategies—modification of a preexisting statute and criminalization of interference with civil rights—did not increase in the 1990s, suggesting that they came to be seen as less desirable approaches to the problem. Interestingly, the three legal strategies that became dominant were the least embedded of the five legal strategies. Thus, states adopting hate crime law in the latter period had greater license to pursue more progressive approaches.

This pattern of policy making suggests a process that is well known to students of diffusion research. During initial periods, an innovation diffuses rather slowly, and the precise model of action is unsettled. As time goes by, however, the rate of diffusion accelerates, and new adopters converge around particular models. The social process implied by this pattern, institutionalization, involves the introduction of an innovation followed by a period of experimentation with various forms of the innovation. Thereafter, as a result of the accumulation of knowledge and experience with the various forms of innovation, one or a handful of forms comes to be hailed as the "best" or "most efficient" way of dealing with the problem the policy is designed to address. Once that consensus is formed, potential adopters tend to select from the "legitimated" options, and as a result a general homogenization occurs. In the long run, states tend to resemble one another as policy makers conform to institutionalized models established in the policy domain. This is referred to as a process of homogenization.

Homogenization, at the level of legal strategy, is not the only observable attribute of the institutionalization process. Some characteristics of the adopters, in this case, state legislatures, make it unlikely that homogenization will ever be complete: legislatures seldom adopt multiple types of laws, and they rarely repeal one law in order to install another based on an entirely different strategy. In the case of state hate crime law, only three states adopted multiple pieces of leg-

**Figure 4.3   Cumulative Frequency of Legal Strategies in States' Hate
Crime Statutes from 1980 to 1999**

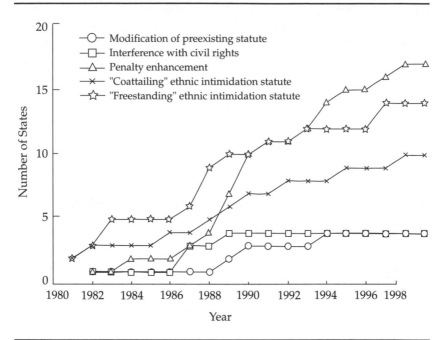

Source: Authors' compilation.

islation: California in 1984 and 1987, Iowa in 1990 and 1992, and Illinois in 1982 and 1988. In the vast majority of cases, states adopted an exclusive remedy at one point and time. If changes were made to the laws, they usually came in the form of amendments rather that wholesale repeals and reenactments.

In organizational theory vernacular, state legislatures exhibit a high degree of "path dependence" (Powell and DiMaggio 1991; Stinchcombe 1965). That is, the courses of action that appear plausible in the present are often limited by decisions made at an earlier point in time. This property of legislatures undermines the complete homogenization of policy in a policy domain because policy makers remain committed to the statutory forms adopted early on. This means that part of the differentiation along methodological lines that appears when viewing the composition of the state laws at present is the result of the fact that states that passed less popular methods early on never changed their strategies.

Motivational Phrasing and Perception Standards

One of the important ways that the statutes differ across jurisdictions is in the way they phrase the motivational requirement. Differences in motivational phrasing shape the breadth of circumstances in which the law can be invoked for prosecutorial or symbolic purposes.

Four general types of wording of the motivational standard are summarized in table 4.1. The most common form—the "because of" wording—represents the broadest conception of motivation. For example, Iowa's statute (Iowa, *Code*, sec. 729A.2) punishes a bias crime, defined as a criminal act "committed against a person or a person's property *because of* race, color, religion, ancestry" [italics added for emphasis]. Such statutes invite little interpretation of the mental state of the perpetrator involved in the crime because they do not require that the precise character of the motive be analyzed. In this formulation of the law, it does not matter whether a perpetrator held virulent racist beliefs or only a mild bias toward the victim's race. Rather, it matters only that the victim was chosen *because of* his or her race. As a result, these statutes are more aptly described as "bias crime" rather than "hate crime" statutes. As Anthony Dillof (1997, 106) explains, "'Bias crimes' is a more accurate term than 'hate crimes.' The statutes under consideration likely apply to many criminal acts in which hate, understood as a particular subjective emotion, is not involved. Likewise, the statutes under consideration do not apply to many criminal acts based upon hate."[4]

The other constructions of motivational phrasing call for more information about the exact quality of the perpetrator's motives and intentions. For example, Florida's 1989 law states that the act must evidence prejudice, Michigan's law specifies maliciousness as a component, and Montana's law requires that the act must be motivated by an "intent to terrify, intimidate, threaten, harass, annoy, or offend." Based strictly on the wording of the statute, the precise nature of the perpetrator's motives matter to a greater extent in these laws. That is, contrasted with the "because of" construction, each of these approaches calls for a deeper inspection of the quality of the perpetrator's bias. In particular, they emphasize the underlying emotional aspects of the act—for example, how intensely felt the bias was, whether the act expressed resentment, and how much fear the perpetrator intended to transmit. Actions not motivated by hatred, hostility, prejudice, and perhaps anything beyond only mild bias would not—under the strict letter of the law—qualify for an increased punishment. Within the "because of" phrasing these qualitative aspects of

Table 4.1   Phrasing Regarding Motivation in States' Hate Crime Statutes

Category	Phrasing
"Because of" or "by reason of"	
Minnesota (1989)	"because of"
Iowa (1990, 1992)	
Maryland (1988)	
Delaware (1995)	
Montana (1989)	
Nebraska (1997)	
North Carolina (1991)	"because of" (ethnic intimidation law); "if any misdemeanor with punishment less than the punishment for the general misdemeanor is committed because of" (penalty enhancement law)
California (1984)	"intentionally killed because of his or her" (homicide enhancement law); "because of" (penalty enhancement law)
Missouri (1988)	"by reason of any motive relating to"
Mississippi (1994)	"by reason of"
Ohio (1986)	
Illinois (1982, 1988)	"by reason of" (ethnic intimidation law, 1982); "because of such person's" (penalty enhancement law, 1988)
Nevada (1989)	"by reason of . . . violates"[1]
Virginia (1994)	"intentionally selects the person against whom the offense is committed because of his"
Wisconsin (1987)	"intentionally selects the person against whom
Kentucky (1998)	the [crime is committed] . . . in whole or in part because of the actor's belief or perception regarding"
Alaska (1982)	"knowingly directed the offense at a victim because of"
Maine (1995)	"The selection by the defendant of the person against whom the crime was committed or of the property that was damaged or otherwise affected by the crime because of"
Alabama (1994)	"was found to have been motivated by the victim's"
Louisiana (1997)	"It shall be unlawful for any person to select the victim of the following offenses against person or property because of"

Table 4.1 *Continued*

Category	Phrasing
Intent to harass, intimidate, or terrorize	
California (1987)	"for the purpose of intimidating or interfering with that other person's free exercise or enjoyment of any right . . . because of the other person's"
Massachusetts (1983)	"for the purpose of intimidation because of said person's"
West Virginia (1987)	"if any person conspires with another person or persons to willfully injure, oppress, threaten, or intimidate or interfere with any citizen because of such other person's"
Oregon (1981)	"intent to cause substantial inconvenience because of" (2d degree); "intentionally, knowingly or recklessly because of" (1st degree)
Tennessee (1989)	"intent to unlawfully intimidate another from the free exercise or enjoyment of any right" or because he or she exercised a right
Montana (1989)	"when, because of another person's . . . with intent to terrify, intimidate, threaten, harass, annoy or offend" (ethnic intimidation law)
New Jersey (1995)[1]	"with a purpose to intimidate an individual or group of individuals because of" (amended penalty enhancement law)
Minnesota (1989)	"with intent to harass, abuse, or threaten . . . because of" (mail harassment law)
New York (1982)	"with intent to harass, annoy, threaten, or alarm another person because of"
Utah (1992)	"with intent to intimidate or terrorize another person"
Colorado (1988)	"with the intent to intimidate or harass because of"
Rhode Island (1982)[2]	"with intent to terrorize by reason of"
"Maliciously" and with intent to harass	
Washington (1981)	"maliciously and with intent to intimidate or harass another person because of, or in a way that is reasonably related to, associated with, [or] directed toward that person's"
Oklahoma (1987) South Dakota (1993) Idaho (1983) Connecticut (1990) Michigan (1988)	"maliciously and with specific intent to harass another person because of"

(Table continues on p. 90.)

Table 4.1 *Continued*

Category	Phrasing
"Prejudice," "hostility," malice	
Rhode Island (1998)[2]	"because of the actor's hatred or animus toward"
Florida (1989)	"evidences prejudice based on"
New Hampshire (1990)	"substantially motivated to commit the crime because of hostility towards the victim's"
New Jersey (1990)[3]	"Contempt or hatred on the basis of" (penalty enhancement law) "ill will, hatred, or bias, and with a purpose to intimidate" (ethnic intimidation)
Pennsylvania (1982)	"with malicious intent toward"
Texas (1993)	"if offense committed because of bias or prejudice"
Vermont (1989)	"who commits, causes to be committed or attempts to commit any crime and whose conduct is maliciously motivated by the victim's"
Arizona (1997)	"evidence that the defendant committed the crime out of malice toward the victim because of"

Source: Authors' compilation.
1. In 1995, wording changed to "willfully violates."
2. In 1998, the Rhode Island legislature repealed its 1982 law and replaced it with a new law containing the "animus" wording.
3. In 1994, the New Jersey Supreme Court struck down its statute's earlier (1990) phrasing.

the affect associated with the conduct are not specified. As a result, they would not be relevant to determining whether or not the act should be punished as a hate crime.[5] Therefore the "because of" wording provides for the broadest possible application.

Motivational phrasing, like the selection of legal strategy, has varied over time. Figure 4.4 maps the frequency of use of the four categories of motivational phrasing in state hate crime statutes. Initially, all four types of terminology were experimented with by legislators as they grappled with how to write the law. After the early 1990s, however, states increasingly gravitated toward the "because of" construction. This pattern reflects the same institutionalization process described in relation to the legal strategies: there is a general momentum toward homogenization, but because of path dependence, states tend to retain the wording contained in their original statutes.

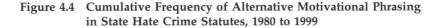

Figure 4.4   Cumulative Frequency of Alternative Motivational Phrasing in State Hate Crime Statutes, 1980 to 1999

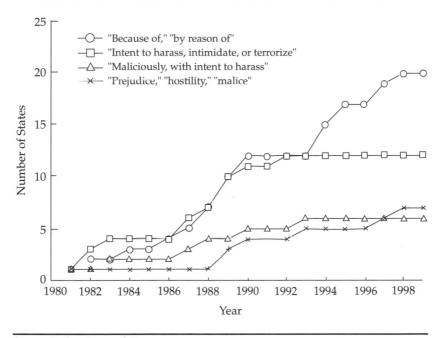

Source: Authors' compilation.

Consistent with this move toward the broadest possible application, recently developed state hate crime law has included a "false perception" standard. Recent laws routinely address cases of misperception of the victim's identity. For example, a California statute amended in 1994 states that "a person who commits a felony or attempts to commit a felony because of the victim's race, color, religion, nationality, country of origin, ancestry, disability, or sexual orientation, or because he or she perceives that the victim has one or more of those characteristics, shall receive an additional term of one, two, or three years in the state prison" (California, *Penal Code,* sec. 422.75).

The perception clause was added because of publicized cases in which the offender mistakenly selected a victim who did not represent the assumed target group. The best-known example involved the murder of Vincent Chin, a Chinese American who was thought by his attackers to be Japanese. A more recent case in southern California involved several men who assaulted a group of Lebanese men. When caught, the perpetrators admitted that the attack was motivated by their perception that the victims were Jewish. In cases like these the "because of" standard, coupled with the "false perception" standard, encourages the expansion of the domain of the law and its potential applications.

Variation in Content: Conduct Provisions and Status Provisions

Consistent with the theoretical framework laid out in chapter 1 and the analysis of the development of federal hate crime law in chapter 2, the question of who and what is covered under state hate crime laws is more directly addressed by examining the two remaining characteristics of state hate crime laws: conduct provisions, which specify the types of criminal activity that qualify as hate crime; and status provisions, which specify the types of intergroup conflicts that are recognized as plausible axes of hate crime.

Conduct Provisions

Although the terms used vary from state to state, three kinds of activities are most commonly cited in state hate crime law: physical attacks against persons (for example, assault, bodily injury), destruction of property (for example, arson, property damage, vandalism), and conduct intended to intimidate a victim (for example, harassment, threat, intimidation). Twenty-eight states have laws that mention some combination of these three kinds of activities. The focus on this trio of activities reflects an awareness of the most stereotypical and well-documented manifestations of intergroup violence. The documentation and the publicizing of hate crimes provided by social movements and social movement organizations has produced an image of the ordinary circumstances under which hate crime—or, to use a more technical sociological term, a "normal" hate crime—occurs (Sudnow 1965). A sample of such images might include an assault outside a gay bar, arson directed at a black family's home, or verbal threats and taunts by skinheads. Scenarios like these have emerged as the "normal" victimization pattern in social movement, and eventually legislative, discourse about hate crime. Such examples draw on and contribute to a portrait of hate crime as involving a specific range of stereotypical victims and conduct.

Moving beyond a focus on the most stereotypical forms of hate-motivated violence, several state statutes expand the domain of the conduct falling under the rubric of hate crime by detailing more activities that qualify as a hate crime. This is generally accomplished in one of three ways. First, some states list additional types of criminal conduct, such as trespass, interference with civil rights, mob action, murder, unlawful use of weapons, and theft. These are typically itemized separately in state hate crime law, positioned in such a way that they differ from the "core" list of concerns. Second, some states expand the domain of conduct that qualifies as hate crime by upgrading the penalties for certain blocks of crime, like felonies or misdemeanors. For example, a 1982 Alaska law and a 1984 California law upgrade all felonies, a 1993 Texas law upgrades all crimes below the level of first-degree felonies, and a 1991 North Carolina law upgrades all misdemeanor crimes that are committed from bias. Finally, eight states have adopted a comprehensive approach to lawmaking in which all crimes can be upgraded to the status of hate crime under identifiable conditions. Vermont's Hate-Motivated Crimes Law declares that

> a person who commits, causes to be committed, or attempts to commit any crime and whose conduct is maliciously motivated by the victim's actual or perceived race, color, religion, national origin, sex, ancestry, age, service in the armed forces of the United States, [or] handicap as defined by 21 V.S.A. s 495 d (7)-(11), or sexual orientation, shall be subject to the following penalties: (1) If the maximum penalty for the underlying crime is one year or less, the penalty for violation of this section shall be imprisonment for not more than two years or a fine of more than $2,000, or both. (2) If the maximum penalty for the underlying crime is not more than one year but less than five years, the penalty for the violation of this section shall be imprisonment for not more than five years or a fine of not more than $10,000, or both. (3) If the maximum penalty for the underlying crime is five years or more, the penalty for the underlying crime shall apply; however, the court shall consider the motivation of the defendant as a factor in sentencing. (Vermont, *Statutes*, Title 13, sec. 1455)

Legislative approaches identifying new conduct provisions, blocks of crimes, or entire categories of crime for penalty enhancement are associated with the later phase of the national campaign to criminalize hate-motivated behavior. As such, they signify a broader coverage of conduct than the "bodily injury, property damage, threat" conception. These more sweeping depictions of conduct, most common in the penalty enhancement form of the law, expand the domain of what counts as hate crime conduct. They presuppose that any criminal conduct, even actions we might not ordinarily associate with normal hate crimes, such as purse snatching and motor vehicle theft, constitute acts that could be motivated by hatred or bias and are thus properly defined as hate crime. One consequence of such an expansion is that the image of a hate crime as a specific range of criminal acts diminishes. There is no typical hate crime conduct presumed under these statutes.

Much of the variation in how the conduct is defined within hate crime statutes occurs over time. Figure 4.5 illustrates a comparison of the categories of conduct covered under state hate crime laws in 1988 and 1998. By the end of 1988, nineteen states had adopted bias-intent hate crime laws. Most laws cover assault, property damage, and threats—the forms of conduct that correspond to the most popular conceptions of how hate crimes "normally" occur. A few other states mention "harassment," "menacing," "trespass," and "mob action"; fewer still extend coverage to the remaining categories listed in figure 4.5.

By the end of 1998, however, forty-one states had passed hate crime laws. In addition to coverage of bodily injury, property damage, and threat, nearly one-third of states now cover all crimes. Also, a number of states created extremely long lists of offenses. For example, Louisiana's 1997 law covers forty-one offenses and includes oral sexual battery, carnal knowledge of a juvenile, contamination of water supplies, and purse snatching. Similarly, Wisconsin passed a law that included seventy-one separate offenses, including gang crimes, terrorism, assisted suicide, stalking, racketeering, and unlawful use of a phone. Both the "all crimes" category and the extensive listing of included conduct considerably expand the scope of activities that qualify as hate crime.

Status Provisions

The demarcation of what we refer to as the "status provisions" of law, including the categories of group affiliations protected (race, religion, national origin, for example), exhibits a similar pattern. Figure 4.6 shows the status provisions included in hate crime laws in 1988 and 1998. In 1988, the most common status provisions were for race, religion, color, and national origin. As is the case with conduct provisions, the more popular elements early on are those associated with the most visible, recognizable, and stereotypical kinds of discriminatory behavior. For example, the stereotypical hate crime involves violence toward or harassment of blacks, immigrants, and Jews. Although other categories, such as gender, ancestry, sexual orientation, creed, age, political affiliation, and marital status, were recognized

Figure 4.5 Conduct Provisions in States' Hate Crime Statutes, 1988 and 1998

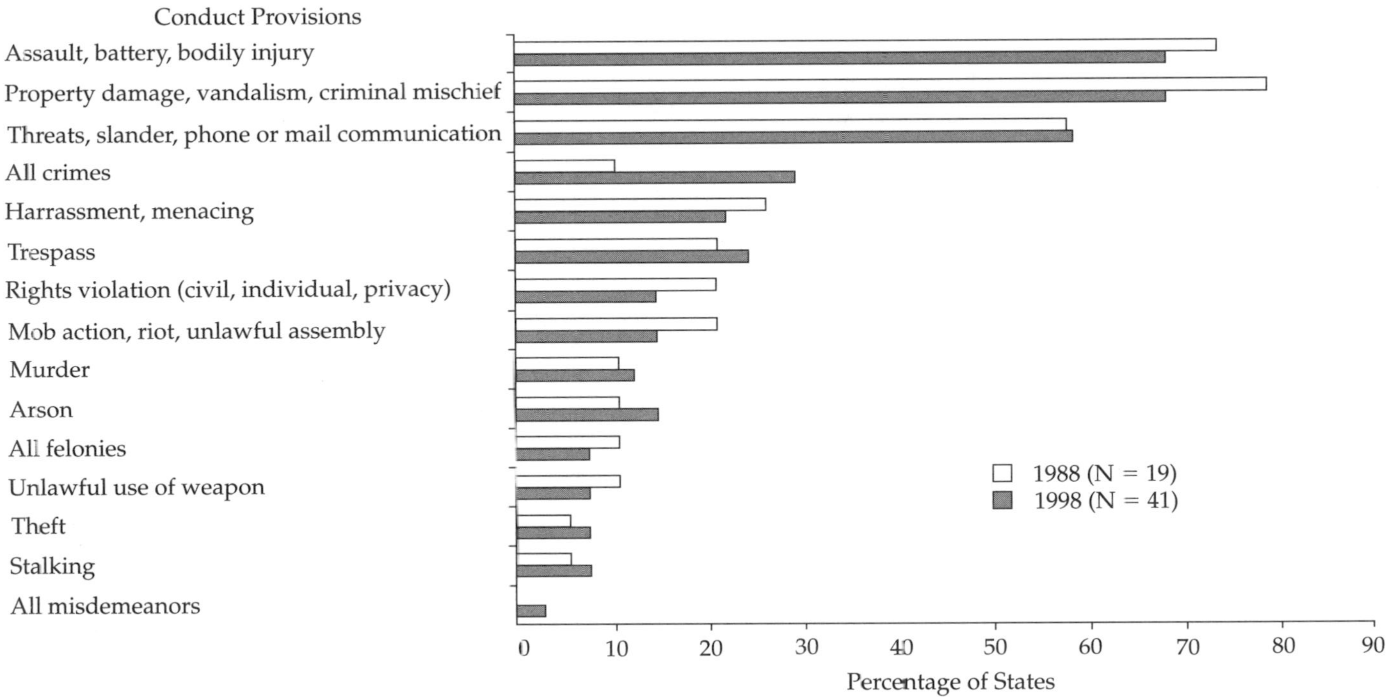

Conduct Provisions

Assault, battery, bodily injury

Property damage, vandalism, criminal mischief

Threats, slander, phone or mail communication

All crimes

Harrassment, menacing

Trespass

Rights violation (civil, individual, privacy)

Mob action, riot, unlawful assembly

Murder

Arson

All felonies

Unlawful use of weapon

Theft

Stalking

All misdemeanors

☐ 1988 (N = 19)
■ 1998 (N = 41)

Percentage of States

Source: Authors' compilation.

Figure 4.6   Status Provisions in States' Hate Crime Statutes, 1988 and 1998

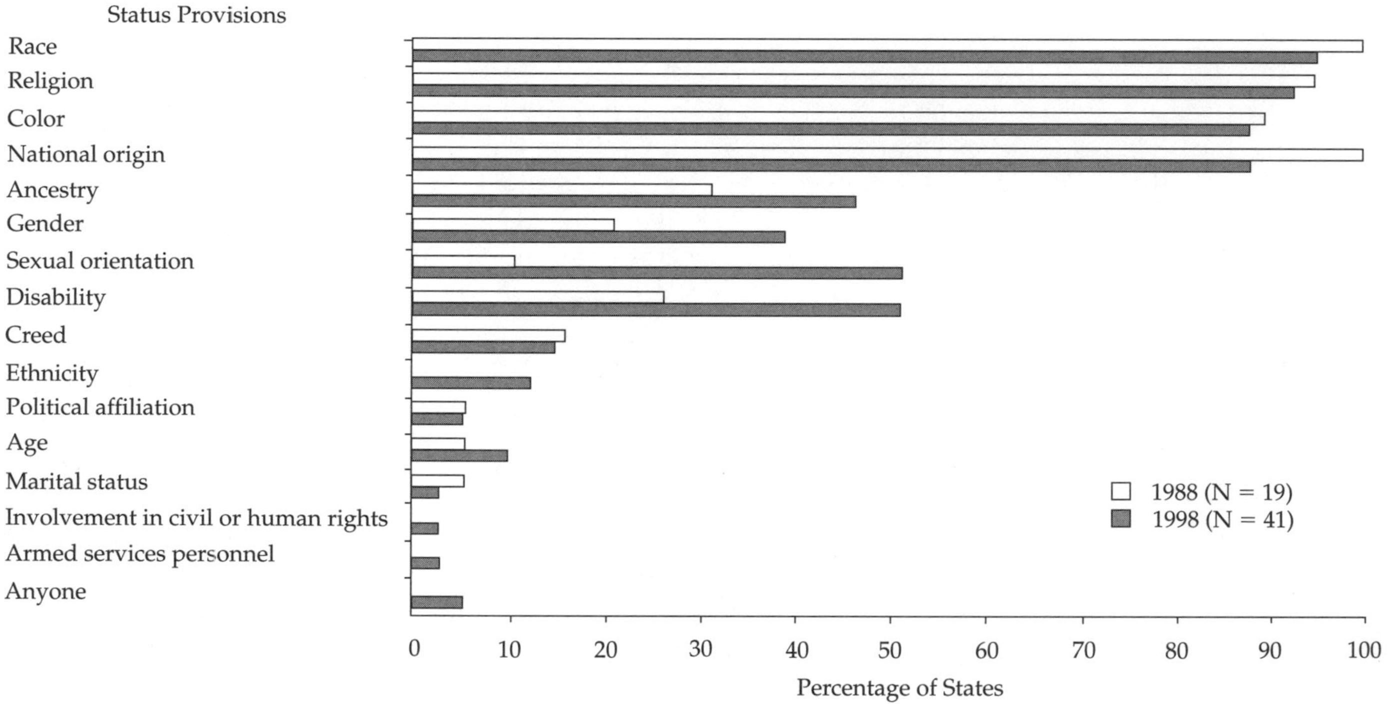

Status Provisions

Source: Authors' compilation.

in the early period, in 1988 they appear infrequently enough to conclude that they were not part of legislators' conception of the "normal" axes along which hate crime occurs.

By 1998, however, a second tier of categories had clearly emerged, with sexual orientation, gender, and disability appearing more often in state hate crime law. Although less stereotypical than their predecessors, these categories have become increasingly recognized as axes along which hate-motivated violence occurs. The respective unfolding of these clusters of statuses—the core and the second tier—reflects the history of various post-1960s civil rights movements in the United States (Goldberg 1991; Jenness and Broad 1997).

As our analysis in chapter 2 demonstrates, race, religion, color, and national origin reflect the early legal categorization of minorities' status and rights. Thus, there is a more developed history of invoking and then deploying the law to protect and enhance the status of blacks, Jews, and immigrants. Because the gay and lesbian movement (Adam 1987; Vaid 1995), the women's movement (Ferree and Hess 1985), and the disability movement (Shapiro 1993) reflect a "second wave" of civil rights activism and "identity politics" (Goldberg 1991; Marx and McAdam 1994), sexual orientation, gender, and disability have only recently been recognized by the law. These are also more heavily contested protected statuses than the "first wave" categories. Not surprisingly, they remain less embedded in hate crime law.

In general, state laws have expanded to cover a broader array of potential victims. Although it is most clearly evident in the particular status provisions included in the laws, the change has occurred in other ways, as well. The most notable example of the evolution of hate crime law is Iowa's law. It defines hate crime as one of a number of public offenses when committed against a person or a person's property because of the person's race, color, "or the person's association with a person of a certain race [or] color" (Iowa, *Code*, sec. 729A.2). This law includes an almost limitless range of "victims by association." One high-profile example of this was a case in Denver, Colorado, wherein Jean Vanvelkinburgh, a white woman, was shot by skinheads as she attempted to aid Oumar Dia, a man from western Africa, after he had been wounded. Another example is a case in Cypress, California, in which a Latino and two of his white friends were attacked outside a pool hall by a group of skinheads. Incidents like these provided the grounds for expanding the provisions of the laws to include victims who were selected not because of their own status characteristics but because they were collateral to the specific targets of the bias conduct.

The statuses that are replicated and those that are not are usually distinguished by their degree of external legitimacy and the support mobilized by mass social movements. Race, religion, color, and national origin are already embodied in antidiscrimination laws and the civil rights movement. Gender, sexual orientation, and physical and mental disabilities are connected to mass social movements that have politicized violence and victimization in recent decades. Marital status, creed, age, service in the armed forces, and political affiliation, however, are not visibly connected to issues of discrimination and victimization by any particular mass movement, although this may be changing with respect to age as increasing attention is given to the problem of "elder abuse" in particular and an aging society more generally. Hate-motivated criminal conduct toward married people, armed services personnel, and Democrats, for example, does not conform to the popular conception of hate crime, and these categories are, therefore, not replicated in state law.

Domain expansion is not limitless, however, and some protected statuses are not replicated. For example, although the first reference to marital status appeared in New York's Interference with Civil Rights statute, adopted in 1982, no other state has adopted that provision. In contrast, provisions for gender and disability were introduced in 1982, for sexual orientation in 1987, and for ethnicity in 1989, and these have been adopted in subsequent legislation. This proliferation and replication of protected statuses continues to the present. By 1998, fifteen protected statuses were referenced by hate crime laws, "anyone" (included in Texas's 1993 and Utah's 1997 laws) and "armed services personnel" (included in Vermont's 1989 law) being the most recent innovations.

Although several of the status and conduct provisions that are introduced are not subsequently replicated by other states, the general trend is toward domain expansion as hate crime law diffuses. The term "domain expansion" refers to a process whereby the substantive reach of the law is extended over time and the substantive territory falling under the rubric of the social problem thereby increases over time. Our examination of state hate crime law suggests that this is a central feature of the development of hate crime law across the United States.

The process of domain expansion has both analytic and substantive import. It is worth noting that precisely how the domain of the law expands determines the kinds of persons and conduct that fall under the law. For example, if a gay man in Mississippi is assaulted because of his sexual orientation, his perpetrators cannot be prosecuted under the state's penalty enhancement statute because the law does not recognize sexual orientation as a protected status. Individuals engaging in hate-motivated theft can be prosecuted under the hate crime laws of Wisconsin and Illinois but not in most other states, because most state statutes do not include theft among the offenses prosecutable as hate crime. Given that the specific combinations of provisions is shaped when (early or late) a state passes a law, the consequences of domain expansion are quite striking.

Countervailing Forces in the Growth of State Hate Crime Law

In large part because hate crime constitutes a fairly recently recognized social problem, it is not surprising that early in the formulation of the concept there was little agreement—first among activists and then among policy makers—on what behaviors we considered instances of hate-motivated violence. Early discussions of the issue by activists, civil rights organizations, and social movements set out somewhat varied definitions and policy solutions for the problem. However, as more and more legislatures have considered the issue, the parameters of hate crime statutes have become more settled. Indeed, a set of "core" attributes of the laws have emerged.

The broader picture derived from our examination of the evolution of state hate crime law is one of an innovation diffusing across time and space and taking on different attributes as it does so. Taken together, the findings presented here suggest that it is useful to examine the specific features of innovation and diffusion at different levels of abstraction (that is, at the levels of method and content). Doing so allows us to see how, as law within a policy domain becomes institutionalized, two seemingly countervailing processes— homogenization and differentiation—operate.

Homogenization

In a period of over twenty years, states converge most around the methods of altering their criminal codes. Policy makers increasingly conform to "preferred" legal strategies as well as the motivational phrasing contained in the law. With respect to method, a pattern can be discerned that involves the ascendancy of two specific ways of making a piece of legislation. With respect to motivational wording, one form has gained increasing popularity. Even so, owing to path dependence, homogenization is not complete. Thus, states appear to be differentiated with respect to method even as two particular methods have attained a high degree of institutionalization.

This finding is consistent with conclusions drawn from other policy contexts. For example, the evolution of equal opportunity laws was similarly shaped by processes of path dependence and mimicry. As a result, the basic principles employed in equal employment opportunity laws were strongly influenced by the earliest proposals (Burstein 1998[1985], 37–38). As was the case with hate crime laws, the "power of the first draft" was such that legislators were unlikely to revisit their initial assumptions in later rounds. Subsequent discussions were structured by the initial formulation, and thus a narrow range of policy alternatives were considered. This winnowing process flows from legislators' desire for familiarity and shared understandings of the nature of the problem.

Similar patterns have been found in other work. For example, a handful of common patterns of diffusion have been identified across diverse social contexts and policy domains. Indeed, one of the recurrent findings in the literature on diffusion processes is that, in the aggregate, units in a social system increasingly come to resemble one another.[6] Such a pattern reflects the institutionalization of a social practice or innovation, which means that the practice has become taken for granted by actors as the most desirable way of accomplishing some task.

Differentiation

At the same time, however, our analysis points to a second tendency: differentiation. Whereas homogenization occurs at the level of method, domain expansion occurs at the level of content. As our discussion of changes in the content of state hate crime law reveals, one of the key features of the development of hate crime legislation is that as the laws have become more established their domain has widened to include more kinds of statuses and conduct. Specifically, more recent statutes possess varying combinations of statuses and conduct, suggesting that as hate crime laws become institutionalized their precise composition becomes more differentiated rather than homogenized. The various permutations of conduct and status provisions constitute the unique signatures of states that are otherwise participating in a more general process of homogenization. This differentiation is highly consequential for the kinds of activities that can be prosecuted and the kinds of statuses that are protected under the rubric of hate crime law. As with homogenization, most of what produces variation in conduct and status provisions is timing in the larger institutionalization process. States that passed laws earlier tend to have a more limited domain of coverage in their laws; in contrast, states that passed laws later tend to have more expansive domains. Notably, this process of domain expansion in state law parallels the development of federal hate crime law.

Although not addressed as such, the twin patterns of homogenization and differentiation are revealed in other studies of legal reform. Herbert Jacobs' (1988) study of the evolution of modern divorce laws shows that although most states embraced the basic no-fault strategy, important differences remained in terms of the substantive details of the laws. Jacobs suggests that divorce laws are like an impressionist painting, which from afar appears to contain broad strokes but upon closer inspection is seen to be composed of small heterogeneous points and dabs. That metaphor nicely captures the diffusion of hate crime laws, as well.

Ultimately, a consideration of diffusion processes in general, and homogenization and differentiation processes in particular, suggests that an exclusive focus on broad structural imperatives or moral entrepreneurs and lobbying activities provides only a limited view of how and why legislatures take action and what kinds of crime policy they design. Legislation is not merely a reflection of issue-specific mobilization. Moreover, issue-specific mobilization is often not necessary once a policy pedigree has been established and circulates across polities. The temporally specific nature of policy domain formation is further emphasized through a consideration of the ways in which the law is interpreted in judicial proceedings. This is the focus of our next chapter, which directs attention to how seemingly "settled" legislative models are justified, challenged, and on occasion altered as a new institutional arena addresses the policy within its domain.

$=$ Chapter 5 $=$

Judicial Decision Making and the Changing Meaning of Hate Crime

A T ANY given moment in time legal rules and categories exist on a continuum from controversial to settled (Friedman 1967, 793–94). There is widespread agreement, for example, about the behaviors and intentional states involved in larceny or fraud but significantly less consensus about what should be included under sexual harassment (Schultz 1998) and computer "hacking" (Chandler 1996). The controversy surrounding these latter categories has resulted in intensive negotiation among politicians, legal officials and experts, collective actors, and others about their meaning: What kinds of behaviors and intentions can be grouped under these categories? What should be excluded? What is the relationship between these activities and those already legally proscribed? What makes the misbehavior involved severe enough to be labeled illegal? All of these questions aim to attach a precise meaning to a broad legal concept and delimit the concept's domain and usage. The centrality of such "meaning-making" activities in constituting a legal category, coupled with temporal variability in the "settledness" of legal categories, underscores a core social process operative in the formation of law: that "determinacy" is a social achievement rather than an inherent quality of legal rules and concepts (Mitchell 1990; Ewick 1992).

Courts have played a central role in the process of fixing meaning to hate crime laws. Legislatures produce the basic templates for this process, but courts are assigned the role of giving authoritative meaning to those templates. Oliver Wendell Holmes once wrote that "the prophecies of what the courts will do, in fact, and nothing more pretentious, are what I mean by the law" (Holmes 1897). Legal rules are not meaningful as collections of words published in statute books;

they take on meaning, in practice, as judges apply them to specific circumstances. Ultimately, much of what constitutes a hate crime is determined by judges in the process of applying statutes to particular "real world" situations. Thus, the cases that come to their attention represent critical moments in the legal construction of hate crimes. Over time, as courts grapple with constitutional issues related to hate crime law they clarify precisely what the laws cover. They also continue to fashion elaborate justifications for the statutes, indicate what constitutes evidence in hate crime cases, invalidate a specific subset of approaches to drafting legislation, and limit the scope of applications of the law.

In dealing with constitutional challenges in particular, appellate courts demonstrate the important role played by the judicial realm in the meaning-making processes around legal constructs. Courts can elaborate or complicate the meaning of a statute, delimit its meaning and application, reject the language of particular statutes, validate or valorize others, work out deeper justifications (that is, link issues to new sources of legitimacy), and decide whether to widen the scope to include new actions. In the legal field, courts often are viewed as the ultimate sense makers of statutes. Their views, expressed in court opinions, serve as authoritative texts that then circulate throughout the legal field, to prosecutors, defense lawyers, presiding judges, and legal scholars. Thus, judges' determination of the scope and meaning of statutes is an important moment in the legal construction of hate crimes.

An early and influential sociological interpretation of meaning making in the judicial realm can be found in David Sudnow's (1965) work on "normal crimes" (see also Cicourel 1969; Daniels 1970; Frohman 1997; McCleary 1977). Sudnow finds that as prosecutors and public defenders negotiate plea bargains they connect offender behavior with a normal crime construct. As a kind of rich folk theory about the ordinary circumstances in which crime occurs, the normal crime construct goes far beyond the narrow specifications of the statutory definition of the crime. Prosecutors and public defenders then use the concept of normal crime, rather than the statutory definition, to derive the charge used in the plea bargain. Thus, both "criminal" actions and statutes are assigned meaning through the interactions of criminal justice officials.[1]

Two things can be added to Sudnow's analysis. First, we need to examine a variety of actors and organizations that contribute to the construction of legal meaning. Meaning is attached to legal concepts at several points: social movements construct "a problem," politicians create legislation, judges interpret statutes, and prosecutors—with the assistance of detectives and other law enforcement officials—decide whether to prosecute (Boyd, Berk, and Hamner 1996; Martin 1995) based on their decisions about how to classify and investigate a crime. Each of these are moments in the circulation of a crime concept within and outside of the justice system, and each moment sets in motion different groups of actors with unique ideologies, interests, and role scripts.

Second, the use of normal crime as a theoretical concept in the work of Sudnow and others (Boyd, Berk, and Hamner 1996; Frohman 1997) has been rather static. A normal crime appears to officials as fully formed, fixed, and a priori. In actuality, the meaning of a criminal statute is temporally variable, and such variability is particularly evident in categories that are new or vigorously contested. Actors must reach consensus over time if the construct is to become more settled. Sudnow provides useful insights into how, once established, a normal crime concept is put into use; however, we also need to understand how normal crime constructs are formed and institutionalized.

With an awareness of both of these issues, this chapter examines the role of judges in attaching meaning to a legal construct, just as previous chapters have examined the roles of social movements and legislators. Although the processes identified here are more generally applicable to other aspects of law, hate crime cases are particularly well suited to an examination of judicial meaning making because it is a fairly new, and thus a comparatively "unsettled," concept. The series of hate crime cases heard over the past decade or so has given judges the opportunity to reach consensus, to delimit and specify what the concept covers. In light of this, we examine how appellate courts have made sense of hate crime statutes and, in the process, assigned new meaning to the concept.

Court opinions provide an ideal arena for examining the role of institutionalization in judicial meaning making because courts use them to communicate their interpretations with interested parties, including other courts, lawyers, law students, advocacy groups, and lawmakers.[2] Although case law is not binding from one state to the next (unless a case reaches the U.S. Supreme Court), courts have generally understood hate crime statutes to share certain common elements, and citation of cases across jurisdiction is frequent. Furthermore, published opinions provide a public forum through which judges articulate the rhetorical strategies, or arguments, used to deny or affirm claims raised by appellants. These arguments are often picked up by other courts as part of an emerging consensus or can be subsequently discarded when such a consensus does not exist. Thus, opinions serve as a key venue through which the authoritative meaning of a legal rule or concept is circulated throughout the legal field.

To systematically analyze the development of the hate crime construct we tracked the following kinds of information from each case. First, we recorded both the types of claims defendants make about the facial validity of a statute and the types of judicial arguments made in response to those claims. Arguments consist of justifications for rejecting or accepting particular claims. For example, in response to the claim that a statute is "unconstitutionally vague," a judge might argue that, in fact, the statute has a plain meaning—that ordinary people can interpret it—or that because the statute requires demonstration of "specific intent" there is little likelihood of arbitrary enforcement. Analyzed over time, the changing combinations of claims and arguments are indicative of the struggle over what the law means, including the kinds of conduct it covers and which form of law represents a legitimate method. In addition to recording information about the claims and arguments present in each case, we also focus specifically on the shifts and changes in the assumptions judges make about what kinds of statutes represent legitimate forms of regulation, why hate crime should be treated more severely than other offenses, and what kinds of acts (and victims) are involved in hate crimes. Taken together, this information allows us to measure the changing features of judicial rhetoric about hate crimes, to trace the development of a "normal" hate crime in the case law, and to follow shifts in the parameters of what is included under the concept of hate crime.

Constitutional Challenges to Hate Crime Law

Although the two U.S. Supreme Court cases on hate crime, *R.A.V. v. St. Paul* (505 U.S. 377 [1992]) and *Wisconsin v. Mitchell* (113 S. Ct. 2194 [1993]), generated much of the public and scholarly attention devoted to determining the constitutionality of these laws, the lower court challenges date back to 1984 and continue into the present. Thirty-six of these cases were decided between mid-1991 and early 1999. In terms of both method and content, a wide variety of laws has been considered by appellate courts.[3] Five courts have rejected specific statutes, one court has invalidated a portion of one state's statute, and in two instances laws have been wholly repealed. Curiously, the growth in court challenges to the laws has lagged behind the passage rate. That is, many states possessed laws long before challenges were mounted. Whether this is attributable to a growth in enforcement or to the atmosphere of the early 1990s—which witnessed the emergence of a highly visible critical reaction to "multiculturalism," affirmative action policies, and other policies that appeared to conservative-leaning intellectuals as extending "special" privileges to some groups and not others—is difficult to determine. In any case, by the late 1990s, enforcement was reaching its highest level, and the frequency of constitutional challenges had dropped off markedly.

Across this series of cases, judges have considered five kinds of constitutional challenges to the laws. These challenges can be summarized as follows:

1. Vagueness (in violation of the Fourteenth Amendment): The statute does not clearly express which acts are proscribed and which acts are not. The lack of clarity is potentially problematic because ordinary citizens will not be able to know when they have transgressed the law and because vague laws allow for arbitrary enforcement, and therefore the statute violates a defendant's right to due process.

2. Punishment of speech (in violation of the First Amendment): The statute punishes motives or thoughts and therefore constitutes a regulation of speech.

3. Overbreadth (in violation of the First Amendment): The statute is so broadly written that it extends to expression protected by the First Amendment. The implication is that such regulations, even if they are not enforced, have a "chilling effect" on the exercise of constitutional rights.

4. Content discrimination (in violation of the First Amendment): The statute regulates speech based upon the content or viewpoint of speech. It is suggestive of an important limiting condition on the state's power to regulate speech—that it can do so only irrespective of the content of the speech itself.

5. Denial of equal protection before the law (in violation of the Fourteenth Amendment): The statute violates the equal protection clause because it grants preferential treatment to minorities.

Each of these claims has been made in multiple cases, and courts have developed a diverse array of responses (mostly rejections, but some acceptances) (Phillips and Grattet 2000). A summary of these claims, along with the frequency with which they have been asserted and select cases that exemplify their assertion, is presented in table 5.1.

Table 5.1   Defendant Claims Regarding the Constitutionality of Hate
Crime Statutes in Appellate Cases, from 1984 to 1999

Claim	Number of Cases	Description	Sample Case
Vagueness	26	Precludes sufficient notice of proscribed act and allows arbitrary enforcement	*State v. Mitchell* (1991)
Punishment of speech	24	Punishes motive or thought, therefore constitutes regulation of speech	*State v. Mitchell* (1992)
Overbreadth	20	Allows application to protected conduct, resulting in "chilling effect" on exercise of constitutional rights	*People v. Superior Court* (1993)
Content discrimination	7	Regulates speech based on content and viewpoint	*R.A.V. v. St. Paul* (1992)
Denial of equal protection	6	Allows preferential treatment for minorities, unequal treatment of offender based on views	*State v. Beebe* (1984), *State v. Mortimer* (1994)

Source: Authors' compilation.

Changes in Judicial Interpretation

The development of the appellate case law regarding hate crimes can be viewed as comprising four stages, as illustrated in table 5.2. This parsing of hate crime appellate case law defines an evolution characterized by early dispositions, constitutional crisis, reclamation of laws, and a shift to peripheral issues.

Early Dispositions

In the first five cases, decided between 1984 and 1991, challenges were rejected by lower appeals courts in Oregon, California, New York, and Wisconsin. The Wisconsin case, which would later reach the U.S. Supreme Court (*Wisconsin v. Mitchell*), involved a black teenager who was given an enhanced penalty for directing several youn-

Table 5.2   Hate Crime Cases, 1984 to 1999

Characteristic	Date	Court
Early disposition		
State v. Beebe	January 20, 1984	Court of Appeals of Oregon
People v. Grupe	August 17, 1988	Criminal Court of the City of New York
State v. Mitchell	June 5, 1991	Court of Appeals of Wisconsin
State v. Hendrix	June 19, 1991	Court of Appeals of Oregon
People v. Lashley	December 16, 1991	Court of Appeals of California
Constitutionality crisis		
R.A.V. v. St. Paul	**June 22, 1992**	**Supreme Court of the United States**
State v. Mitchell	**June 23, 1992**	**Supreme Court of Wisconsin**
State v. Wyant	**August 26, 1992**	**Supreme Court of Ohio**
Reclamation		
State v. Plowman	August 27, 1992	Supreme Court of Oregon
Dobbins v. State	September 24, 1992	Court of Appeals of Florida
People v. Miccio	October 20, 1992	Criminal Court of the City of New York
Richards v. State	**November 17, 1992**	**Court of Appeals of Florida**
People v. Joshua H.	March 8, 1993	Court of Appeals of California
People v. Superior Court	May 19, 1993	Court of Appeals of California
Wisconsin v. Mitchell	June 11, 1993	Supreme Court of the United States
State v. Ladue	July 1, 1993	Supreme Court of Vermont
In re M.S.	August 17, 1993	Court of Appeals of California
State v. Talley[1]	**September 9, 1993**	**Supreme Court of Washington**
People v. Richards	November 2, 1993	Court of Appeals of Michigan
People v. Baker	December 15, 1993	Court of Appeals of California
State v. McKnight	January 19, 1994	Supreme Court of Iowa
State v. Vanatter	January 25, 1994	Supreme Court of Missouri
State v. Stalder	January 27, 1994	Supreme Court of Florida
Reeves v. State	February 11, 1994	Court of Appeals of Florida
Groover v. State	March 1, 1994	Court of Appeals of Florida
State v. Mortimer	May 26, 1994	Supreme Court of New Jersey
Shift to peripheral issues		
State v. Kearns	**May 26, 1994**	**Supreme Court of New Jersey**
Richards v. State	October 5, 1994	Court of Appeals of Florida
People v. McKenzie	May 9, 1995	Court of Appeals of California
In re M.S.	July 3, 1995	Supreme Court of California
People v. Superior Court	July 3, 1995	Supreme Court of California
Washington v. Pollard	December 11, 1995	Court of Appeals of Washington
In re Vladimir P.	September 20, 1996	Court of Appeals of Illinois
Illinois v. Nitz	November 15, 1996	Court of Appeals of Illinois
Wichita v. Edwards	May 23, 1997	Court of Appeals of Kansas
Montana v. Nye	July 23, 1997	Supreme Court of Montana
New Jersey v. Apprendi	August 19, 1997	Superior Court of New Jersey
Boyd v. Texas	March 25, 1999	Court of Appeals of Texas

Source: Authors' compilation.
Note: Cases in bold were ruled unconstitutional on appeal.
1. Section 1 is constitutional because it regulates conduct; section 2 is unconstitutional because it proscribes speech based on content.

ger boys to assault and rob a white teenager. The defendant's attorneys argued that the enhancement was both vague and overbroad. This basic line of attack—on grounds of vagueness, punishment of speech, and overbreadth—was followed in each case.

This first period is notable because opinions tended to be short and simple. They do not contain multiple or in-depth justifications for the statutes. The courts endorsed the statutes as though the issues at stake posed little controversy. They dismissed the challenges with the simple argument that the laws cover conduct, not speech. Also, courts applied the "compelling interest" argument to these cases. This argument, which later became an important rhetorical plank in justifying the laws, holds that even if the laws were found to constitute a punishment of speech, upholding them would be justified on the basis of the state's "compelling interest" in reducing the harms of hate violence.

Constitutional Crisis

The second period is marked by a series of cases in which existing laws were declared unconstitutional. The case that set off this period was *R.A.V. v. St. Paul*, involving a white teenager who burned a cross on a neighboring black family's front lawn. The boy was prosecuted under a city ordinance that prohibited the "display of a symbol which one knows or has reason to know arouses anger, alarm or resentment in others on the basis of race, color, creed, religion or gender." The U.S. Supreme Court heard the case in 1991 and ruled the St. Paul ordinance unconstitutional, in the majority view, on the grounds of content discrimination and overbreadth and, in the minority concurring view, on overbreadth alone. One day later, the Wisconsin Supreme Court declared its penalty enhancement law unconstitutional although this decision was subsequently overturned by the U.S. Supreme Court. Two months later, the Ohio Supreme Court, reviewing a case involving an aggravated menacing conviction stemming from a dispute between white and black campers in a state park outside Columbus, declared its ethnic intimidation law unconstitutional; in light of the Wisconsin decision, this ruling was subsequently vacated and remanded by the U.S. Supreme Court.

These latter cases in Wisconsin and Ohio, dealing with quite different forms of statute, rejected the laws on the basis of punishment of speech. Notably, the punishment of speech grounds differ from the content discrimination claim that was central to *R.A.V.* Nevertheless, the judges in both the Wisconsin and Ohio cases cited *R.A.V* in support of their decisions. Also, the Wisconsin and Ohio judges rejected the arguments used in previous cases to defend the laws, maintaining that the penalty enhancement and ethnic intimidation forms inappropriately punished offenders for their thoughts, motives, and speech. Because most other statutes in the country resembled either the Wisconsin or the Ohio laws, the punishment of speech issue centrally occupied much of the discussion in the remaining cases.

Besides declaring the laws unconstitutional, the Wisconsin and Ohio cases represent the first time hate crime laws had reached the state Supreme Court level. The opinions in these cases were considerably longer and contained more justifications and external references than previous cases (Phillips and Grattet 2000). Thus, even the formal characteristics of opinions attest to the crisis in the meaning of the laws. Indeed, some commentators forecasted the end of hate crime statutes (Justice 1993).

Reclamation

The third period is characterized by a period of reclamation of the laws. In a relatively short period of time, stretching from mid-1992 to mid-1994, eighteen cases prompted consideration of the laws. In each of these cases, a constitutionally valid account for hate crime law was elaborated. A key case was the Florida case, *Dobbins v. State* (605 So. 2d 922 [1992]). This case involved a Jewish youth who had joined a skinhead group to anger his parents; he was beaten by the other members of the group when they discovered he was Jewish. It demonstrated that it is neither the status of the victim (a skinhead) or the perpetrator (a group of skinheads) nor the type or the extent of their bigotry that is covered by the laws. The court maintained that hate crime laws are appropriately invoked when criminal conduct reflects racial, religious, or other statutorily defined bias. The court's interpretation in *Dobbins* restated the earlier argument that hate crime laws punish only conduct. However, it also advanced a new argument; namely, that hate crime laws are comparable in strategy and meaning to antidiscrimination laws. This argument served to situate hate crime law within other more established laws that also regulate motive. In addition, during this period a consensus emerged that some forms of law are illegitimate strategies. Most notably, statutes that use wording similar to the phrasing found in the St. Paul ordinance, such as New Jersey's law and a portion of Washington's law (*State v. Kearns* 136 N.J. 56 [1994] and *State v. Talley* 122 Wash. 2d 192 [1993], respectively), were deemed illegitimate, whereas statutes using wording similar to that found in Wisconsin's penalty enhancement law were deemed legitimate (*People v. Joshua H.*, 13 Cal. App. 4th 1734 [1993]). Opinions grew shorter, and a set of patterned responses to each major claim arose (for example, punishment of speech, vagueness, and over-breadth), suggesting that as a consensus emerged around the meaning of hate crime statutes judicial responses became more streamlined, more economical (Phillips and Grattet 2000).

Shift to Peripheral Issues

The fourth and final series of cases, stretching from mid-1994 to the early 1999, have been marked by a shift to more peripheral issues. Many of the cases replay issues raised earlier, which by the fourth stage are easily disposed. Four particular issues have characterized these cases: What qualifies as harassment or threatening behavior? What kind of evidence is legitimate (for example, are racist utterances made during the course of a crime sufficient to establish motive)? To what degree is victim preselection necessary for a crime to qualify as a hate crime? And what proportion of the motivation needs to be biased in order for an act to qualify as a hate crime? These issues suggest that by 1994 the core legitimacy of hate crime law was taken for granted, having been established across prior cases.

Moreover, each of these issues moved the focus of concern away from the central preoccupation with whether the entire statute represents an infringement on speech to more peripheral issues that could potentially be resolved by simply changing the wording of the statute such that key components of the law are clarified. For example, a California case, *In re M.S.* 10 Cal. 4th 698 (1995), which involved a female minor who took part in an attack on a group of gay men in San Francisco, focused specifically on whether the intimidation portion of the law covers all threats or just those with a high likelihood of being carried out. Had the court eliminated all threats from the law, it would still cover things like assault and vandalism. Thus, it would not have caused the law to be overturned entirely.

Using quantitative measures of the number of words used to deal with specific claims and the number of citations, Scott Phillips and Ryken Grattet (2000) demonstrate that early cases reflect a heavy volume of rhetorical work to justify statutes or to justify striking down statutes. Later, the techniques for disposing of unconstitutionality claims became increasingly taken for granted, and the volume of rhetorical work decreases. However, the pattern is not a simple "linear decay" in the volume of rhetorical work, which would suggest that a single point of contention was raised and resolved in an increasingly efficient manner across cases. Instead, the pattern Phillips and Grattet observe is what they term a "diminishing peaks" model of institu-

tionalization. The diminishing peaks model involves a general settling
of the law, punctuated by periodic controversies that are increasingly
less substantial (Phillips and Grattet 2000).

Substantive Changes in Hate Crime Law

The chronological breakdown of case law is useful in characterizing
the general development of the law. However, it does not address
changes in the substantive meaning of the hate crime construct. As
hate crime has become increasingly institutionalized in judicial rhetoric, two general processes have contributed to the substantive meaning of the concept: construct elaboration and domain expansion.

Elaboration of the Construct

As more and more cases are subject to the scrutiny of appellate
courts, the legal definition of a hate crime has become richer and
more developed. Over time judges compose increasingly elaborate
practical theories about what hate crime statutes mean. Although the
text of the individual statutes changes little across the series of cases,
judges gradually invest more complex meanings, including theories
about the practical or normal circumstances under which such crimes
occur and a more specific understanding of particular phrasing in the
statute. The development of more complex meanings is intimately
connected to negotiation around ideas related to the state's compelling interest, speech and motive, proportionality of motive, and expressive conduct.

State's Compelling Interest   Courts have consistently argued that states
have a "compelling interest" in curbing hate crime; legally speaking,
this justifies limited infringements on first amendment protections of
free speech *(United States v. O'Brien* [391 U.S. 367 (1968)]).[4] Tracing the
development of the compelling interest argument reveals the emergence of an increasingly elaborate depiction of the nature of hate
crime and the normal circumstances under which it occurs. The argument is based on knowledge and information presented by extralegal
sources—such as interest groups, scholars, experts, government officials, and special task forces—that delineate the parameters of hate
crime.

Throughout these decisions, various groups were cited. Some argued that there is a "rising tide" of hate-motivated violence, sometimes described as reaching "epidemic" proportions *(People v. Joshua*

H., State v. Kearns). *People v. Grupe* 141 Misc. 2d 6(1988). An early case in New York City, mentions the reported "increase" in bias crime five times in a six-page opinion. Others argued that hate crimes are more harmful to society than conventional crimes because they threaten entire groups and often produce cycles of retaliatory violence and community unrest. In *State v. Plowman* (314 Ore. 157, 165 [1992]), for example, the court argued that "such crimes—because they are directed not only toward the victim but, in essence, toward an entire group of which the victim is perceived to be a member—invite imitation, retaliation, and insecurity on the part of persons in the group to which the victim was perceived by the assailants to belong." Finally, some surmised that hate crimes lead to more serious injuries, involve multiple offenders who are not typically strangers, and are more psychologically debilitating than conventional crimes for the victim and the victim's group (see, for example, *People v. Joshua H., Wisconsin v. Mitchell, In re M.S., State v. Slulder*).

Yet the image of hate crime in case law that emerges from these citations is selective in that all statutes cover a variety of groups and activities for which the assertion of an epidemic could not hold (see our description of federal and state hate crime laws in chapters 3 and 4). For example, there is little systematic evidence that property damage directed at the physically and mentally disabled is on the rise (cf. Waxman 1991), yet statutes including physical and mental disability as protected statuses have been justified using the compelling state interest argument. Similarly, although rates of victimization toward Hindus or Seventh Day Adventists do not appear to be increasing, the statute nonetheless protects all religious groups equally, even those for whom the compelling interest argument seems implausible.

Acceptance of the compelling interest argument requires that judges have a mental image of the "normal" circumstances in which hate crime occurs. These circumstances include stereotypical kinds of conduct and victims, such as "gay bashing," terrorizing a black family that has moved into a new neighborhood, and vandalism of synagogues. Indeed, these stereotypical hate crimes are more plausibly perceived to be widespread and increasing "exponentially."[5] Although it narrows the possible meanings of hate crime, the exclusion of particular imagery from association with the concept elaborates the concept by infusing it with a much richer and more complex set of meanings about what kinds of things inspire hate crimes, where they usually occur, and who constitutes the typical perpetrator and victim. These examples illustrate the ways that extralegal sources of knowledge shape the meaning-making and rhetorical practices of judges.

The elaboration of hate crime occurs as external sources propose—and judges adopt—an increasingly rich, albeit selective, imagery of the normal hate crime.

Speech and Motive   The negotiations around the role of speech and motive as components of hate crime are not purely questions of the constitutionality or appropriateness of the law, although they often are presented as such. These negotiations also have implications for the legal construction of hate crime, most notably what is and is not included in the concept. The earliest judicial decisions attempted to impose a simple solution: hate crime statutes criminalize conduct, not speech. To support this argument courts contended that hate crimes statutes are not meant to police expression. Moreover, they argued, for example, that bigoted thoughts and expression alone are an insufficient basis upon which to invoke a hate crime penalty enhancement, because bigoted thoughts and expression are not already (and could never be) criminal acts. Furthermore, early courts argued that offensive speech was not even necessary to demonstrate that a hate crime occurred. Judges could use routine behavior, such as a person repeatedly visiting a Korean neighborhood and picking fights with Koreans, to conclude that a hate crime had occurred. Inferring the defendant's intention from such evidence, the court found, is entirely appropriate (*State v. Plowman* 314 Ore. 157).

Behavior alone was not a sufficient basis upon which to deem some action a hate crime. For example, the fact that victim and perpetrator were of different races or religions did not in itself signify that a hate crime had taken place. In fact, an appeals case in Illinois involved a religiously motivated attack by one Jewish youth on another (*In re Vladimir P.* 283 Ill. App. 3d 1068 [1996]). The motivation had to reflect bias toward the victim because of his or her race, religion, national origin, and so forth. This certainly narrows the application of law and limits the contexts to which it can be applied; but it also deepens the judicial understanding of what is excluded from the concept in ways that are not entirely clear from the wording of the statutes alone. For example, an incident involving racist speech alone is excluded, as are offenses for which motivation cannot be shown—by speech or otherwise. These meanings contribute to the accumulating judicial sense of the terrain covered by the laws.

The controversy surrounding motive also helps to further refine the kinds of mental states included and excluded from the concept. Earlier courts envisioned hate crime as conduct contingent on specific motives and evidenced by speech and other kinds of expression (see "Hate Is Not Speech" 1993; Dillof 1997; Grannis 1993). Thus, thought processes (and speech) themselves were not criminalized; rather, only offensive conduct that stemmed from those thought processes was implicated in hate crime law. In the three consecutive cases in 1992 in which certain forms of hate crime statutes were declared unconstitutional (*R.A.V. v. St. Paul, Wisconsin v. Mitchell, State v. Wyant* [64 Ohio St. 3d 566 (1992)]), this conception was challenged. In the Wisconsin and Ohio cases, challengers relied heavily upon Susan Gellman's (1991) critique of hate crime statutes to argue that the statutes punish motives. Following Gellman, they argued that since the criminal conduct involved in hate crime is already punished under existing statutory law, the enhancement can only mean that there is an extra punishment if the defendant has unpopular motives. In other words, the challengers to the laws conceptualized hate crimes as separable into independent units of conduct and motive, with ordinary criminal sanctions corresponding to the conduct and the hate crime penalty enhancement corresponding to the motivation.

Advocates of Gellman's view further argue that although criminal laws may consider intent to commit a crime, they may not consider the offender's motives. In other words, statutes may not regulate all of the possible mental precursors to crime but must be restricted to intent. To punish motive shades into punishing beliefs and political ideology and is inconsistent with the principles of criminal law.[6] Following the Wisconsin and Ohio cases, there was considerable uncertainty as to whether Gellman's conceptualization of motive or the earlier view of hate crimes as conduct contingent on specific motives should prevail.

Which conceptualization of motive has triumphed? The conventional view is that the U.S. Supreme Court simply intervened, applied the "proper" analysis, and clarified this issue. In so doing, it declared the conclusions of the Ohio and Wisconsin courts invalid. In fact, six appellate cases (*State v. Plowman, Dobbins v. State, People v. Miccio* [155 Misc. 2d 697 (1992)], *Richards v. State, People v. Joshua H., People v. Superior Court* [10 Cal. 4th 735 (1993)]) occurred between the Ohio and Wisconsin cases and before the U.S. Supreme Court decision in *Wisconsin v. Mitchell*. All the judicial arguments used to dispose of the overbreadth and punishment of speech claims in *Wisconsin v. Mitchell* had been employed by lower courts in the previous six cases. Thus, *Wisconsin v. Mitchell* might be better thought of as replicating arguments made in the previous cases rather than crafting a truly innovative solution.

The key factor shaping the rejection of the Ohio and Wisconsin courts also served to elaborate a specific meaning of motive in hate crime statutes. That meaning came from a parallel drawn by the

Court of Appeals of Florida *(Dobbins v. State)* between hate crime statutes and antidiscrimination statutes. Using the framework of antidiscrimination law allowed for a specific understanding to be attached to the issue of motive and speech: "It does not matter why a woman is treated differently than a man, a black differently than a white, a Catholic differently than a Jew; it matters only that they are. So also with section 775.085 [Florida's hate crime statute]. It doesn't matter that Dobbins hated Jewish people or why he hated them; it only mattered that he discriminated against Daly by beating him because he was Jewish" *(Dobbins v. State,* 925).

Drawing an analogy between hate crime law and antidiscrimination statutes served not only to situate the laws within a pre-established body of legal principles, it also resolved the issue of the propriety of considering motive in such cases. Antidiscrimination statutes are understood to provide little scrutiny of motives. The only thing that matters is whether there is evidence that the victim was intentionally selected because of his or her race, religion, national origin, and so on. In other words, it is not the prejudice of the perpetrator but rather the act of discrimination that is punished. The *Dobbins* decision adopts and extends the understanding provided by the earlier courts that hate crimes statutes punish only conduct, and it incorporates the narrower conception of the mental states demanded by critics like Gellman.

The implication here is that hate crimes are not "thought crimes" any more than other forms of discrimination are "thought crimes." In both cases, the precise characteristics of the perpetrator's attitudes are irrelevant; the act of discrimination is all that matters. To reflect this change in the conception of hate crime, some subsequent commentators have shifted to describing the subject of these laws as "bias crime" rather than "hate crime." Anthony Dillof (1997, 1,016), for example, argues that "'bias crimes' is a more accurate term than 'hate crimes.' The statutes under consideration likely apply to many criminal acts in which hate, understood as a particular subjective emotion, is not involved. Likewise, the statutes under consideration do not apply to many criminal acts based upon hate." Ironically, this conception broadens the applicability of the laws in that hate does not need to be present, only bias. In other words, hate requires a higher evidentiary standard than bias.

In some instances, this elaborated conception of motive was imposed on statutes that appeared to require more information about the offender's state of mind than is implied in the "because of" construction. For example, Florida's statute, which enhances penalties if the crime "evidences prejudice based upon race, religion," et cetera, invites an investigation of the precise character of the offender's motivation.[7] However, the Florida Supreme Court (*State v. Stalder*) narrowly interpreted the statute as providing for enhancement when the victim was *intentionally selected because of* race, religion, et cetera. In other words, ignoring the specific terms included in the statute (that is, that prejudice was required), the court aligned its interpretation with the discrimination parallel.

Proportionality of Motive   Courts have also elaborated the conceptualization of motive with respect to the question of proportionality. Starting with *People v. Superior Court* (15 Cal. App. 4th 1593) in May 1993, courts began to consider what proportion of the motive needed to be oriented toward bias for a crime to qualify as a hate crime. Courts recognized that victims are often selected for multiple reasons: presumed level of guardianship, location, appearance, potential for material gain. Because none of the statutes spells out the degree or proportion of the motive that needs to be bias related, it was up to courts to attach a specific interpretation along these lines. A California court introduced the notion that bias should be a "substantial factor" in the selection of the victim; all of the other courts considering the issue followed suit (*People v. Baker* [31 Cal. App. 4th 889 (1993)], *In re M.S.* [10 Cal. 4th 698(1995)], *People v. Superior Court* [15 Cal. App. 4th 1593 (1993)], *Wichita v. Edwards* [Kan. App. LEXIS 90 (1997)]).

Interestingly, the test of bias as a "substantial factor" could have been more narrowly drawn. Courts could have required that bias be the sole factor. That is, they could have relied upon a "but for" standard, which requires that the crime would not have taken place "but for" the race, religion, or sexual orientation of the victim. In fact, some law enforcement training programs employ a "but for" criterion by instructing officers to question whether the crime would have happened without the presence of the element of bias. Richard Berk, Elizabeth Boyd, and Karl Hamner (1992, 130–31) note that "our experience with law enforcement officials, however, suggests that, for a crime to be categorized as hate-motivated, a 'but for' criterion is commonly applied: But for the hate-motivation, the crime would not have occurred." This conception of hate crime includes acts in which bias is the sole or substantial factor and excludes circumstances in which bias is a trivial factor in the selection of the victim. For example, shouting a racist epithet during the commission of a crime might reveal the perpetrator's bias toward the victim, but that bias might be a trivial factor relative to the other reasons the crime took place. These criteria are crucial to understanding the developing legal conception of hate crime, and, once again, they add considerable depth and breadth to the meaning of the statutes.

Expressive Conduct   In addition to assumptions about normal hate crime and the reconceptualization and elaboration of motive, courts also have fleshed out the understanding of what kinds of expressive conduct can be regulated under a hate crime statute. For example, although the *R.A.V.* decision appeared to signal considerable limitations on the incorporation of expressive conduct into hate crimes, most other states' statutes contained wording that seemed to shade into expressive activity, such as harassment, menacing, terrorizing, and intimidation. The subsequent decisions spelled out the circumstances under which such conduct should be deemed punishable. The key notion is that of "true threats." As the California Supreme Court explained in its decision in *In re M.S.*, for such acts to be punishable the perceived threats must constitute "true threats" in the established legal sense. That is, the speaker must have the ability to carry out the threat and must also be likely to do so.

On the one hand, the "true threat" factor expands the domain of coverage of the law by incorporating conduct other than bodily injury and vandalism, which were emphasized so strongly in early decisions. However, it restricts the meaning of the hate crime construct, as well. Notably, it does not permit punishment of hate speech that is unconnected to "true threats." Even when hate speech is connected to a threat the court could conceivably evaluate, it does not in itself qualify as a "true threat."

The elaboration of the hate crime construct appears to be headed in several other directions. The role of premeditation and victim preselection has been addressed in *Washington v. Pollard* (80 Wash. App. 60 [1995]). The defendant argued that the motivational standard applied in hate crime presupposes planning and forethought on behalf of the perpetrator. In rejecting this argument, the court allowed that hate crimes sometimes occur spontaneously. Other cases limit the degree to which prior speech, tattoos, and preexisting organization affiliations can be considered suggestive of motive in particular instances of hate crime. If these interpretations hold in other cases, like the courts' interpretations of the state's compelling interest, speech as indicative of motive, and proportionality of motive, they will refine and contribute to the evolving concept of hate crime.

More generally, the rhetorical strategy employed in restricting the meaning of threats corresponds to the way the courts dealt with motive. It involves situating a more specific interpretation into a pre-established mode of legal analysis. Doing so elaborates and enriches—but at the same time limits—the legal meaning of the concept.

Domain Expansion

From the preceding discussion it is clear that the elaboration of the hate crime construct occurred mostly as a restriction of the possible meanings of the term, but it also occurs in expansive ways. Over time, judges often are presented with a more diverse array of behavior and circumstances to be reconciled with a particular legal concept. New circumstances provide an opportunity to demonstrate the reach or the limitations of a concept. Although the numbers of hate crime cases are small and any conclusions drawn must be tentative, it appears that the expansion of the domain of the hate crime concept is well under way. From the beginning, most hate crime cases have involved acts resulting in bodily injury to a specific victim (see figure 5.1). A few cases appeared that involved property damage (see figure 5.2). However, a growing number of cases contained little or no physical violence or property damage but instead consisted primarily of harassment and threatening behavior (see figure 5.3). Thus, one way of contrasting the early and late cases is with respect to the kinds of conduct involved in the case. The general pattern is toward a higher quotient of expressive action as opposed to the physical violence involved in the early cases. This suggests that hate crimes involving physical violence were first embedded in the concept: cases involving bodily injury were perceived by prosecutors (and perhaps by judges) to be "easier" to apply the laws, given the centrality of concerns about whether or not the laws punish expression. Once the easy cases had been upheld, prosecutors began to push the envelope by pursuing increasingly ambiguous circumstances. Thus, the domain of law was expanded to incorporate matters that were once ambiguous or questionable as to whether they should be included under the law.

This shift makes both theoretical and logical sense. As the concept of hate crime becomes more cemented, courts are increasingly willing to entertain a broader array of possible circumstances in which they can occur. This is consistent with the arguments put forth in chapters 3 and 4. More theoretically, domain expansion reflects a high degree of institutionalization of a legal construct because in order for it to be applied to novel contexts the core elements of the construct must be firmly established.

Figure 5.1   Cumulative Frequency of Hate Crimes Court Cases Involving Bodily Injury, 1984 to 1999

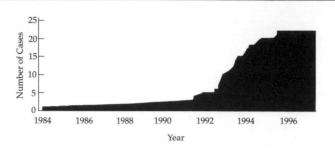

Source: Authors' compilation.
Note: Data as of first day of indicated year.

Figure 5.2   Cumulative Frequency of Hate Crime Court Cases Involving Property Damage

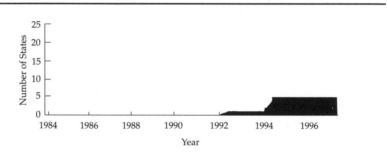

Source: Authors' compilation.
Note: Data as of first day of indicated year.

Figure 5.3   Cumulative Frequency of Hate Crime Court Cases Involving Harassment, 1984 to 1999

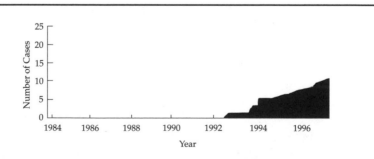

Source: Authors' compilation.
Note: Data as of first day of indicated year.

The Formation of Constitutional Forms of Hate Crime Law

Because considerable debate has revolved around the constitutionality of hate crime law, it is important to note that—despite construct elaboration and domain expansion—courts have not endorsed any one strategy (for example, the penalty enhancement or ethnic intimidation forms of law) for drafting hate crime law. They have, however, rejected laws that specify coverage of noncriminal expressive conduct. Thus, an emergent baseline requirement of hate crime statutes is that they cover only criminal acts. The St. Paul ordinance, the New Jersey statute, and a portion of the Washington state statute— the only statutes that have been successfully invalidated—were all struck down because, although they covered many acts that are criminal, they also targeted expressive conduct that was not already criminalized. According to the majority opinion in *R.A.V.*, a statute that created penalties for the entire class of "fighting words"—that is, one that did not restrict the penalty to expressions of hatred on race, religion, and the like—would be constitutional. From the point of view of the Supreme Court, such a statute would regulate the manner, not the content, of expression. No such statute currently exists; moreover, there is no evidence of an inclination within the activist community for developing such a remedy. Nor would such a statute, if it did exist, accomplish the symbolic goals of promoting tolerance and understanding along known axes of intergroup conflict. Instead it would, by definition, ignore those axes.[8]

Courts have also steered legislation toward more desirable forms of law with respect to motivational phrasing. In the wake of the *R.A.V.*, *Wyant*, and *Mitchell* cases, courts have elaborated a discrimination parallel to understand the way motivation properly figures into hate crime statutes. They have increasingly thought about hate crime as a discriminatory act, one in which the offender discriminates in the selection of his or her victim. The role of motive in hate crime cases becomes the same as the role of motive in discrimination cases. Namely, the abstract beliefs of the discriminator or the hate crime offender are irrelevant to the determination of whether a discriminatory act has taken place. All that must be shown is that the victim was selected because of his or her (real or imagined) social group characteristics. Under such a standard, Klansmen are not distinguished from people who hold mild negative stereotypes about blacks or Jews. The statutory phrasing that is both succinct and corresponds most closely with the discrimination logic is the "because of" construction. Consistent with the findings presented in chapter 4, in the course of the appellate cases this phrasing has been elevated to the "model" formula.

The failure to take seriously the discrimination parallel has led Jacobs and Potter (1998, 128) and other critics to reject hate crime statutes on the grounds that they punish "politically incorrect opinions and viewpoints." If hate crime laws punish viewpoints, however, then so too do all discrimination laws, and the same logic would imply that discrimination laws should also be repealed. Jacobs and Potter put forward the argument that hate crime laws are fundamentally different from civil rights laws and that the discrimination parallel should not be extended to criminal law. They argue that "the harms hate crime laws are designed to remedy are not clearly identifiable. The harm to the victim is already punished by generic criminal law" (Jacobs and Potter 1998, 128).[9]

Consistent with other forms of antidiscrimination law, courts have not specifically ruled on which status provisions should be included in hate crime law. However, court opinions often contain assumptions about which categories of persons constitute the "normal" victims of hate crime. Recall that courts assume an image of the "normal" hate crime in their application of the compelling interest argument. The compelling interest argument breaks down when and if statutes begin to identify status categories for whom hate violence is, arguably, neither widespread nor increasing. Thus, a limitation on which status provisions courts are likely to accept is implied in those discussions. Minimally, status provisions should reflect long-standing historical axes of discrimination and intergroup conflict upon which significant inequality is built and in which violence or threats of violence have historically been a means of maintaining inequality (see Lawrence 1999). Status provisions also tend to be universal categories: the terms race, religion, and sexual orientation, for example, cover all religions (or even the lack thereof), all races, and all sexual orientations (as the term is usually meant in legal discourse: heterosexuality, homosexuality, bisexuality). This construction blunts possible equal protection challenges, in that penalty enhancements are offered to all groups simultaneously. In other words, blacks, gays, and Jews are not given protections by the laws that are not also given to Caucasians, heterosexuals, and Christians. Extending this logic, it would seem unlikely that we would see laws that include provisions for Democrats, octogenarians, or Yankees' fans, because these are historical axes of neither discrimination nor violence and, if included, would give special protections to one group rather than to an entire category. Thus, the court cases suggest that the two criteria governing the inclusion of status provisions are that they reflect a historical pattern of conflict and discrimination and that they protect inclusive, universal categories. The importance of this observation is taken up more fully in the concluding chapter of this book.

Convergence of Meaning and Repertoires of Justification

The controversy surrounding hate crime has centered on the meaning that should be attached to the concept. This meaning is assigned not only at the moment when political actors and legislators formulate statutes or when law enforcement and prosecutors determine whether the behavior they confront can be plausibly interpreted within those statutes. Hate crimes are also given meaning within court cases, particularly the kinds of cases analyzed here—all of which deal with the constitutional standing of particular statutes.

Like all appellate cases on constitutional issues, the cases analyzed in this chapter reflect a struggle by the parties involved to give meaning to the statutes. Judges intervene in this process to assign an authoritative meaning. The judicial opinion is the primary vehicle by which this meaning is transmitted to other members of the legal field. Thus, looking across a group of opinions that deal with roughly the same species of law and behavior we can observe the broader process by which statutes are made meaningful and the connected process by which judges converge around repertoires of justifications.

The institutionalization of hate crime is reflected in several features of judicial interpretations of the substantive meaning of the statutes. The meaning has been elaborated over time, in four stages. First, judges employed a conception of normal hate crime to justify statutes in the face of constitutionality challenges. This conception is more narrow than the possible statutory meanings. Second, they refined and reconceptualized the role of motivation to mean bias rather than the hatred, ill will, or hostility. Third, judges restricted and elaborated the relationship between the concept of hate crime and expression in such a way that intimidation, harassment, and menacing must constitute "true threats" to be included offenses under hate crime law. Finally, in contrast with these restrictions on the meaning of hate crime, the concept is currently expanding the domain of coverage at the judicial level.

Taken together, these properties of judicial decision-making on hate crime suggest that the institutionalization of a legal concept occurs through construct elaboration. In this case, construct elaboration, which mostly restricts and delimits the meaning of hate crime, has, at the same time, expanded the range of its application. Much like David Sudnow's concept of a normal crime, hate crime statutes take on a much more complex cluster of ideas than is indicated in the statutory definition. Judges create practical theories that constitute the "working" meaning of statutes, which, at best bear only a loose resemblance to the handful of signifiers assembled within the statute. In addition, the elaboration of the hate crime construct occurs through both a restriction and an expansion of meaning. The general trajectory of domain expansion in hate crime laws has been toward the accommodation of more expressive forms of conduct. Whereas early cases emphasized violent conduct as the basis of hate crime, later cases have addressed the question of speech as bias crime. Such an elaboration only becomes possible once the core of the hate crime construct has been institutionalized.

A key question remains unanswered: How open are the meaning-making processes to external social influence? With respect to hate crime law, it is possible to identify at least two kinds of influence on the courts' statutory interpretation: social movement "framing" and the opinions of legal experts. Consistent with our portrayal of the development of an anti-hate-crime movement in the United States, it is useful to consider the role of social movement groups in transmitting constructions of hate crime to judges. For example, recall that the courts have routinely emphasized the "compelling state interest" as a justification for the laws. That is, even if there exists some potential First Amendment infringement in hate crime laws, the laws remain justifiable because states have a compelling interest in managing the arguably deleterious social effects associated with this widespread and increasing problem. As we and others have suggested, the portrait of hate crimes as increasing, or as reaching the oft-noted "epidemic proportions," is the product of a handful of interest groups like the Anti-Defamation League, the Southern Poverty Law Center, and the National Gay and Lesbian Task Force. Although the empirical grounds for this claim are debatable, it has been treated as "fact," first by lawmakers and then by the courts. The courts have implicitly and explicitly accepted this claim in order to advance the compelling state interest argument. This suggests that social movements can influence judicial reasoning by shaping the baseline constructions of "reality" that judges then take for granted as credible representations.

A second area of potential external influence is the analysis of the laws within scholarly circles. It is often difficult to gauge the influence of scholarship and commentary on law because we cannot determine the degree to which judges are aware of and attentive to scholarship. Even when court opinions cite law review articles, for example, they tend not to do so proportionate to the amount of scholarship available. Instead, opinions cite one or two of the major pieces. They are, after all, legal opinions, not reviews of the literature. The implication of this, however, is that scholarship may have little impact on the development of legal interpretation.

Indeed, hate crime law can serve as an interesting empirical referent in the examination of the role of scholarship in shaping judicial meaning making. Despite the fact that the legal literature on hate crime law exploded during precisely the same period as the constitutionality cases (1991 to 1994), there is little evidence that this work was considered in the development of the law. One important exception to this is the legal controversy precipitated by Susan Gellman's *UCLA Law Review* article published in 1991. Gellman's charge that the laws punish speech was subsequently the topic of a heated symposium, entitled "Penalty Enhancement for Hate Crimes," in *Criminal Justice Ethics* (11[2]: 1992). Since then, a steady stream of articles for and against the hate crime concept have appeared in law reviews debating its constitutionality and other policy issues (Bader 1994; Brooks 1994; Dillof 1997; Gaumer 1994; Grannis 1993; "Hate Is Not Speech" 1993; Kagan 1992; Lawrence 1994; Maroney 1998; Morsch 1992; Strossen 1993; Tribe 1993; Winer 1994). Gellman's contention that the laws punish speech appears to be the only one that has been directly engaged by the courts. Used extensively in *State v. Wyant* (64 Ohio St. 3d 566 [1992]) to strike down the Ohio law, her analysis was rejected by the U.S. Supreme Court in *Wisconsin v. Mitchell*. Other scholars have suggested alternative foundations for the laws (for example, Tribe 1993; Dillof 1997), but the courts have yet to employ these arguments. Finally, the law review articles are overwhelmingly critical of the hate crime laws—much more so than the courts. After a point, the courts do not seem to have paid much attention to the scholarly literature.

As to the larger questions of how and when scholarly commentary and social movements influence the development of legal doctrine, it appears from the example of hate crime law that they are most likely to be influential early in the institutionalization process of a legal construct or during periods in which the construct is "unsettled." During those moments, judges often reach for external legitimation, particularly scholarly commentary, for their opinions. Once a concept is institutionalized, opinions are more likely to be embedded in existing case law, and scholarly commentary is likely to have little impact.

Quite apart from their multiple and changing sources of influence, courts have been consequential in defining hate crime as a policy domain. The courts represent yet another arena of meaning making, one that is authoritative relative to other parts of the criminal justice system and, thus, carries considerable weight. Our analysis of how the courts' influence has been felt suggests striking similarities with the influence of the legislators responsible for the development of state and federal laws. The meaning of hate crime has shifted and changed across time: it has become increasingly elaborated, the scope of its application delimited, and yet it also appears to be undergoing domain expansion. Combined, these processes ensure that the concept will become more settled over time. As we discuss in the next chapter, this process repeats itself as the concept enters the domain of law enforcement agencies as police officers and prosecutors attempt to understand the law and apply it to concrete circumstances.

═ Chapter 6 ═

Law Enforcement Responses: Policing and Prosecuting Hate Crime

ONCE LEGISLATURES and courts have spoken, legal constructs must be applied in concrete day-to-day circumstances by officials on the front lines of the criminal justice system. What sociologists refer to as the "labeling" process occurs at the point of contact between the criminal justice system and the victims and perpetrators of crime. It is the moment at which the statutes that constitute the body of law are set into operation, applied to concrete events, and inserted into the lives of specific individuals. It is also the moment at which what we have previously referred to as "the determinacy of law" is once again accomplished by state officials in a position to fix its meaning. As they do so, some events are deemed hate crime, some individuals are deemed victims of hate crime, and some individuals are deemed perpetrators of hate crime. The interactional and bureaucratic accomplishment of these assignments are crucial to the social construction of hate crime; thus they invite examination of another institutional sphere: law enforcement.

If the efforts of legislators to respond to bias-motivated violence peaked in the late 1980s and the court challenges to established hate crime law played out mostly before 1995, then the late 1990s witnessed enormous attention to policing and prosecution as the principle "problem areas" with respect to hate crime. At this point in the history of the concept, the legislative issues regarding who and what should be covered by the laws, as well as the judicial issues regarding the legitimacy and constitutionality of the laws, gave way to pragmatic issues about the organizational changes required to enforce the laws. Efforts along these lines are currently in process in policing institutions at all levels.

In 1999, law enforcement officials at federal (Reno 1999), state (Bill Lockyer, "Announcement of Civil Rights Commission and Rapid Response Protocol for Combating Hate Crimes," press release, State of California, Attorney General's Office, August 16, 1999), and local (Bettina Boxall, "D.A. Seeks to Expand Hate Crimes Unit," *Los Angeles Times*, February 13, 1998, B3) levels announced plans to redouble efforts designed to enforce hate crime statutes. This is perhaps most pronounced in the creation of special bias crime units across the nation. According to the Law Enforcement Management Administrative Statistics (LEMAS) 1997 survey of the operations of American police and sheriffs departments, 40 percent of cities with populations of more than a half million and 30 percent of cities with populations of more than a quarter million have specialized bias crime units with full-time personnel (Department of Justice 1999). Bias crime units in Los Angeles, New York, and Chicago have ninety, twenty-three, and sixteen full-time sworn officers, respectively.

Further characterizing this trend, the same type of special units are being established in prosecutors' offices across the country. In 1998, for example, the Los Angeles County district attorney Gil Garcetti announced plans to expand his office's hate crimes prosecution unit. "I'm asking for more specially trained hate crime prosecutors to handle these cases," he explained. "These hate crime prosecutors will also work with communities and all law enforcement in L.A. county to encourage the understanding and reporting of hate crimes" (quoted in Boxall, "D.A. Seeks to Expand Hate Crimes Unit"). The Los Angeles Police Department has also implemented a Hate Crimes Monitoring System. This system allows officers to assess hate crime patterns, such as when and where potential bias-motivated crime incidents occur, and to adjust policing accordingly ("Tackling the Haters," *Los Angeles Times*: July 21, 1999). Finally, Los Angeles supplemented and enhanced their hate crimes training program, which was originally implemented in the late 1980s (Boxall, "D.A. Seeks to Expand Hate Crimes Unit"). Similar to these organizational responses occurring in Los Angeles, police in many jurisdictions are joining forces with local community leaders and school systems to respond to tensions between groups before they erupt into acts of violence and to assist with the creation of victim services to be made available when such acts do occur (Bruce Muramoto, detective, West Sacramento Police Department, personal communication, June 14, 1999).

These organizational changes, as well as the social processes that underlie them, reflect many of the dynamics of the broader hate crime policy domain discussed in previous chapters, such as the diffusion of the concept of hate crime, the homogenization of what is understood to constitute a hate crime, and the expansion of the domain over time to include a wider array of persons, conduct, and institutional practices. In this chapter we discuss these developments, keeping in mind the core issues set out in the preceding chapters. As in other parts of the hate crime policy domain, many of the concerns about the concept of hate crime have centered on issues of ambiguity, lack of uniformity, and uncertainty as to what is included in the concept. How these issues are managed represents a fundamental problem in the enforcement of hate crime laws and thus looms large in the present discussion.

However, limited existing data suggest that the policing of hate crime is far from impossible or erratic. Despite the fact that the concept represents a fairly new—and, some have said, inherently problematic—criminal category with which both police and prosecutors must contend, they are doing so with predictable results. What was once highly unsettled is becoming more settled. Although the preliminary and limited data are mostly suggestive at this point, hate crimes are apparently being policed and prosecuted with success equal to other crimes. This chapter details how this occurs and, at the same time, what enforcement success means for the continued development of the policy domain.

Because police and prosecutors, as two interlinked clusters of law enforcement officials, manage the front lines of the criminal justice system, our discussion of the factors influencing law enforcement's capacity to recognize and classify specific forms of conduct as hate crime focuses on these players. Law enforcement constitutes the last phase of the formation of a policy domain (see table 1.1) and thus operates with the least-settled definitions and attendant organizational routines. Moreover, because it is the institutional sphere on which we have the least amount of valid and reliable data, we are left to hypothesize to a greater extent than in previous arenas. As more data, especially longitudinal data, become available, a clearer picture of law enforcement's response to hate crime will emerge. For now, however, we turn to what is presently known.

The Demands on Law Enforcement and the Policing of Hate Crime

Without an understanding of policing as a social practice, our examination of hate crime as a social problem and policy domain is incomplete. As Boyd, Berk, and Hamner (1996, 848) eloquently put it, "From the initial response of the patrol unit to the institutional structure of the division to the individual determinations made by the detectives, the constitution of a hate crime is deeply intertwined with the social context in which detection, investigation, and classification occur." At every step, classification is dependent upon meaning-making processes enacted by law enforcement officials.

The classification of incidents as hate crimes falls first and foremost to police officers and detectives. As Susan Martin (1996, 459) explains in her work on law enforcement's response to hate crimes, "the initial identification of a case as possibly bias motivated is likely to rest with patrol officers." Prior research on policing indicates that discretion is inherent to the administration of justice, with more discretion being employed at the bottom of the organizational hierarchy than at the top (Wilson 1970). Moreover, discretion contributes greatly to a well-documented lack of uniformity in policing. Officers on the street in different contexts make different decisions regarding when to arrest, whom to arrest, and how to officially record the arrest for statistical reporting purposes (Black 1980). Similarly, the investigators to whom cases are forwarded also exhibit variability in philosophy and investigative approaches (Martin 1996).

The routine use of discretion is a common feature of police work even when the definitions of a particular crime are clear and well understood by officers. In hate crime cases, however, discretion is coupled with definitions and rules that are not always clear to officers because of the relative newness of the criminal category (Boyd, Berk, and Hamner 1996; Martin 1996). Martin (1995) argues that this situation places unique burdens on officers who are confronted with determining whether an ordinary crime (assault, vandalism, arson) has been committed or whether a hate crime has been committed. This is often a difficult determination to make because, by definition, hate crimes contain "parallel crimes" (Lawrence 1999). Moreover, the subjective judgments made by police officers are necessitated by the recurrent problems of reconciling partial as opposed to sole motives, assessing conflicting reports, identifying the intended target, separating the multiple statuses of the victim, and understanding provocation (Boyd, Berk, and Hamner 1996).[1]

These seemingly special requirements of hate crime combine with ordinary discretion in police work to potentially undermine the enforcement of hate crime law and exacerbate the problem of heterogeneity in law enforcement responses. However, the allowance of discretion and the presence of ambiguity do not free officers from enforcing hate crime law, nor do they free them to classify acts in any way they deem appropriate. Rather, the classification of both ordinary crime and hate crime varies according to an array of factors, most notably the officers' general attitudes toward policy innovation, the social organization of police work, and the presence and content of specific training practices. Each of these considerations is relevant to how the determinacy of hate crime is fixed at the level of policing.

Resistance to the Category

In light of the "newness" of hate crime as a criminal category and the "subjective judgments" it necessitates, it is not surprising that police officers both complain about the concept of hate crime and also comply—to greater or lesser degrees—with the mandate to enforce the laws that define it. Early research on the topic finds varying degrees of receptivity to hate crimes on behalf of law enforcement personnel (Boyd, Berk, and Hamner 1996; Martin 1996).

Some officers merely proceed as if hate crimes can be easily incorporated into existing police practices and are puzzled by others' view of the crimes as problematic. In their view, the categorization processes that surround the enforcement of hate crime are fundamentally no different from the enforcement of other kinds of crimes and attendant police work. In particular, officers committed to the community policing philosophy view hate crime laws as a useful tool for managing tensions between groups in their communities (Muramoto, personal communication). Martin's (1995) work reveals that bias crime units are compatible with the growth of a community policing philosophy to the extent that they assume that jurisdiction-wide standards exist, embrace values of tolerance rather than prejudice, and are based on a sharing—or at least an understanding—of such values on the part of the police.

In contrast, however, some officers register the same kinds of complaints lodged by law professors and law enforcement personnel alike about domestic violence laws in the 1970s and 1980s and stalking laws in the 1990s—namely, that hate crime laws are hopelessly vague and too ambiguous to be enforced. Moreover, law enforcement personnel have more serious problems with which to contend (Walker and Katz 1995). As a result, "hate crimes were dismissed as 'overkill,' 'mostly bull,' 'a pain in the ass,' 'media hype,' and 'a giant cluster fuck'" (Boyd, Berk, and Hamner 1996, 827).

Early research on hate crime policing emphasizes the reluctance of police officers, particularly street-level patrol officers, to fully embrace the concept of hate crime. As Samuel Walker and Charles Katz (1995) point out, police officers often are the least likely members of the system to be sensitive to the needs of hate crime victims. Some officers view hate crimes as a distraction from more serious crimes and a reflection of the influence of naive policy makers and administrators who are more concerned with "political correctness" than with effective crime control (Boyd, Berk, and Hamner 1996). Officers also often resent expansion of their responsibilities to include such crimes at a time when there are not enough resources to fight what they consider to be more pressing offenses and when the pursuit of "parallel crimes" involved in hate crime can be more effectively investigated and prosecuted (Lawrence 1999). Finally, for some law enforcement personnel, resistance is bound up with a more general opposition to "special treatment" for particular groups in society and community policing (Jacobs and Potter 1998), which threatens to transform the role of the police from crime fighters to social workers.

Although concerns are frequently expressed by rank-and-file police officers—especially the question of "how to get inside the offender's head"—in practice officers overcome the ambiguity of the concept and increasingly enforce the law. Understanding how police accomplish this is not a trivial matter; after all, it is only through the officers' interpretive work that hate crimes come to be recognized, classified, and recorded as official occurrences. Therefore, we turn to two pieces of research to articulate the parameters of this process.

In their ethnographic study of the situated decision-making practices of police detectives in two divisions of a large urban police department charged with enforcing hate crime law and collecting hate crime data, Boyd, Berk, and Hamner (1996, 821) conclude that "far from finding it problematic to interpret and classify specific incidents, police detectives engage in certain routine practices in order to determine the hate-related status of an incident." Specifically, they "rely on typifications and commonsense reasoning regarding the attributes of hate crimes and estimations of the proper role of the police as a basis for their interpretive decisions" (Boyd, Berk, and Hammer 1996, 821). This allows them to apply general principles encoded in statutes to concrete events and thus proceed with the work of policing hate crime.

Complementing Boyd, Berk, and Hamner's work, Martin's (1995, 316) quantitative research comparing two police units that rely upon different organizational structures to enforce hate crime laws demonstrates that detectives assigned to evaluate reported incidents of hate crimes found most cases extremely easy to classify. Obvious cases— for example, cases in which a religious facility or minority family's property is vandalized and racial or religious slurs are left as graffiti, or those in which the perpetrator of the crime admits to a bias motivation—provoke little dispute and are routinely classified as hate crimes. By contrast, in circumstances in which the centrality of bigoted beliefs is unclear, officers devise reasonable approaches for making relevant determinations. In these situations—for example, situations in which racial epithets are shouted but are secondary to some other motive or the offender and victim are simply of different races or religions—officers render conservative decisions, generally classifying such events as "ordinary" crimes. These observations are paralleled in Boyd, Berk, and Hamner's study. They find that many bias unit officers "expressed [a] desire to eliminate all other possible explanations before categorizing an incident as a hate-motivated crime, thereby helping deflate what they believe to be the 'inflated statistics' regarding hate crime in the area" (1996, 833). Other officers treated bias crimes as "just like any other kind of crime" (842).

When combined, the empirical studies conducted by Martin (1995; 1996) and Boyd, Berk, and Hamner (1996) provide evidence that counter a common complaint about the enforcement of hate crime law: that the policing of hate crime is hopelessly flawed because the core concept—hate crime—is inherently ambiguous and riddled with political tensions that make the classification of every case an enormous struggle (Jacobs and Potter 1998). As Boyd, Berk, and Hamner (1996, 846) argue, "Hate crimes are not oriented to by the police detectives we observed as any more problematic than any other type of crime, despite their unique definitional and bureaucratic features." In the face of the ambiguity of the concept, and given the ordinary discretion involved in police work in general, why do we not see more obstacles reported in these initial studies? As with other kinds of criminal behavior, especially those that implicate categories of behavior that also contain ambiguity—for example, sexual harassment, stalking, domestic violence, and white-collar crime—over time police develop a set of routine practices that organize their responses. As social actors, police officers operate with a folk theory about how, when, where, and to whom hate crimes occur. This heuristic device references the ordinary circumstances and markers of hate crime. With this working construct in mind, police officers classify incidents that come through the system according to their similarity with the normal hate crime construct.

As with other "normal crimes" (Frohmann 1997; Sudnow 1965), the notable feature of this working construct is that it is much richer and more elaborate than the corresponding statutory definition. The empirical studies available suggest that the normal hate crime construct is made up of key elements the officers consider to represent an ordinary occurrence of hate crime: namely, the facts of the crime reveal no provocation by the victim, no prior encounters between the victim and the perpetrator, a specific target, accompanying derogatory insults, observable graffiti or other hateful words or epithets, the victim's fears about the perpetrator or beliefs about the crime, and recognizable indications of association with known, organized hate groups. These, in turn, suggest that "the perpetrator is reacting to the victim solely on the basis of his perceived racial, ethnic, religious, or sexual identity and the accompanying slurs reveal the nature of the perpetrator's feelings—hatred as his motive" (Boyd, Berk, and Hamner 1996, 835; see also Martin 1996). At the factual level, these elements are perceived to be the most easily discernable characteristics; thus, from the point of view of police officers, the elements closely correspond to the attributes of a normal hate crime precisely because they appeal to the obvious, clear, easily discernible characteristics of cases that qualify for hate crime status.

The fact that the normal hate crime construct is shared among police officers within the department and often with the prosecutors with whom they work resolves the apparent ambiguity of the concept. However, it is important to note that because this concept is part of the local knowledge of a particular segment of the criminal justice system, it can be variable across units within the same statutory jurisdiction as well as across units in different jurisdictions. For this reason, a consideration of how different normal crime constructs arise in different locales is in order.

Organizational Structures and Practices

Reflecting the major current of social science research on policing, much of the work on hate crimes focuses on the multitude of ways police departments are responding to the legal mandate to pursue bias-motivated crime (Boyd, Berk, Hamner 1996; Martin 1996; Walker and Katz 1995; Wexler and Marx 1986). Conducted in the early 1990s, when the precise definition of hate crime was still being negotiated in legislatures and courts, these early studies reveal that the policing of hate crime is quite variable across jurisdictions and across divisions within the same jurisdiction. This variation is, in large part, attributable to differences in the philosophies and the routine practices in the different departments as well as the newness of the criminal category itself.

In their study of a large urban police department, Boyd, Berk, and Hamner (1996) find that two of the most active divisions of the department employed quite different procedures for dealing with potential hate crime incidents. In the first division, the commanding officer considered hate crime as distinct from other kinds of crimes; thus he assigned a single senior detective the responsibility of investigating potential hate crimes. This detective handled all of the hate crime cases that came through the department over the course of several years. Also reflecting the department's commitment to the enforcement of hate crime law, patrol officers were routinely reminded at roll calls of the definition of hate crime and were given a "checklist" of distinguishing characteristics, such as victim accounts and testimony about hateful expressions made during the crime (ibidem, 833). Thus, in this division, the leadership's commitment to thoroughly investigate incidents as potential hate crimes was quite high, the expertise of the detective in charge of investigating potential hate crime was pronounced, and the officers' familiarity with the parameters of hate crime was strongly encouraged by police administrators.

In contrast, the second division made few changes in departmental policies in light of the mandate to enforce hate crime law. The commanding officer did not think that hate crimes were a problem in the part of the city over which his division had jurisdiction. Therefore, officers were not routinely briefed about the definition of hate crime, nor were they given instructions on how to identify and process them. Responsibility for investigating hate crimes rotated from detective to detective over the course of several years. The detective assigned to investigate hate crime also had responsibility for investigating other crimes. The second division, unlike the first, treated hate crimes as comparable to other kinds of crimes, not as a special kind of crime. Whereas the detective in the first division focused his investigation on gathering evidence relative to the specific motive involved in the crime (to determine whether there was evidence of bias motivation), the detective in the second division largely accepted the characterization of the patrol officer and focused her attention on developing evidence related to the basic factual information of the incident in order to establish that a crime took place—much like she would have in any other crime. As a result, the second division was less likely both to recognize when hate crimes occurred and to engage in the further investigative efforts that might disconfirm the original officer's assessment of the incident. In addition, whereas the operations of the first division were likely to produce evidence that could be useful in the prosecution stage, the second division left much of that evidence gathering to prosecutors themselves.

A comparison of these two divisions suggests that the statistics they produced are largely incommensurable—an "aggregating of apples and oranges" (Boyd, Berk, and Hamner 1996, 847)—because of the differences in the underlying set of practices that generated them. It also suggests that the problems resulting from the ambiguity of the concept are less consequential in terms of the detection, verification, and recording of hate crimes when there is more information given to officers (specific definitions and checklists, for example), when detectives focus on establishing the evidence for bias motivation, and when the entire organization is committed to pursuing hate crimes as legitimate crimes. As Boyd, Berk, and Hamner (1996, 846) conclude, "Although these differences between Division A and Division B represent, in some sense, two extreme opposites, they are generalizable to other divisions in the department as well as to other police departments in the country."

Martin's (1995, 1996) comparative study of police practices in Baltimore County, Maryland, and New York City points to a similar set of organizational factors that influence how hate crimes are identified, verified, and recorded. Although the police in both locations have been among the leaders in law enforcement initiatives to identify and focus attention on offenses defined as bias-motivated crimes, they have employed different organizational structures and procedures to do so. As a result, the New York City police department generates higher arrest percentages for hate crime cases than for other kinds of crimes in the city, as well as higher arrest percentages than those reported by the Baltimore County police department. From 1982 through 1988 the arrest rates for bias cases involving confrontational and property crimes in New York City were double those for nonbias cases for the same category of offense; in harassment cases the arrest rate was eight times as high. As for comparisons between New York City's and Baltimore County's arrest rates for bias crime, no matter how the data are analyzed—by type of offense, locale, or target group—the New York City police department detects, verifies, and records more hate crime than the Baltimore County police department (Martin 1995).

In large part, New York City's higher percentages are an outgrowth of the commitment of the agency to the goals of hate crime policing and the creation of a Bias Incident Investigative Unit (BIIU). This commitment translates into the expenditure of much greater effort on the investigation phases, particularly with respect to follow-up work, which, in turn, generates more information about offender motives and thus more frequent confirmation that a hate crime has occurred. In addition, the BIIU employs a definition of hate crime commensurate with the normal hate crime construct described in the previous section: "the NYPD's definition of bias crimes requires only that the offender's bias motivation be responsible *in part* for the offense, without defining motivation" [italics added for emphasis] (Martin 1995, 460). Beyond this central standard, the department's criteria for identifying incidents as hate crime include consideration of the perpetrator's motivation; the absence of any other motive; the perception of the victim; the display of offensive symbols, words, or acts; the date and time of occurrence (for example, corresponding to a significant holiday, such as Hanukkah or Martin Luther King's birthday); statements made by the perpetrator; and a commonsense review of the circumstances surrounding the incident (Martin 1995, 461–62).

Clearly, the criteria utilized by the New York City BIIU signal an elaboration of the concept, one that exceeds the statutory definition. This finding is corroborated in Boyd, Berk, and Hamner's (1996, 824) work, which finds that the parameters of hate crime specified by the department exceeded those stipulated by law by defining hate crime as "any malicious or offensive act directed against an individual or group based upon their race, religion, ethnic background, culture or lifestyle, including criminal and noncriminal acts." Notably, "culture or lifestyle" and "criminal and noncriminal acts" do not appear as provisions in a single hate crime law, much less in the law for the jurisdiction examined in the study.

The Baltimore County police department does not have a specialized unit comparable to New York's Bias Incident Investigative Unit. Instead, patrol officers are responsible for evaluating incidents not only for their "crime potential" but for their "hate crime potential," as well. Individual officers were provided fewer incentives by departmental policy to engage in the follow-up investigations that would enhance the likelihood of an arrest (Martin 1996). This decentralized approach to detecting hate crime relies upon a definition of hate crime that is as robust as that employed by the New York City BIIU. "Criteria for reporting," Martin (1995, 462) explains, "rest on a 'commonsense approach.'" The key criterion is the "motivation behind the act" directed at any racial, religious, or ethnic group. As in New York City, criteria for verification include consideration of the offender's motive; absence of another motive; display of offensive symbols, words, or acts; the totality of the circumstances surrounding the incident; the effect on the victims; statements by suspects or victim; a history of similar incidents in the area or against the same victim group; and violation of certain statutes that specifically prohibit burning a cross or other religious symbol, bomb threats, destruction of another's property, assault, unlawful use of the telephone, and common-law offenses pertaining to acts of racial, religious, and ethnic intimidation or harassment (Martin 1995, 462). Like the standards employed by the New York City police department's BIIU, these criteria clearly signal an elaboration of the parameters of the concept, one that exceeds the statutory definition of hate crime.

In both New York City and Baltimore County the proportion of cases in which an arrest was made was greater for hate crimes (Martin 1996) than for other categories of crime. Beyond this finding, however, stark differences emerge in terms of the "screening thresholds" applied to individual cases and the likelihood that any individual case will be labeled a hate crime (Martin 1995, 1996), despite the fact that the two departments in the study operate under similar statutory definitions of hate crime. As Martin (1996, 476) observes, "[The findings presented here] illustrate the effects of two alternative policing strategies for addressing hate crimes. By devoting additional time and attention to investigating such crimes, the police (particularly in New York City) generated a higher arrest rate, especially for relatively minor offenses that ordinarily receive very limited police attention." This suggests that hate crimes are not more difficult to enforce than other laws; rather, their differential enforcement is, at least in part, a function of the organizational structures and practices that underlie the enforcement. Martin concludes that the effectiveness of bias crime law enforcement is contingent upon the awareness of victims and their willingness to report incidents and the awareness of officers and their willingness to properly report and investigate such crimes. The latter is directly tied to the emergence of bias crime units, mandatory reporting efforts, and specialized police training within the department and reflects the degree of the organization's commitment to the enforcement of hate crime law.

Bias Crime Units

As of the early 1990s, the organizational commitment to hate crime policing in American police departments, as reflected in the creation of specialized bias crime units, the generation of knowledgeable officers and detectives, and well-developed departmental training policies, was questionable (Walker and Katz 1995). Even today, most departments have no specialized bias crime unit, no personnel assigned to routinely deal with bias crime incidents, and no formal policy on the definition, identification, and policing of hate crime.

However, the 1997 LEMAS survey (U.S. Department of Justice 1999) suggests that the level of adoption of hate crime policies and programs is comparable to other kinds of innovations. Figure 6.1 shows data on recent organizational innovations adopted in municipal police, sheriff, and county police departments. These data suggest that innovations, across the board, are fairly uncommon, and the adoption of specialized hate crime units in particular lags behind other areas. This fact is offset somewhat by the comparatively high level of commitment to designing specialized hate crime policies and to the prac-

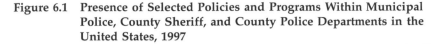

Figure 6.1   Presence of Selected Policies and Programs Within Municipal Police, County Sheriff, and County Police Departments in the United States, 1997

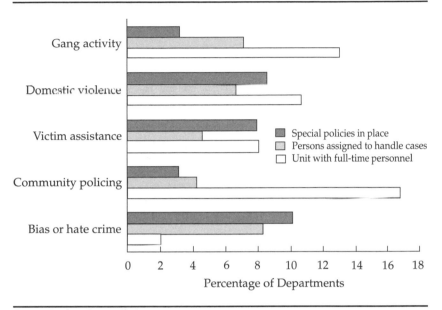

Source: Authors' compilation.
Note: N = 2,907.

tice of designating certain officers to handle hate crime cases on a part-time basis. The reluctance to create full-blown units at comparable levels reflects the perception that because of the low frequency of hate crimes, the need for a unit is less pressing than for these other innovations.

It remains unclear whether these data accurately reflect the level of commitment to the policing of hate crime. Based on their study of sixteen police departments in the Midwest, all of which reported having special bias crime units in the 1990 LEMAS survey (Department of Justice 1992), Walker and Katz (1995, 42) find that "even among the departments that have either a special unit or special procedures related to bias crimes, the level of commitment appears weak." This is not surprising, given that law enforcement, as one of many institutional spheres relevant to the policy domain, emerges in the last phase of the formation of the hate crime policy domain (see figure 1.1). Therefore, we would expect policing, compared with other institutional spheres—especially social movement mobilization, lawmaking, and judicial decision making—to operate with the least coherent set of meanings and attendant practices.

However, with the continuing growth of interest in hate crimes triggered by recent high-profile incidents and reflected in President Clinton's and Attorney General Janet Reno's proposals to increase the effectiveness of hate crime laws, the awareness and organizational commitment to the policing of hate crime has arguably increased in recent years. For example, in October and November 1998, the Department of Justice published a four-volume report designed to spell out the procedures for each step in the law enforcement process. Volume 1 offers guidelines for responding officers, volume 2 addresses detectives and investigators, volume 3 sets out the curriculum for training, and volume 4 advises commanding officers. This report, produced through the collaboration of the Department of Justice, the National Association of Attorneys General, the International Association of Directors of Law Enforcement Standards and Training, the Federal Law Enforcement Training Center of the Department of the Treasury, and the Anti-Defamation League, serves as a standardized curriculum for law enforcement across states and within the federal government (U.S. Department of Justice 1998). The degree to which awareness and attendant organizational changes are occurring can be assessed by examining two sources of data: measures of participation in the hate crimes reporting system and archival evidence that speaks to the degree to which departments are pursuing specialized training for rank-and-file officers.

Hate Crime Reporting

The national database on participation in the hate crime reporting system, which was created by the Hate Crimes Statistics Act of 1990, reveals a steady increase in the level of involvement by local law enforcement departments. As figure 6.2 illustrates, the steady increase in the incidence of hate crimes as reported by local police correlates with the increases in the proportion of the population whose police departments participate in such reporting efforts. From 1992 to 1998, the number of police departments participating in the national effort to gather hate crime statistics rose from 4,558 to 7,755, representing a 70 percent increase in six years. The population covered by those reporting units increased almost 30 percent during the same six-year period. These figures demonstrate that, at the aggregate level, law enforcement's commitment to hate crime policing as measured by reporting practices is generally on the rise.

Figure 6.2   Law Enforcement's Participation in Hate Crime Policing, from 1992 to 1998

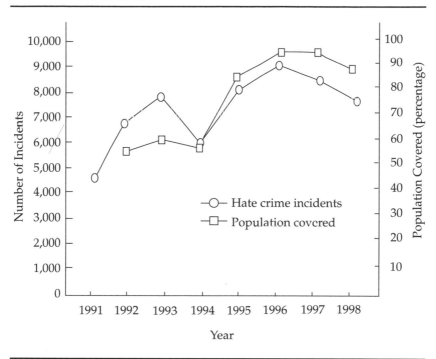

Source: U.S. Department of Justice.

Although participation in the national effort by the Federal Bureau of Investigation (FBI) to gather hate crime data is voluntary, state legislatures increasingly mandate data collection. This mandate provides yet another measure of the degree to which law enforcement's commitment to policing hate crime is growing. In 1986, Pennsylvania became the first state to mandate collection of data on hate crime. By 1999, twenty-four states had adopted similar laws. Like the national figures, these numbers suggest that, at the aggregate level, law enforcement's commitment to hate crime policing is increasing. A typical approach is Florida's Hate Crime Reporting Act, passed in 1989, which requires the state's Department of Law Enforcement to "collect and disseminate data on incidents of criminal acts that evidence prejudice based on race, religion, ethnicity, color, ancestry, sexual orientation, or national origin" (Florida, *Statutes*, sec. 877.19).

Police Training

The degree to which awareness and attendant organizational changes related to the policing of hate crime are occurring can also be assessed by examining the history and status of relevant specialized training for rank-and-file officers. Many states have laws mandating training of police in procedures for reporting hate crimes, Pennsylvania being, once again, the pathbreaker in 1986. Such laws require the generation of educational materials and programs for instructing police officers about the legal definition of hate crime, victim services, and the proper procedures for processing cases. In 1992, California passed a law requiring its Commission on Police Officers Standards and Training to "develop guidelines and a course of instruction and training for law enforcement officers who are employed as peace officers, or who are not yet employed as a peace officer but are enrolled in a training academy for law enforcement officers, addressing hate crimes" (California, *Penal Code*, sec. 13519.6). The program resulted in the publication of a training manual in 1995 for statewide distribution (California 1995).

Moving beyond state statutory mandates, at the federal level the Department of Justice has devised a standardized curriculum for law enforcement training McLaughlin et al. 1997 [1995]. For example, the *National Bias Crimes Training Guide for Law Enforcement and Victim Assistance Personnel* was funded by the Office for Victims of Crime of the Department of Justice and developed by the Education Development Center, in partnership with the Massachusetts Criminal Justice Training Council. The purpose of this much-cited curriculum is to "familiarize law enforcement and other victim services personnel with the nature of bias crimes, appropriate actions to deter and respond to such crimes, and effective ways of assisting victims" (McLaughlin et al. 1997 [1995]). Guided by input from key members of law enforcement, prosecution, and victim assistance fields, "this training package builds upon the best efforts and practices to date to provide a two-and-a-half-day program designed to strengthen the knowledge and skills of individual professionals in law enforcement and victim assistance" (ibidem, 2).

The program is designed to accomplish four goals: (1) to provide law enforcement officials with up-to-date information and strategies for identifying bias crime and taking appropriate actions to deter and investigate such crime; (2) to provide victim assistance professionals with up-to-date information and strategies for use in assisting the victims of these crimes; (3) to strengthen the capacity of professionals in both fields to contribute to successful investigations and prosecutions of bias crime and to changing community norms that presently foster a tolerance and indifference toward bias crimes; and (4) to provide professionals in both fields with the perspectives and strategies that will enable them to work more effectively within their own departments and agencies and with one another, as well as with their broader communities (ibidem, 2). Notably, although the training program was developed in the late 1990s, it hinges on the definition of hate crime provided by the federal government in the 1990 Hate Crimes Statistics Act rather than the definition used in the 1994 Hate Crimes Sentencing Enhancement Act. Thus, it does not rely upon the most expansive definition of the concept.

In addition to the federal training standards, some states have devised their own standards for specialized policing training. To assess these standards, we examined the training manuals, bulletins, and orders produced and disseminated by local law enforcement agencies throughout California, one of the largest, most heterogeneous, and innovative states in the country. Although these archival materials do not speak directly to the issue of the organizational changes and the degree to which training improvements affect officers' awareness and practices, they do provide a window through which to view the stated goals and practices of police departments in a state that has been on the forefront of the hate crime policy domain. As Walker and Katz (1995, 43) remind us, "Special training and formal screening procedures are factors that can be observed and measured; they serve as indirect indicators of the level of organizational commitment to enforcing hate crime law." In short, these documents articulate local department policies about hate crime, thus embodying law enforcement's response to the issue and its position in the policy domain.

Our research reveals great diversity across police departments in terms of how much knowledge and training about hate crime police officers throughout the state of California receive. A sergeant from a midsize police department in northern California informed us (in personal communication on August 15, 1999) that "our officers don't get trained in hate crimes. We don't have hate crimes here, those are mostly in other parts of the state, like San Francisco and Los Angeles. Those are your problem areas." Other officers, such as a captain from a larger police department in southern California, acknowledged (in personal communication on August 30, 1999) that "we do not currently have any hate crime guidelines, but we're developing them. They should be in place soon—the sooner the better." Many California law enforcement agencies have not adopted general orders that define departmental policing priorities for hate crime, provide officers with a definition of hate crime, or detail the protocol for identifying

and processing such incidents. Thus, officers are left to deploy their
normal hate crime constructs, which have yet to be informed by official state policy and subject to attendant police training.

In contrast with the foregoing comments and the many police departments that have undergone little organizational change in the
name of enforcing hate crime law, some police departments have
training procedures of one form or another—from simple orders and
bulletins to day-long workshops and the development of other curric-
ula—designed to inform officers of the newly institutionalized criminal category of hate crime and its consequences for law enforcement.
Most notably, California police departments have increasingly
adopted general orders regarding hate crime. These typically include
a working definition of the concept, often accompanied by definitions
of key terms, such as "race," "ethnic group," "sexual orientation,"
and "bias"; a list of the kinds of evidence that suggest a hate crime
has occurred, along with an articulation of how to weigh the rele-
vance of various sources of evidence; and a set of procedures for processing cases that might be classifiable as hate crime, including preliminary and follow-through procedures. The production and
dissemination of such orders is not surprising given that, from the
point of view of law enforcement, hate crime constitutes a relatively
new criminal category of which many officers are now aware.

Our examination of police bulletins and general orders related to
the enforcement of hate crime in California reveals that when policy-
related orders do exist, they appear to vary considerably with respect
to how hate crime is defined; what procedures departments have
adopted to deal with them; and how rank-and-file officers are expected to identify, classify, and record such incidents. At the same
time, however, our examination of such material also suggests that
the general trajectory is toward greater levels of organizational commitment to policing hate crime and convergence in how that policing
is expected to unfold. This is evident in the content of police bulletins
and orders in California along three dimensions: the degree to which
local policy aligns with federal policy, provides a definition of hate
crime, and details how officers should handle potential incidents of
hate crime.

Some California police departments have revised and updated
their police training guidelines to reflect changing definitions and judicial interpretations of the law and to bring their guidelines into
alignment with those of the FBI. More often than not, California police departments' guidelines demonstrate an awareness of the judicial
rulings relevant to the question of how to classify cases in which bias
is only one of several motivations. Reflecting recent court decisions in

Figure 6.3   Status Provisions Included in Hate Crime General Orders of California Police Departments, 1994 and 1999

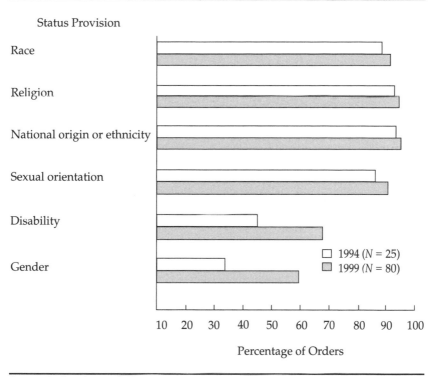

Source: Authors' compilation.

California, both sets of guidelines—California's and the FBI's—stipulate that an incident should be classified as a hate crime when it appears to have been caused "in whole, or in part" by race, religion, and so forth. In other words, at both the state and federal levels, training is being altered to reflect the more recent conceptualization of hate crime law, suggesting that policies, and perhaps practices as well, are becoming more homogeneous.

More than half (58 percent) of the California police department's general orders we examined provide a definition of hate crime by referencing the "in whole or in part" phrasing of the FBI and broader state policing guidelines as a way of defining the intent standard inherent in hate crime (California 1995). Some police orders, using the conceptual distinctions introduced in chapter 5, invoke the notion of "hate crime," whereas others employ the notion of "bias crime." Moreover, many explicitly advise officers to ask themselves whether there were other factors that might explain the crime, suggesting a conservative approach to defining the concept. In addition, few of the general orders cite anything other than race, religion, sexual orientation, and ancestry as relevant status provisions in their definitions of hate crime. This signals a return to the most restrictive conceptualization of hate crime, despite the fact that California law has one of the most extensive lists of status provisions, including most recently an innovative provision for transsexuals. However, as figure 6.3 illustrates, the definitions employed in the orders have broadened in recent years. In 1994, hate crimes tended to be defined as conduct motivated by race, religion, national origin or ethnicity, and sexual orientation. The first three of these provisions were included in roughly 95 percent of the orders, and sexual orientation was mentioned in 88 percent of the orders. By 1999, sexual orientation, gender, and disability were included more frequently. Of course, further research is necessary to determine whether differences in these definitions and phrasings translate into differences in policing.

Finally, the general orders indicate some variation in how hate crime cases are to be handled. Sixty-one percent of the orders direct officers to forward the cases to a supervising officer for further investigation, and 14 percent direct officers to pass the case to a special officer or unit whose duties include acting as a specialist in hate crime case processing. The remaining orders fail to specify what is to be done once an officer confronts a hate crime incident.

In essence, our examination confirms Walker and Katz's (1995) finding that police department approaches to hate crime policing are far from uniform, although there is evidence that uniformity is increasing. The newness of the concept as a criminal category to be reckoned with in the world of policing has increasingly been recognized through police orders and bulletins. Programs are now being designed and implemented in an attempt to standardize officers' understandings of hate crime. Presumably, as officers come to share definitions and awareness of what counts as evidence, their interpretations and policing practices will converge. Although preliminary, our investigation of general policy orders from California municipal police and sheriff departments suggests that this process, while under way, is far from complete.

At this point, further research is needed specifically gauging the future trends and trajectory of hate crime policing. In addition, more research is needed that compares hate crime enforcement and investigation to the policing of other kinds of crime, including crimes that—like hate crimes—are newly created and therefore at the same stage of "unsettledness." Without such comparisons it is difficult to conclude whether hate crime policing actually faces any unique problems or is instead subject to the same ordinary ambiguities and processes of discretion as other kinds of crime. The same question can be asked of the prosecution of hate crime, to which we now turn our attention.

The Demands on Prosecutors and the Prosecution of Hate Crime

The other side of law enforcement, the prosecution of hate crime, is in roughly the same shape as the policing. Prosecutors express mixed opinions about the viability and value of enforcing hate crime law. Some prosecutors view hate crime laws as a meaningful response to community strife insofar as they provide an extra tool with which to manage crime and intergroup conflict in their communities (Boxall, "D.A. Seeks to Expand Hate Crimes Unit"). Other prosecutors, however, have gone on record rejecting hate crime laws as useless and unenforceable (Jacobs and Potter 1998).

Prosecutors' objections to hate crime law are multifaceted. At least in the abstract, hate crime implies greater evidentiary burdens, increased effort to spell out the intricacies of the law to juries, and, generally, more time and energy to prepare cases. For prosecutors who are understaffed and burdened with heavy caseloads, the task of prosecuting hate crimes may represent an extra set of duties they prefer to avoid in an occupation in which one's worth is measured in terms of conviction rates. Besides, as the argument goes, hate crime perpetrators can usually be convicted for their parallel crimes.

To date, however, no empirical studies on the prosecution of hate crimes have been published. This, no doubt, is in large part a function of the newness of the criminal category and of the lag time between changes in the legal world and scholarship devoted to understanding such changes. In the absence of systematic data on the prosecution of hate crime, however, we turn to the broader research literature on prosecution for clues to the potential problems. This literature focuses on many of the same themes discussed earlier with respect to policing. Like policing, prosecutorial discretion provides a lens through which to examine hate crime prosecution. Like policing, the presence of increased bureaucratic controls often has little effect on the uniformity of prosecutorial decision making. Finally, like policing, the presence of prosecutorial discretion does not result in prosecutors' behaving in an unpredictable and haphazard manner (Baumgartner 1992; Carter 1974; Feeley 1973; Feldman 1992; Johnson 1998; Ohlin 1993).

Lief Carter (1974) argues that despite the appeal of constraining prosecution with clear-cut rules, a criminal justice system characterized by such constraint is impossible to achieve and would be undesirable even if it were possible. It is impossible to achieve because of the complexity and uncertainty of the matters faced by prosecutors, and undesirable because it would leave prosecutors with little flexibility to tailor justice to particular circumstances and would encourage them to remain ignorant of the details of the criminal acts they confront (for example, the seriousness of the crime, mitigating circumstances, appropriateness of the punishment, integrity of the evidence and the gathering process that generated it, and community expectations). Such ambiguity prompts the prosecutors to adopt a 'learning' orientation in which prosecutors adapt to a variety of extra legal sources of information rather than merely the law and the conduct at hand. Thus, uncertainty is not an extraordinary characteristic of prosecution unique to hate crime, but something that prosecutors routinely face and overcome.

Building on Carter's approach, others have argued that prosecution is principally oriented toward "individualized" justice (Ohlin 1993). Here the decision-maker places a premium on selecting charges that are appropriate to the unique circumstances of incidents, placing great emphasis on determining the fairest solution in a particular case. Often, this requires that prosecutors recognize their role as actors within a local community and make choices regarding the importance of the instrumental good that law enforcement provides within that community (Wilson 1973). Such an orientation explains why some researchers have found that broad categories like "social harm" determine the likelihood of prosecution (Baumgartner 1992) and why media coverage of a case affects prosecutorial decision-making (Haynie and Dover 1994). Clearly, this view would also see hate crime laws as enhancing the ability of prosecutors to be responsive to these extralegal influences and to individualize justice.

Other work focuses on the social organization of the prosecution in a somewhat different way. Some argue that prosecutors' decisions are largely made in relation to self-interest and efficiency. That is, prosecutors frequently privilege career advancement and the efficient processing of cases over strict adherence to formal rules (see, for example, Frohmann 1997, on the prosecution of rape cases). Abraham Blumberg (1967), for example, argues that much of prosecutorial conduct is traceable to bureaucratic pressures to process cases and achieve high conviction rates. Similarly, Celesta Albonetti (1987) argues that prosecutors are fundamentally oriented to the reduction of uncertainty, which leads them to focus on the pragmatic features of cases, most notably, the quality of evidence and testimony. Wherever there is ambiguity, there is less likelihood of prosecution, and thus prosecutors are motivated to avoid ambiguous cases.

From this perspective, hate crime cases are not attractive crimes to prosecute because they create additional burdens for prosecutors, consequently lowering the likelihood of successful prosecution. A prosecutor choosing to prosecute a case as a hate crime rather than an assault, for example, might need to extend greater effort to gather evidence to show that the victim was selected because of his or her race, religion, or sexual orientation. Although this might be easy to do, it nonetheless involves extra work. In addition, prosecutors may view hate crime as a concept that is highly controversial and ambiguous and thus more difficult to prove to a judge or jury and perhaps even more easily defended against. These two characteristics make it much more difficult to predict the success of a prosecution strategy. In such circumstances the prosecutor would be likely to take a more conservative approach, pursuing the simpler prosecution of the parallel crime (Lawrence 1999).

A final strand of work focuses on the patterned ways discretion is wielded by prosecutors. Classic work by Sudnow (1965) and recent work by Frohmann (1997) show that prosecutors organize their work around informal rules about normal crimes—in particular, stereotypes of the location of the crime (Frohmann 1997), evaluations of the standing and characteristics of the victim (Stanko 1981), and assessments of the moral worth of the victim (Baumgartner 1992; Frohmann 1997). Arguably, these features may not be good for hate crime prosecution, especially when the victim is a member of a targeted group toward whom prosecutors hold negative views or assume that others hold negative views. Alternatively, minority victims might be perceived to be in greater need of legal protection. Either way, hate crime policy might be thought of as promoting a reconsideration of precisely the question "who is a worthy victim?" (Jenness 1995a; Jenness 1999).

Although no empirical social science research has been published on hate crime prosecution, the publications of initial statistics on hate crime prosecutions, convictions, and plea bargains are beginning to be reported. Jacobs and Potter (1998) report that few bias crime incidents are prosecuted. For example, only 12 percent of reported complaints in Brooklyn, 11 percent of incidents in California, and 7 percent of complaints in San Francisco were prosecuted in 1992, 1995, and 1995, respectively (Jacobs and Potter 1998). At first glance, these statistics appear striking, but when compared with ratios of incident to prosecution for other crimes they are not so extraordinary.

As we argue with respect to policing, the prosecution of hate crime must be analyzed longitudinally and comparatively with other kinds of crimes. Unfortunately, we have few longitudinal data points on hate crime prosecution from which we can undertake such an analysis. Initial data, however, suggest that—as in the development of legislation and judicial interpretation and, to some extent, in policing—prosecution strategies may become more convergent and more uniform over time as officials within these arenas become more familiar with the concept. In particular, recent data on prosecution in California begin to tell the story. From 1995 to 1998 all of the major indicators of hate crime processing varied. Only about 6 percent of hate crime incidents in 1995 and 1996 led to successful convictions. In 1997, that figure rose to more than 17 percent, but in 1998 it fell back to 10 percent. On the surface, these percentages may seem dismal. However, to put them in perspective, consider that data for 1996 and 1997 actually fall about halfway between the percentages for aggravated assault (a crime known to be comparatively easy to police and prosecute) and vandalism (a crime known to be fairly difficult to police and prosecute). Of course, hate crime runs the gamut from assault to vandalism, and it is therefore not surprising that it falls somewhere between the two in terms of the ratio of incidents to convictions. However, these data only tell us about the slippage between the police's classification of incidents and the ability of prosecutors to obtain convictions.

Perhaps a more useful way of evaluating the prosecution of hate crime is to determine the proportion of hate crime case filings that have led to convictions. Again, data along these lines are limited and preliminary. Although there is much variability in hate crime conviction rates, in general, the ratio has improved and falls within the range of other crimes. This suggests that once prosecutors decide to prosecute a crime as a hate crime, obtaining a conviction is no more difficult than in other crimes. When 70 to 90 percent of cases lead to convictions, as in California from 1996 to 1998, the argument that the laws are unenforceable is difficult to maintain. A final piece of evidence worth contemplating is the proportion of guilty pleas in hate crime cases. If, as some have contended (Jacobs and Potter 1998), hate crimes are considerably more ambiguous and contestable than their "parallel crimes" and thus represent a misuse of justice system resources, then we would expect plea bargains to be rare. Cases would be protracted, and charges would most likely be contested by defendants. However, as with most crimes, the majority of hate crime cases in California result in guilty pleas rather than trials; moreover, that number has increased in recent years, from 40 percent in 1995 to almost 70 percent in 1998.

In sum, a limited—but growing—amount of evidence suggests that the pessimistic view of hate crime prosecutions as causing enormous problems for prosecutors is problematic at best and unfounded at worst. Initial data indicate that although only a small portion of incidents produce convictions, when prosecutors do decide to file cases as hate crimes they are comparatively successful in obtaining prosecutions, often by guilty plea. This suggests that the prosecution of hate crime is proceeding in a conservative rather than liberal or indiscriminate fashion, as could be expected from a newly initiated policy anchored around an unsettled concept.

Moreover, hate crime prosecutions are beginning to resemble patterns for other crimes as the concept becomes more settled in the law enforcement arena. The California data suggest that since the mid-1990s, after the constitutionality of its hate crime law had been confirmed, California prosecutors have increased the frequency with which they file hate crime complaints.[2] Conviction rates and guilty pleas are also increasing, which suggests that prosecutors are becoming more comfortable invoking and enforcing hate crime laws and criminal defense attorneys are less likely to effectively interfere with their doing so.

The Future of Law Enforcement as the Least Settled Arena of the Policy Domain

Policing and prosecuting represents the most recent phase of the legal construction of hate crimes. Accordingly, law enforcement is the least "settled" or the least institutionalized of the phases we have considered. As a result, data on the policing and prosecuting of hate crime is only now beginning to surface; thus it is preliminary and limited, and published empirically grounded social science research is even more sparse. At this point, it is not surprising that the central concerns of researchers and practitioners revolve around the viability of policing and prosecuting hate crime and the lack of uniformity in the responses of law enforcement to hate crime.

However, evidence from recently published studies of hate crime policing, coupled with our own research on the topic, indicate that despite the ordinary discretion involved in police work and the apparent ambiguity of the concept, policing of hate crime is not impossible or unpatterned. Rather, the policing of hate crime is highly contingent upon predictable personnel and organizational characteristics. In places where there is a high degree of organizational commitment to the enforcing of hate crime law and a set of organizational routines built around detecting and processing hate crime cases, there is greater likelihood that hate crimes will be recognized, verified, and classified as such. In contrast, where there is less commitment to and few or no organizational routines built around enforcement, police officers are less likely to identify hate crime and less likely to forward cases for prosecution. Moreover, there is also evidence that the organizational commitment among police departments generally has increased in recent years. Thus, although there is considerable variability in the way police departments define hate crime, such variability may be lessening and, in fact, may never have been significantly greater than in other kinds of criminal policing.

Although there is even less research and empirical evidence available relevant to the prosecution of hate crime, initial official statistics and the available research literature on prosecution paints a picture that is largely favorable to supporters of hate crime law. Arguments presented elsewhere have exaggerated the problems hate crime poses for prosecutors. Although limited and preliminary, existing data suggest that prosecutors are using hate crime law and often doing so in an appropriately conservative fashion. They are prosecuting only those cases in which evidence is compelling and success is likely, as indicated by our comparison of conviction rates for hate crime and other types of crime. Specifically, the rates of conviction and guilty pleas for hate crime are similar to those for other kinds of crimes; moreover, the rates are improving as cases continue to accumulate. Thus, prosecutors do not appear to view the concept as overly ambiguous or unusable.

The implications of the research literature on prosecution provide a somewhat more mixed set of expectations. One strand of the research on prosecution suggests that prosecutors who are oriented to bureaucratic efficiency or career self-interest through high conviction rates are unlikely to see hate crime law as a useful tool because of the perceived costs and risks associated with its use. However, another strand of literature suggests that prosecutors are receptive to hate crime law in the spirit of seeking a broader conception of justice, one that permits a certain amount of sensitivity to the unique characteristics and the broader political significance of these crimes. As with policing, any conclusions about exactly how hate crime law will work must be provisional until more empirical data are available on the unique characteristics and costs of hate crime prosecution and data, as well as how prosecutorial use of the law changes over time.

For now, the data that are available emphasize the viability of policing and prosecuting hate crime. This is not surprising, given the findings of classic and contemporary social science studies of policing and prosecution that demonstrate that officers frequently deal with circumstances that are difficult to classify and require them to understand complex motivations and the interpersonal dynamics of the persons involved. Moreover, as the key concept that defines the crime—in this case, bias motivation—becomes increasingly settled, the work of police departments and prosecutors becomes more routine and less problematic. Thus, the question that must be asked about hate crime is this: does the variation we currently see correspond to other innovations in crime policy at this stage of their development? In other words, the appropriate comparison for hate crime policing and prosecution is not crimes like theft, which is a deeply settled concept in American law; rather, crimes like stalking, domestic violence, sexual harassment, and white-collar crime—all of which began as highly contested legal concepts but have become increasingly settled in recent years—constitute appropriate comparisons.

There is growing evidence that much of the variation in the policing and prosecution of hate crime is, in large part, attributable to the newness of the criminal category itself. Given that this is only a temporary feature of the policy domain, there is reason to believe that variation in the policing and prosecution of hate crime is decreasing and will continue to do so as the concept becomes settled. Indeed, we hypothesize that just as social movement activism, lawmaking, and judicial decision-making around hate crime have done over the past two decades, newfound police practices related to hate crime will become established and taken for granted. Just as we have demonstrated with other institutional sectors of the hate crime policy domain, over time the definition of hate crime has become broader and more inclusive in the law enforcement arena. Again, the underlying processes are best characterized as simultaneous domain expansion, homogenization, and elaboration. Because these processes underlie the social organization of hate crime as a public policy, we conclude this book with a discussion of their theoretical importance and policy implications.

= Chapter 7 =

Conclusion:
Empirical Findings, Theoretical
Interpretations, and
Policy Implications

O VER THE past three decades hate crime has been defined, promoted, and addressed as a contemporary social problem. As Senator Edward Kennedy has proclaimed, "Civil rights are still the unfinished business of America. Hate crimes are uniquely destructive and divisive, because their impact extends far beyond the victim. They poison entire communities and undermine the ideals for which America stands. They deserve to be punished with the full force of law" (Lawrence 1999). Interestingly, it was not until the end of the twentieth century that statements like this were issued by senior elected officials and policy reform designed to combat discriminatory violence was put forward and institutionalized. This marks an important moment in the history of crime control efforts, the development of criminal and civil law, the allocation of civil rights, and the symbolic status of select minorities in the United States.

Given this, we conclude this book as we began, with a question: how have the many changes that accompany this moment come about such that an entirely new policy domain has emerged to redefine age-old conduct—discriminatory violence—as a crime problem? Moreover, what are the structure, content, and consequences of this policy domain? By addressing these related questions, this book is first and foremost about the birth and structure of an entire domain of public policy, its key players, practices, and substantive focus. This study forms a backdrop against which the behavior and consequences of what is now commonly referred to as hate crime can best be understood by social scientists and addressed by activists, policy makers, and concerned citizens.

As with other social constructions, especially those imbued with criminal meaning, the concept "hate crime" can, in the first instance, be seen as an outgrowth of the interplay between social movement activism, policy making, and the law (including judges, police, and law enforcement) and the meanings they engender. The law in particular has played a major role in defining hate crime as a social problem. Through legislative activity, judicial activity, and policing and prosecutorial activity, "hate crime" has become a meaningful term. After all, the law delineates hate crime from other forms of bias-motivated behavior, as well as other forms of criminal and noncriminal activity that is seen by some as sinful, inhumane, deviant, or malicious. By demarcating specific forms of bias-motivated intimidation and violence as hate crimes, the law—a highly visible and binding form of public policy—has created new categories of violent crime and new categories of crime victims. The evolution of this social fact has been the central concern of this book.

Empirical Findings

As identified in the first chapter and analyzed in subsequent chapters, multiple institutional spheres have contributed to the invention, development, and institutionalization of the term hate crime and of attendant policy responses. Table 7.1 provides a summary of these influences. Social movement organizations and their representatives invented and promoted the concept of hate-motivated violence. Politicians have enacted legislation defining the parameters of hate crime, as opposed to "ordinary" crime. Judges have fixed more elaborate and complicated meanings to the law produced by legislators. Finally, enforcement officials continue to engage in categorization work that serves to classify only some conduct as hate crime. The ideologies, interests, and practices of these players have constituted and reconstituted the parameters of hate crime in the United States.

Social Movements and the Development of Hate Crime

Although what is now commonly referred to as bias- or hate-motivated violence is as old as humankind, the emergence of an anti-hate-crime movement proved crucial to initiating the policy domain. Consistent with a central tenet of new social movements theory (Johnston and Klandermans 1995; Morris and Mueller 1992), our study suggests

Table 7.1   The Formation of a Policy Domain Regarding Hate Crime: Summary of Key Findings

Institutional Sphere	Empirical Findings	Theoretical Import
Social movements	• Convergence of established rights movements • Establishment of anti-hate-crime movement • Documentation of select forms of discriminatory violence • Dissemination of "horror stories" and epidemiological portraits of hate crime	• Discovery of a "condition category" • Establishment of empirical credibility of condition category • Development of collective action frames that define the condition category • Initiation of issue creation
Legislatures	• Attention to newly defined condition category • Emergence of hate crime as statutory concept • Establishment of core elements of a statutory template • Proliferation of common and differing elements	• Translation of social movement goals into legal discourse • Negotiation of key parameters of policy • Expansion of the domain of the problem • Homogenization of the policy response
Courts	• Questioning of the legal standing of the statutes • Development of a constitutional crisis around the law • Elimination of particular statutory responses • Development of legally defensible theoretical foundations for the law	• Affirmation of the legitimacy of the policy concept • Delineation and demarcation of the concept • Continuing expansion of the domain • Restriction of the parameters of the concept's applicability

Table 7.1   *Continued*

Institutional Sphere	Empirical Findings	Theoretical Import
Law enforcement	• Variation in definition and response to problem • Changes in organizational structure initiated to confront ambiguity • Expansion of the working definition • Increasing streamlining in processing of cases	• Translation of abstract concept into practice • Development and institutionalization of "normal" constructs • Homogenization of organizational practices • Reduction of the ambiguity of the concept through routinization

Source: Authors' compilation.

that at least four social justice movements converged around a common concern about discriminatory violence directed at minority constituencies. Each movement contributed its own antiviolence project to the emergence of a new sector of social movement organization in the United States—the anti-hate-crime movement—which prompted the transformation of the social and legal status of select groups of individuals and, more generally, the emergence of the hate crime policy domain.

Capitalizing on the material and discursive resources generated by the modern civil rights movement, the contemporary women's movement, the gay and lesbian movement, and the victim's rights movement, the anti-hate-crime movement emerged in the latter part of the twentieth century to identify, name, and respond to violence born of bigotry. In an effort to represent the interests of diverse constituencies—people of color, Jews, women, gays and lesbians, and people with disabilities, among others—the anti-hate-crime movement called attention to the many atrocities committed because of racism, anti-Semitism, sexism, homophobia, and prejudice toward those with disabilities. In so doing, it brought newfound attention to age-old conduct—it "discovered" hate crime in the United States. The most significant contribution of these movements was the gathering, compiling, and publicizing of anecdotal and statistical information on the victimization of members of minority groups (Jenness and Broad 1997). Epidemiological reports and single case overviews, what John Johnson (1989) calls "horror stories," generated by the anti-hate-crime movement continue to be distributed to law enforcement agencies, government officials, members of minority communities, the general

population, and policy makers. This information highlights undetected and unreported hate-motivated violence, purports a well-documented rise in violence motivated by bias, and portrays an epidemic
of discriminatory violence. Taken as a whole, this information be-
stows empirical credibility on a now identifiable social problem in
need of official response and remedy (Jenness 1995a; Jenness and
Broad 1997).

The establishment of empirical credibility was accompanied by the
development of collective action frames that defined the parameters
of the condition-category.[1] In social movement analyses, "the framing
perspective has been at the forefront of renewed interest in cultural
and ideational processes" (Johnston 1995, 217; see also Benford 1997)
precisely because of a recognition that the mere discovery of a condition-category is not sufficient to warrant government response and
policy change (Benford 1997). Rather, the successful framing of the
condition-category as a particular type of problem is required. In this
case, the master frames of crime, discrimination, and civil rights violation were deployed to constitute a single collective action frame: hate
crime (Best 1999; Jacobs and Potter 1998; Jenness 1995a, 1999). This
framing of the condition-category was the first step in what Burstein
(1991) refers to as issue creation and a necessary precursor to making
demands on the larger political system. But the question remains,
what demands?

Federal and State Law and the Development of the Concept of Hate Crime

Activists, educators, community representatives, and other interested
claims makers continually point to the law as the primary institution
responsible for addressing discriminatory violence. Most notably, social movement mobilization translated into the demand for legal reform, with sympathetic legislators generally agreeing with Representative John Conyers that "hate crime[s], which can range from threats
and vandalism to arson, assault and murder, are intended not just to
harm the victim, but to send a message of intimidation to an entire
community of people" (*Congressional Record* 1988, 11393). Therefore,
"hate crimes motivated by intolerance need to be distinguished from
other crimes motivated by other factors"(Congress 1988c, 8). The general justification for legislation developed by the anti-hate-crime
movement—that harassment and intimidation, assault, and destruction of property assume a particularly dangerous and socially disruptive character when motivated by bigotry—was presented to state
and federal lawmakers, who were in a position to make public policy.

Sympathetic and not-so-sympathetic legislators quickly confronted a seemingly simple but ultimately complex question: what manifestations of violent conduct and what types of people should occupy center stage in legal battles against bigotry, and why? Lawmakers were faced with the dilemma of determining what distinctions to inscribe into law and how to justify those distinctions. Consistent with the constructionist framework laid out in chapter 1, our detailed analysis of how "people-categories"[2] in particular were determined in federal hate crime law demonstrates that what becomes recognizable as socially problematic is the product of practical and political activity. As ethnomethodologists in particular have asserted, the orderly and recognizable features of social life are "talked into being" (Heritage 1984, 29), in this case as victims are designated and dramatized in congressional talk (Chock 1995).

Federal Law   Since 1985, every U.S. Congress has considered the question of hate-motivated violence. Thus far, hundreds of hours of congressional hearings and debates have culminated in three major reforms: the Hate Crimes Statistics Act (1990), the Violence Against Women Act (1994), and the Hate Crimes Sentencing Enhancement Act (1994). The legislative histories of these laws reveals how the inclusion of status provisions (such as race, religion, ethnicity, sexual orientation, and gender) in hate crime law ensured that the substantive character of federal law was shaped in racialized, sexualized, and gendered ways but not in ways that attend to violence organized around age, occupation, political affiliation, and other status categories.

Consistent with the recommendation of the Coalition on Hate Crimes, early claims from local, regional, and state-level activists and experts focused on the scope and consequences of race-, religion-, and ethnicity-based violence, thus articulating the parameters of the problem in comparatively narrow terms. A growing awareness of this type of violence became grounds for promoting federal hate crime legislation by a limited number of activist organizations and their representatives. This activity cemented a trio of statuses—race, religion, and ethnicity—as the anchoring provisions of all hate crime law. This occurred without contestation over the legitimacy of these status provisions and in light of the fact that race, religion, and ethnicity were already institutionalized as legitimate subjects for federal discrimination law.

The character of hate crime law was reshaped when the domain of the law expanded to include additional provisions. Shortly after federal hate crime law was introduced, proposals were made by activist groups to add sexual orientation to the proposed federal hate crime law. Through direct and sustained testimony in federal hearings, movement representatives were able to bestow empirical credibility upon the violence connected with this provision, just as other movements had previously bestowed empirical credibility upon violence organized around race, religion, and ethnicity. In addition, they successfully engaged in discursive tactics that rendered the meaning of sexual orientation, as a protected status, similar to the meanings already attached to race, religion, and ethnicity. By successfully engaging in these linking strategies of persuasion, gay and lesbian movement activists proved crucial to the expansion of hate crime law to cover sexual orientation. The addition of sexual orientation was contingent upon the presence and viability of direct, sustained social movement mobilization. This proved crucial despite the fact that sexual orientation had not been recognized as a legitimate provision in previous federal discrimination law.

In contrast, other provisions initially recommended for inclusion in the law, but not added to the bill before its passage, did not attract significant, sustained social movement mobilization in congressional hearings. Before the passage of the HCSA, for example, legislators made passing references to the possibility of including the protection of octogenarians, union members, children, the elderly, and police officers under hate crime law. In the absence of formal hearings on violence against these groups, however, there was never a structural opportunity for their representatives to establish the problem's empirical credibility. Neither was there a structural opportunity for representatives of these groups to engage in the categorization work required to legitimate these provisions. As a result, provisions for these constituencies have not been written into federal hate crime law.

For comparative purposes, an examination of the legislative history of gender as a provision in federal hate crime law is instructive. It reveals that later in the history of federal lawmaking around hate crime, the importance of collective action, as measured through the presence of activist organizations at congressional hearings and in congressional debates and reports, declined. Once select provisions were cemented in the law, new provisions were adopted without direct pressure from women's organizations and their representatives and despite the fact that gender was purposely excluded from law earlier in the lawmaking process. Although many federal hearings on violence against women have been held, they were neither initiated nor sustained by feminist organizations. Instead, as lawmakers coalesced around the meaning of hate crime law in previous hearings, established policy templates were institutionalized. This, in turn, shaped federal hate crime law by distinguishing yet another element of the people-category, in this case, women. This occurred without much fanfare and without relevant organizations' engaging in decisive categorization work but in light of the fact that gender—like race, religion, and ethnicity—was already a standard subject of federal discrimination law: the concept of gender as a legal subject parallel to race, religion, and ethnicity has been commonplace for more a quarter of a century.

This mechanism of domain expansion, particular to the later phase of lawmaking, is further evidenced by the history of the disability provision in hate crime law. Disability was added to the reauthorization of the Hate Crimes Statistics Act, the original and final version of the Hate Crimes Sentencing Enhancement Act, and the current bill pending in the Congress, the Hate Crimes Prevention Act (S. 1529/ H.R. 3081). Its inclusion, however, did not result from vigorous lobbying on behalf of persons with disabilities at the federal level. In fact, there never has been a formal hearing, or even testimony, regarding hate crimes against people with disabilities. Nor has there ever been any explicit opposition voiced to the inclusion of the disability provision in federal hate crime law. Regardless, the category "disability," and thus persons with disabilities, have found a home within the legislation. This occurred because disability—like race, religion, and gender—was already a standard subject of federal discrimination law, in large part because of the earlier passage of the Americans with Disabilities Act in 1990 (Shapiro 1993).

State Law   Once developed, how do legal concepts circulate, take shape, and become institutionalized across distinct but interrelated polities? To address this question, our analysis of the macro processes of diffusion and institutionalization reveals the patterned way in which state law has developed over time.

As of 2000, criminal hate crime laws had passed in forty-one states (Soule and Earl 1999). Although these laws differ in important ways, they share core elements: they all create or enhance penalties for criminal behavior motivated by some combination of status categories, such as race, religion, national origin, sexual orientation, gender, and disability. Variation in the distribution of status provisions is extensive, but it is also patterned. In particular, the approach individual states took was largely shaped by the timing of adoption.

Statutes generally have converged in terms of the basic methods by which they alter the penal code. The process of convergence around a specific approach—what we call legal strategy—and the ways of depicting the motivational requirements reflect legislative dynamics that are well known to students of state policy making and the diffusion of innovations (Gray 1973; Strang and Meyer 1993; Walker 1969). Within the system of state governments, innovative policies evolve through a series of phases. The initial phase is characterized by a diversity of approaches because there are no clear models or guides upon which to base action. As time passes, other states begin to respond; however, they no longer operate in the absence of precedent and are instead confronted with various options and the experience of their predecessors about what works and what is a constitutionally or politically legitimate approach. Subsequent policy making results from informed mimicry of early innovators, which often leads to one or two approaches emerging as optimal. In the aggregate, this suggests that a period of experimentation and diversity of approaches tends to be followed by a convergence, or homogenization, of approaches. State hate crime law certainly follows this pattern of homogenization over its life course insofar as approaches to the law, once diverse, are increasingly convergent.

Despite the convergence in method, however, hate crime statutes have become more expansive in terms of content—the categories of persons and the kinds of acts they cover. Categories of race, religion, and national origin generally form the core provisions of the early statutes. Sexual orientation, gender, and disability were added later in several states, and a few categories, such as creed, marital status, political affiliation, and service in the armed forces, have been included on an idiosyncratic basis. The interpretation of this pattern is clear. The most pervasive categories reflect the oldest, most established, and most recognized axes of oppression. The salience of these categories reflects the success of the 1960s-era civil rights movement in galvanizing particular categories in the public consciousness and in legal discourse (Grattet, Jenness, and Curry 1998). Legislators by and large do not contest the prevalence and seriousness of hate crime motivated by these categories (Jenness 1999). Sexual orientation, gender, and disability provisions reflect the interests of more recent, and therefore less embedded, rights movements; thus, these provisions still face considerable opposition when claiming a place in issues like hate crime law (Jenness 1999). Finally, the miscellaneous categories have little or no history to sustain claims for inclusion in the laws and therefore have made much less systematic advancement into the issue.

Thus far, we have seen that the hate crime concept undergoes a common process within each new institutional arena into which it is placed. The institutionalization of the concept of hate crime has been accompanied by a refocusing of the concept relative to constraints of each new arena into which it moves; its meaning is thereby sharpened, expanded, and elaborated in novel ways. Indeed, the twin processes that characterize the evolution of the concept within the legislative arena, homogenization and domain expansion, are reiterated as it moves into the judicial realm.

Courts and the Development of the Concept of Hate Crime

From 1984 to 1999, U.S. appellate courts considered the constitutionality of hate crime statutes thirty-eight times (Phillips and Grattet 2000). During this period, hate crime statutes were embroiled in a highly visible constitutional crisis (Bader 1994; Brooks 1994; Gaumer 1994; Grannis 1993; Kagan 1992; Morsch 1992; Strossen 1993; Tribe 1993; Winer 1994). By 1997, however, that crisis was largely resolved, and the frequency of hate crime cases and attendant legal commentary subsided dramatically, indicating that the rules governing hate crime are becoming more "settled" in judicial discourse (Phillips and Grattet 2000).

Before being resolved, however, the constitutional crisis had important effects on the legal conception of hate crime. Appellate judges rejected certain approaches to formulating hate crime law and endorsed others, thus creating a jurisprudential foundation for the statutes. Although the statutes are quite broad and potentially cover all sorts of things, courts have restricted their meaning in such a way that the concept of hate crime has become increasingly delineated and demarcated. Courts have narrowed the meaning of hate crime statutes to cover only a limited range of expressive conduct: that which constitutes a "true threat." The particular interpretation courts have given to the motivational requirements of the law, however, has served to expand the potential range of coverage. By reframing hate crime as acts of discriminatory violence, courts have subsumed the statutes under antidiscrimination laws. With an intent standard comparable to that of antidiscrimination laws, hate crime law can now actually be enforced in circumstances in which hate is absent. Thus, the meaning of the law has been expanded.

In sum, as hate crime statutes came under the scrutiny of the courts, yet another reworking of the concept was set in motion. As with the social movement and legislative arenas, a refocusing and sharpening of the concept resulted from its circulation within courts. Once again, the institutionalization of hate crime as a socially constructed fact is reflected in its refinement and the emergent consensus about what the laws do and do not cover. The remaining empirical question, then, is this: what happens to the concept once the law is legitimated by the courts and placed in the hands of law enforcement, especially police and prosecutors?

Law Enforcement and the Development of the Concept of Hate Crime

Ultimately, the concept of hate crime must be translated into the day-to-day practices of law enforcement officials. Police officers and pros-ecutors are charged with applying the abstract judicial and legislative conception of hate crime to concrete factual circumstances surround-ing human conduct. Because this represents the theoretical and em-pirical endpoint of the diffusion of the hate crime concept across the various institutional arenas (see table 7.1), it is the least institu-tionalized aspect of the hate crime policy domain examined in this book. That hate crime is least settled within this arena is reflected in the early social science research on the subject, which highlights the variation in commitment to hate crime policing and investigative pro-cedures and a lack of consensus among frontline officers about what the concept of hate crime means (Boyd, Berk, and Hamner 1996; Mar-tin 1995, 1996; Walker and Katz 1995; Wexler and Marx 1986).

However, these initial studies of the policing of hate crime were conducted relatively early in the formation of the hate crime policy domain, before appellate courts had refined the meaning of statutes, before law enforcement had instituted uniform training guidelines, and before many police departments had adopted the general orders relative to hate crimes. In large part police officers and departments vary in terms of how they define hate crime because a consistent enforcement criterion for translating the general statutes into concrete circumstances was less established in the early 1990s. Accordingly, we have argued for a longitudinal view of policing and prosecution.

The evidence suggests that the ambiguity of the concept is decreas-ing; moreover, hate crime may not pose anticipated unique or extraor-dinary difficulties in enforcement. The recent increases in attention given to training and curriculum guidelines are likely to reduce some of the variability in understandings across jurisdictions. Many aspects of the federal guidelines are being replicated in some state curricular materials, and local police departments increasingly are establishing their own general orders relative to hate crime. These guidelines and orders specify a definition of the concept and articulate procedures for detecting, classifying, and recording hate crimes. Moreover, many larger cities have established special hate crime enforcement units so that judgments can be made by law enforcement agents who routinely deal with the subject. As these efforts continue, police practices related to hate crime enforcement are likely to reach a greater degree of convergence—and at an accelerated rate.

Similarly, prosecution practices in relation to hate crime are also highly variable. Consideration of the broader research literature on prosecution provides a mixed assessment of the viability of prosecuting hate crime perpetrators. One strand of work suggests that hate crimes statutes will not be attractive to prosecutors insofar as extra evidence gathering is required. Under such circumstances prosecutors are likely to perceive hate crime cases as riskier than the "parallel crime" prosecutions. In contrast, other work suggests that the prosecution of hate crime perpetrators is a highly attractive pursuit because it allows prosecutors to send a powerful moral message to their communities.

Regardless of its perceived attractiveness, the prosecution of hate crime may fall within the range of variability of other kinds of crime. As it stands, the little data that are available suggest that many of the incidents of hate crime reported to the police are never prosecuted as such. However, ratios of incidents to prosecutions of hate crimes are not extraordinarily different from those for other crimes. Once prosecutors decide to file a case as a hate crime, they are generally successful in obtaining a conviction. In addition, offenders enter guilty pleas at rates that are comparable to those for other kinds of crimes rather than contesting the legitimacy and constitutionality of the laws.

Although evidence is only recently beginning to emerge and accumulate, it appears that the hate crime concept is becoming settled within law enforcement. At least at the level of the policing and the prosecution of hate crime, this process mimics what we have observed in social movement, legislative, and judicial realms: police and prosecutorial practices are becoming more uniform even though there remains significant heterogeneity in organizational and personnel responses. We anticipate that as the ambiguity surrounding the laws lessens police and prosecutors alike will continue to develop a familiarity with the concept and establish case-building routines that facilitate successful policing and prosecution.

As a result of the dynamic described in table 7.1, what was once identifiable as either a private injury or, at best, an "ordinary crime" has been transformed into a delimited category, hate crime. This transformation has resulted in the increased visibility of the victims of bias-motivated violence, institutional changes accompanying this recognition, and the establishment of official policies in multiple arenas that constitute the policy domain. Beyond these empirical details, however, what does this research tell us about the processes that generate and reflect these empirical realities? What does this work suggest about more general processes by which policy domains form and their content is determined?

Theoretical Implications

The history of hate crime as a policy domain contains important implications for the way policies and problems are constructed in the U.S. political system. The birth and structuring of the hate crime policy domain occurred as a sequence of stages, beginning with the discovery of a condition-category and concluding with the institutionalization of that category within social movement discourse and legislative, judicial, and law enforcement practice.[3] Moreover, the institutionalization of hate crime is occurring both within and across these arenas. Finally, hate crime is an increasingly settled category of politics and policy making in the American political marketplace. Initial questions about the legitimacy of the concept have shifted to questions about how to elaborate and extend current policies. This achievement resulted from the settling of the concept within the select institutional spheres examined in this book.

Using hate crime as a microcosm of the broader institutionalization process, within each arena the concept begins as an imprecise multivalent concept whose definition and attendant policy implications become more refined and settled over time. In its journey from social movement frame to legislative concept to judicial principle to law enforcement practice, the meaning and policy significance of hate crime has undergone a series of transformations. Each change reflects the unique demands placed upon the concept in the different institutional arenas. The meaning of hate crime has been pushed and pulled in new directions within each new institutional arena, retaining some previously established meaning and, at the same time, adopting new meaning along the way. As the concept was formulated in social movement discourse it was used to reference violent conduct directed toward specific historically targeted groups: blacks, Jews, immigrants, and gays. As it entered the policy-making process it was reframed in terms of generic categories associated with the major modern civil rights laws and, ultimately, extended to cover forms of intimidation and harassment. As it was considered by courts, the precise role of speech and motives was defined and the range of application further elaborated to exclude certain forms of political speech and to include intimidation that constitutes a "true threat." Finally, as law enforcement and prosecution have encountered the concept they have, in many ways, returned to the social movement conceptualization by emphasizing blacks, Jews, immigrants, and gays as the "normal" targets.

The settling of the policy concept has taken two seemingly contradictory paths, each of which reflects countervailing forces evident within select institutional spheres as well as across these spheres. On the one hand, the concept becomes more specified and restricted in terms of the circumstances in which it is applicable; that is, it becomes possible to exclude certain behaviors and circumstances from the domain of the concept. The concept becomes more exclusive, more focused, and more delineated in terms of what it references. On the other hand, as the concept becomes more embedded and more established, it is often increasingly applied in novel circumstances; thus, its domain expands as new phenomena are assembled under its rubric. In our documentation of the different arenas we have provided examples of both the restrictive and expansive aspects of the institutionalization of hate crime.

Recognizing the limitations of theoretical contributions drawn from a single case study, we can nonetheless make a claim to generality by pointing to similar processes operative in other policy domains. For example, stalking (Lowney and Best 1995), sexual harassment (Schultz 1998), child abuse (Best 1990), and domestic violence (Dobash and Dobash 1992) are all categories that, on the surface, have experienced dynamics comparable to the ones described here. All generated significant controversy when they were initially introduced. As with hate crime, such controversies were fundamentally concerned with how to define the limits of the concept. What conduct should be covered, and what conduct excluded from coverage? Concerns about ambiguity and enforceability were also raised in each case. However, over time, each body of law became more specified, and its policy implications more determinate. Finally, institutionalization of each concept was also staggered across the phases of the policy process.

As policy concepts traverse various institutional spheres, it is subject to many of the same demands identified here with respect to hate crime. Social movements create issues and vie for ownership of the problem. Legislators craft statutes in increasingly homogeneous ways. Courts refine the meaning of the policy concept relative to constitutional principles and other legal traditions. Law enforcement officials develop protocols and routines for processing cases, including the development of normal crime constructs applicable to each category of crime. Moreover, as policy concepts get applied in novel circumstances there are clear consequences for the concept. First, its domain expands to include an increasingly wide range of phenomena. Second, the concept gets elaborated in ways that restrict its usage. In other words, the sequence of events that characterized the formation of the hate crime policy domain is paralleled in these other issues areas. In addition to these generalizable characteristics of the policy making process, the hate crime example contains implications for theories of policy making. Traditionally, those theories have emphasized three kinds of factors: demand factors, interest groups, and political context.

Demand Factors

The most common arguments about policy making start with the hopeful premise that legislation responds more or less mechanically to the emergence of pressing social problems; as problems surface, legislators and other policy makers spring to action to craft a solution. Given the perspective we have sketched here, it should be clear that we consider this view highly problematic insofar as it presupposes that public problems are self-evident and legislators are willing to address issues in the absence of interest group or other political pressures and opportunities. Nonetheless, applied to hate crime legislation, this perspective points to two considerations, each of which can be explored empirically.

First, it suggests that hate crime policy is best understood as a response to increases in hate-motivated behavior. Certainly, many of the proponents of hate crime legislation have made such arguments in the process of bestowing empirical credibility on the condition-category. However, there is significant reason to question whether hate-motivated conduct was greater in the late 1970s and through the 1990s than in earlier decades; similarly, there is significant reason to question whether hate-motivated conduct continues to worsen (Jacobs and Henry 1996; Jacobs and Potter 1998; Petrosino 1999). There is no readily available and dependable data source with which to evaluate the "rising tide of bigotry" argument (Levin and McDevitt 1993), in large part because agencies have only recently begun to collect data. Even as data are beginning to be collected, the way in which bias-motivated violence is defined by data collection agencies varies considerably. Moreover, most data sources are assembled by groups with a vested interest in portraying the situation as epidemic and worsening. Any changes observed in such data sources are difficult to distinguish from a refinement of reporting techniques and the increasing willingness of victims to come forward, problems that continue to plague government-sponsored data collection.

Given the difficulty of gathering quantitative data with which to evaluate the claim that discriminatory violence is on the rise, one alternative is to consider some historical evidence to contrast with the present period. It is unlikely that hate-motivated violence would have accelerated or surpassed some threshold in the late 1970s and early 1980s that prompted social movement organizations and other interested parties to lobby for policy reform and thus inspired the federal and state legislation described in chapters 3 and 4. A consideration of the history of lynching and violence toward immigrants and gays, for example, suggests that the turn to the twentieth century saw much higher rates of discriminatory violence than the present (Jacobs and Henry 1996; Jacobs and Potter 1998; Katz 1976; Newton and Newton 1991; Petrosino 1999).

The second demand argument leads to a more specific expectation: where the prevalence and incidence rate of some undesirable behavior is high, there will be a greater demand for legislation designed to enhance punishments for this type of behavior. Stated this way, a demand argument has implications for the interstate variation in the development of hate crime law. States with comparatively high rates of discriminatory violence will attempt to curb that violence with legislative reform. Although it is difficult to measure the extent of some criminal activity before its criminalization, most studies suggest that official rates of offensive behavior constitute a weak predictor of escalating public concern and increased legal control. For example, Edwin Sutherland's (1950) early work on the diffusion of laws punishing sexual psychopathy, Mark Fishman's (1978) work on "crime waves as ideology," and Joachim Savelsberg's (1994) assessment of the relationship between the crime rate and the incarceration rate in Germany and the United States, as well as work by Goode (1990), Reinarman and Levine (1989) and Beckett (1994) on the relationship between the rate of drug use, public hysteria surrounding "the drug problem," and social control efforts designed to curb drug use, all cast doubt on rates of conduct as predictors of legislative reform. In the case of bias-motivated violence, the existing empirical work suggests that, contrary to popular opinion, the official statistics and logical proxy measures of hate violence weakly affect or do not affect at all the passage of state hate crime laws (Jenness and Grattet 1996; Haider-Markel 1998).

One last demand argument put forward both in the popular media and some social science sources is the notion that intergroup conflicts escalate during periods of economic downturn and working-class job loss (Green and Rich 1998; Levin and McDevitt 1993; Pinderhughes 1993). Several high-profile cases of immigrant bashing by white working-class perpetrators provide the mental imagery for this effect (Green and Rich 1998). However, it does not appear to be the case that hate crime legislation is a response to the demands of economic strain. Early efforts to empirically test this commonly posited and often uncritically accepted argument have failed to find support for the hypothesis that hate crime policy is a response to economic demands. In particular, states with attributes like high income inequality, high black-to-white income inequality, and loss of or low growth in manufacturing jobs are no more likely to adopt a hate crime law than those with opposite values on those same variables (Jenness and Grattet 1996). Ironically, there is some evidence that prosperity, rather than hardship, may actually encourage the passage of hate crime law (Soule and Earl 1999).

Regardless of the empirical form demand factors assume, there is little evidence to support the notion that they alone can account for the initiation, evolution, content, and institutionalization of the hate crime policy domain. To the degree that they play a role in the birth and formation of a policy domain, demand factors do so in conjunction with other factors, such as the activities and social products of moral entrepreneurs and interest groups.

Interest Group Models

The inability of demand factors to predict legislative reform is often interpreted as evidence that moral entrepreneurs and associated interest groups are at the heart of the processes underlying policy formation. Interest groups are central to the construction of social problems. They are influential to the degree that they can persuade lawmakers to accept those constructions and get their proposals placed on the policy agenda and, ultimately, passed into law. This process relies heavily on the social constructions of collective actors who discover and name condition-categories, frame them as social problems of a particular type, and propose solutions that are deemed desirable and viable. Although this view helps explain some aspects of hate crime policy formation, it neglects others. Thus, here we discuss both the strengths and weaknesses of an interest group orientation toward the understanding of policy domain formation.

Interest group models envision the policy process as a competition between differentially empowered groups of actors who define a problem, dramatize its importance, and promote solutions to remedy it. Interest groups not only initiate policy domains, they also determine the characteristics of policy, the success or failure of policy reform, and whether—and how—the policy is enforced; often, these activities and the processes that underlie them are largely autonomous from the immediate demands and desires of the citizenry. Although interest groups may be spurred into action by disruptive social change that results in various types of demand factors, the influence of demand effects on policy making is contingent upon the workings of interest groups or moral entrepreneurs who translate a grievance into a social problem. Accordingly, much of the social science literature conceives of social problems as social movements and vice versa (Bash 1995; Mauss 1975, 1989; Mauss and Jenness 2000).

The power and authority of interest groups to influence policy making is considered to derive from their material resources, organizational capacity, and expertise, each of which is relevant for our analysis of hate crime policy. First, material resources are mobilized through campaign and party contributions and through the capacity of interest groups to finance the collection, publication, and dissemination of information that reveals the condition-category at issue, frames it in compelling ways, and justifies preferred policy positions. Simply put, in the long run, groups with large amounts of material resources are more likely to have their interests, their framing of the issue, and their proposed solutions expressed in policy.

With regard to hate crime, the cluster of social movement organizations that typically lobbied for hate crime law are mostly civil rights organizations of one kind or another. These groups are not known for having particularly "deep pockets" or stocks of material resources (Minkoff 1995). However, the key organization responsible for creating and promoting the legal concept of hate crime, the Anti-Defamation League, is the most powerful domestic-policy-oriented Jewish organization in the United States. With regional offices in most states, the ADL engages in a wide spectrum of activities, including collecting and publishing information about anti-Semitism and developing and promoting model hate crime legislation. As a result, the ADL's efforts continually have been applauded by lawmakers. Most states now have hate crime laws that resemble the ADL model statute, and the modal form of hate crime law—promoted by the ADL—has withstood the test of constitutional challenge. In addition, law enforcement training often relies upon curriculum and training videos developed and disseminated by the ADL. These accomplishments have been crucial to the development of the policy domain.

Although the ADL and the other movement organizations involved in hate crime policy making historically have worked on legislative campaigns relevant to anti-Semitism and antidiscrimination (Burstein 1998, 7), they cannot be considered "insiders" when it comes to formulating crime legislation and policy at either state or federal levels. Their efforts historically have been focused outside criminal law policy domains. Instead, the interest group politics most

intimately connected to the hate crime policy domain is best characterized as an alliance across race-based rights organizations, women's
rights groups, gay and lesbian organizations, and other groups interested in enhancing the status and welfare of minority groups. This
pattern suggests that the importance of material resources can be su-
perseded by the second interest-group factor: organizational networking. The anti-hate-crime movement and its advocates were successful
in doing what the earlier civil rights organizations did. They mobilized preexisting yet disparate collective actors to pursue a single
goal: to secure the passage of hate crime legislation in the United
States. The pursuit of this goal was made easier by the absence of
sustained organized opposition and the deployment of expertise.[4]

The deployment of expertise, a third source of interest group influence, was pivotal in the development of the policy domain. Although
not the exclusive province of experts, problem framing is the primary
way experts exert influence on lawmaking campaigns. Experts—in
this case, movement organization representatives—affect policy by
providing frameworks for describing and analyzing problems that are
then adopted by lawmakers, the media, and citizens. Social movement scholars use the terms "problem framing" and "diagnostic
framing" to refer to the process whereby movement proponents define the nature of a problem, theorize about its causes and consequences, and select and promote some policies rather than others.
"Frames, like metaphors, are ways of organizing thinking about political issues" (Gamson 1992a, 71). Drawing on this idea, David Snow
and his colleagues (Snow and Benford 1988, 1992; Snow et al. 1986)
use the verb "framing" to conceptualize the signifying work claims
makers engage in to bring attention to extant social conditions and
incite social change. They "frame, or assign meaning to and interpret,
relevant events and conditions in ways that are intended to mobilize
potential adherents and constituents, to garner bystander support and
to demobilize antagonists" (Snow and Benford 1988, 198). This process is critical to the negotiation of the larger sociopolitical environment in which organized community activism is embedded and to
which it responds; moreover, it provides a theoretical and an empirical link between micromobilization and macrostructures (Jenness and
Broad 1994). In large part, the success or acceptance of expert framings of a problem are contingent upon whether their explanations and
proposals resonate with policy makers and the public.

To summarize, the development of hate crime legislation nicely illustrates the ways that interest groups can affect policy making without substantial material resources. Thus, to the extent that some earlier interest group arguments focus exclusively on material factors,

they are inadequate to account for hate crime campaigns. Similarly, arguments made within popular political discourse that echo the materialist interpretation that money determines all political outcomes are also inadequate when applied to the case of hate crime legislation. In contrast, to the degree that interest group accounts focus on the importance of organizational networking, and the role of experts, they appear more fruitful.

In the end, however, a focus on interest group politics cannot fully explain the formation of a policy domain or the policies and practices that define it. To that end, we must turn to the contextual factors that facilitated the growth and acceptance of hate crime policies. Accordingly, we put forward a broader theoretical conceptualization of political context and discuss the importance of considering the role of political context in the formation of a policy domain.

Political Context

Political theories of policy making start with the assumption that demand factors and interest groups are, at worst, irrelevant to lawmaking and, at best, contingent upon the structure and organization of political institutions and policy sectors. These arguments emphasize the importance of political parties in creating opportunities for issues to get placed on the policy making agenda. Such arguments emphasize the role of party strength, organization, competition, and ideology in shaping what policies make it to the legislative agenda. Adoption is likely to occur when a proposed policy is clearly identified with a particular party ideology, when a party has sufficient strength to impose that ideology, and when a political party has stable long-term ties to specific interest groups that generate policy proposals (Skocpol and Amenta 1986). As such, this perspective focuses on political parties as the engines of policy reform. Our research, however, shows little evidence that state legislatures with Democratic majorities are more likely to have passed a hate crime law than those with Republican majorities (Jenness and Grattet 1996). Nor is hate crime legislation clearly identified with a particular party ideology (Grattet, Jenness, and Curry 1998; Haider-Markel 1999; Jenness and Grattet 1996; Soule and Earl 1999). In fact, hate crime law has enjoyed bipartisan support, suggesting that party variables are not particularly helpful for predicting policy outcomes in the area of hate crime laws.

Instead, we focus on the conditions of the political environment that are most pertinent to the spread of state hate crime legislation: cultural opportunities and institutionalization processes. In the social movements literature, "political opportunities" refers to structural conditions that facilitate the emergence and growth of social movements. Doug McAdam (1996, 27) notes that the term references "the relative openness or closure of the institutionalized political system, stability or instability of the broad set of elite alignments that typically undergird a polity, the presence or absence of elite allies, and the state's capacity and propensity for repression." Although these factors reflect general characteristics of polities (usually at the national level), recent work has taken the concept in the direction of more policy-specific kinds of factors and has emphasized cultural dimensions (Gamson and Meyer 1996; McAdam 1994). By "cultural opportunities" we mean to point to both legal culture, which is an available set of symbolic resources that can be used to express a proposal in terms policy makers are likely to respond to (that is, a legalistic framing), and policy making traditions, the set of particular ideologies and strategies toward a public problem that have evolved over time. As elements of the cultural environment, traditions and legal culture provide both a resource that interest groups and policy makers can use to their advantage and a constraint that limits the ways in which policy proposals can be articulated.

The role of experts and the deployment of expert knowledge highlight some of the deficiencies of examining policy domain formation in purely interest group terms. That is, interest groups often cannot be successful without a supportive political context that allows social movement actors and legislators alike to achieve resonance. Achieving resonance is itself a social process insofar as what typically sounds "sensible" to policy makers and citizens is a function of dominant ideologies and traditional modes of analysis. One consequence of this is that policy innovations embedded in established ways of thinking about problems and policy stand a better chance of survival.

In this work, the achievement of resonance is evident in two ways. First, categories that are most likely to be embedded in the law are also those with which policy makers are most familiar (for example, race, religion, ancestry, and national origin). That familiarity results from the long-term work of social movement actors who publicize and make empirically credible claims for inclusion under the hate crime rubric. In other words, certain categories resonate with legislators because of the historical efforts of the preceding movements. Second, in the early 1980s, for example, the receptiveness of policy makers to the expansion of civil rights policies was low compared with that in previous decades. Thus, transferring the concerns of the civil rights movement into criminal law capitalized on a prevailing environment supportive of "get tough on crime" laws, policies, and practices. In this environment, conservatives who might otherwise object to civil rights reforms would have difficulty opposing legislation mandating more severe penalties.[5] The design of many hate crime policies as penalty enhancement laws capitalized on a different opportunity present within the 1980s policy context, as well. As a result of the decreasing discretion of judges, since the 1970s many states have enacted extensive sentence enhancement laws that spell out the conditions under which judges may increase an offender's sentence.[6] Thus, before the emergence of hate crime law, the basic logic of enhancing penalties based upon the presence of certain offense characteristics already had become a familiar way of sensitizing the sentencing process in a context of decreasing discretion. In short, though hate crime statutes add new substance to the practice, the practice itself of enhancing punishments was well established.

Clearly, then, the ways activists, experts, and policy makers have conceptualized and drafted hate crime legislation reflects the constraints and benefits of using law to address systemic conflicts and inequalities. Such constraints and opportunities are a fundamental feature of American legal culture. For example, a basic assumption of American lawmaking, expressed in the equal protection clause and echoed in innumerable other locations, is that laws must apply equally to all groups and individuals in society. For the most part, "equal" treatment historically has implied "sameness" of treatment (Minow 1990). That is, a law must not give one group benefits or protections that it does not extend to others. The norm of sameness is so pervasive that it structures the way interest groups and policy makers orient to particular problems. Although the civil rights movement was fundamentally organized as the black civil rights movement, the laws that were put forward did not specifically outlaw discrimination against blacks but instead proscribed discrimination on the basis of race. By using terms like race, religion, and gender, instead of blacks, Jews, and women, lawmakers did not give benefits to particular groups that were not also extended to all others within the same category.

This same logic is embedded in hate crime politics. The dominant conception of hate crimes, evident in legislative debates, popular media sources, and the testimony of interest group actors, is one in which the targets of hate crimes are minorities who historically have been victims of racism, nativism, heterosexism, and religious persecution (blacks, Jews, gays and lesbians, and Mexicans, for example). However, the laws are written in a way that elides the historical basis and meaning of hate crime by translating specific categories of persons into all-encompassing and seemingly neutral categories (such as race, religion, sexual orientation, and national origin). In doing so, the laws do not offer any remedies or protections to particular groups that are not simultaneously available to all other races, religions, genders, sexual orientations, and nationalities.

This feature of American legal culture created a unique opportunity for hate crime proponents to make laws that could be easily fit into the existing structure of American law. With the success of earlier antidiscrimination legislation, reformers did not have to look far for a template that was compatible with the ways policy makers had approached similar problems. However, the sameness norm limits the possibilities of using law as a focused instrument for resolving some specific problem or range of problems because, technically speaking, all groups must be considered and protected. In the end, working within the sameness norm subtly changes the meaning activists and some policy makers attach to the concept of a hate crime. Sameness in the context of hate crime has meant that laws have been written in a way that equates a hate crime against a black with one against a white (within category sameness). Similarly, hate crimes against persons with disabilities are rendered equivalent to hate crimes against Muslims (across category sameness).

Thus, the consequence of legal culture is twofold. First, it channels interest group and policy making actions. Second, it provides those groups with a formula for making law while also limiting the specific forms of law that can be imagined and justified. Although legal culture, specifically the predominance of the sameness norm, helps us understand why hate crime legislation has assumed its general form, its influence is not likely to vary much across the smaller governmental units, which are both the principal site of criminal lawmaking and the place where most hate crime policy making has occurred.

To further conceptualize the way cultural opportunities shaped variations in the adoption of hate crime laws across the United States, we now turn to the notion of policy making traditions. "Policy making tradition" refers to the observable patterns of responses policy makers in a jurisdiction develop toward specific policy domains (Grattet, Jenness, and Curry 1998). Given that state policy making mostly deals with ongoing policy issues executed through state bureaucracies with a fair measure of built-in inertia or "path dependence" (Arthur 1988), it should not be surprising that even when a "new" policy proposal emerges it tends to be conceived in relation to preexisting modes of analysis and available strategies (Burstein 1998). Our research on the timing of state adoption of hate crime legislation offers empirical support for this idea by showing that the early adopters tended to be more innovative in a wide variety of other policy domains than those that adopted later or not at all (Grattet, Jenness, and Curry 1998).

The political factors that most strongly shape policy making are institutionalization and diffusion processes. Diffusion refers to the process by which policy ideas circulate within and across governmental units. Several characteristic patterns of diffusion reveal distinctive underlying social processes. First, diffusion is usually temporally distributed. A typical pattern is the S-shaped cumulative frequency distribution: states are initially slow to adopt a policy innovation, but once a general consensus is reached about its appropriateness to the particular problem at hand—that is, once it becomes institutionalized—it diffuses rapidly. After a period of rapid adoption, as states conform to the social pressures to have a law, the rate of adoption tends to slow, and there remains a group of states that are more resistant to change and may never adopt a law. This temporal pattern is structured both by attributes of the potential adopters—that is, openness or reluctance to change—and the overtime variation in the degree to which a policy idea is institutionalized. As our presentation in chapter 4 suggests, the diffusion of hate crime laws reflects this temporal pattern.[7]

Once a policy becomes institutionalized, interest group politics become less crucial in shaping laws (Jenness 1999; Ramirez, Soysal, and Shanahan 1997). In addition, once a certain amount of momentum is generated around an innovation, subsequent adoption becomes less a product of interest group pressure than an act of conformity of a legislature to intergovernmental norms. This suggests that state legislatures might be best thought of as part of a broader social system of similar units. As their "reference group," other states provide social pressures to conform to particular kinds of activities.

At the same time, states individuate themselves from the system by attempting to flag their uniqueness. However, this process also appears to be time dependent. The states that pass laws early on tend not to pass the most progressive or expansive laws. In addition, states rarely take on significant revisions once they have passed their first laws. Much like Burstein (1998) has found in the history of equal opportunity laws, early reforms limit the kind of discussions that can occur later on. On the other hand, laws that are passed once the basic template has been established elsewhere (the laggards, in terms of timing) often build on the template in such a way that new kinds of behavior are encompassed under the law. This balancing act of conforming while deviating is only possible once the basic template has been established, and it is reflected in the pattern of homogenization and differentiation of hate crime laws. The irony is that leaders with respect to passage may be laggards in terms of content.

As for what shapes these processes, hate crime legislation is best understood in terms of both interest group politics and political factors. As a legal concept, hate crime initially emerged as a result of interest group activity, and it made its way to the legislative agenda because it was framed in terms of penalty enhancement and discrimination law, approaches that were already familiar to policy makers. Once the concept had been institutionalized—after it became accepted wisdom—states that were concerned with the problem of hate violence and discrimination could turn to an established policy solution and proceed rapidly to adoption.

Similarly, interest group effects on the precise content of hate crime laws was greatest when the inclusion of a particular category was most questioned. Now that several states have adopted laws protecting gender, sexual orientation, and disability, when a new state considers adopting a law these categories tend to be included, often without much interest group mobilization. In short, the history of hate crime legislation reveals that interest group effects are highly variable over time and contingent upon cultural opportunities and institutionalization processes.

Moving Beyond Hate: Implications for Politics and Policy

With these empirical and theoretical themes in mind it is possible to confront some of the major concerns related to current hate crime policy. Jacobs and Potter (1998) echo much of the critical commentary about the laws. At the core of their criticism is a rejection of laws for being rooted in "identity politics." "The passage of hate crime law in the 1980s and 1990s," they note, "is best explained by the growing influence of identity politics. Fundamentally, hate crime laws are symbolic statements requested by advocacy groups for material and symbolic reasons and provided by politicians for political reasons" (Jacobs and Potter 1998, 65). Hate crime laws, they argue, are a perfect example of legislators' ceding the policy-making process to interest groups. As a result, the laws merely represent an exercise in symbolic politics. As such, hate crime policy is more likely to engender divisiveness than to ameliorate pressing problems and is problematic as a result.

Although it is fair to characterize hate crime legislation as highly symbolic and somewhat open-ended, the criticism of such laws as "interest group politics as usual" is not entirely persuasive. First, interest groups were only part of the reason hate crime politics emerged when and how they did and why they took root. Among other things, existing legal culture affected the way those interests were expressed and consequently the way law was formulated. Because of the norm of sameness, for example, no "special rights" were given to one group that were not simultaneously extended to other identity-based groups. As a result, the notion that such politics engender divisiveness could only result from a misperception of the laws as providing special protections. It also raises the question of whether other criminal reforms, such as laws against domestic violence and stalking, clearly driven by the women's movement and "identity politics" (Dobash and Dobash 1992; Lowney and Best 1995), have created such divisiveness. This is, of course, an unanswered empirical question. The larger issue may be whether highlighting or ignoring the difference of hate-motivated criminal conduct through the criminal law engenders more divisiveness or simply renders manifest what has thus far been invisible or latent.

Jacobs and Potter's (1998) critique also assumes that symbolic effects are not worth pursuing through policy reform. Yet criminal justice policies are seldom justified purely by their instrumental value, especially their deterrent effects. In addition to the oft-cited goals of incapacitation and retribution, they also must be seen, in Durkheimian terms, as expressions of collective sentiments. Hate crime laws, in this regard, have a function similar to that of laws enhancing penalties for attacks on teachers or police officers. In addition to punishment, they seek to use state authority to reinforce prosocial values of tolerance and respect. More broadly, criminal laws always express symbolic valuations; thus to oppose hate crime law on these grounds is dubious at best.

Consider, for example, three well-accepted criminal categories: burglary, robbery, and theft. Burglary and robbery are distinguished from theft, even though each are forms of property expropriation, and are treated more severely by the criminal justice system because of the different moral meanings attached to the circumstances in which they occur. Burglary is treated more harshly than theft because it involves a transgression of the "private sphere." Robbery is treated more harshly because it involves threats to the physical safety of the victim. Over centuries of criminal law history, both of these have been deemed necessary to emphasize the seriousness of the crime and the moral culpability of the perpetrator. In other words, the same net conduct, the expropriation of property, has different moral significance. Each prosecution reinforces these differences.

The fact that criminal law contains these distinctions is not based narrowly on their deterrent value or the harms entailed by the crime but also on the cultural meaning these acts imply. Perhaps more relevant to hate crimes legislation, law also routinely distinguishes crimes and punishments on the basis of the intentional states of the perpetrator (for example, distinctions between manslaughter and murder) or the characteristics of the victim (for example, laws in several states enhance penalties for violence directed at paramedics, jurors, trial witnesses, police officers, lawyers, and teachers). These distinctions are made not just to deter future deviance but also to reflect and reinforce broadly held values that define these acts as more serious than their parallel crimes because of their specific circumstances and purported consequences.

Another central concern has been that hate crime is by definition a highly subjective and vague concept and will therefore lead to resource waste as officials strain to determine how best to implement the laws. The examination presented in this book suggests that the ambiguity of the concept is decreasing over time in all of the institutional spheres relevant to the formulation of the concept. Specifically, social movement players have generally reached agreement on how to define the concept. A dominant model of hate crime has emerged in the legislative arena; judicial interpretations of the law have largely converged; and the law enforcement practices appear to be solidifying. To critique a concept because it appears ambiguous to specific officials within the criminal justice system amounts to a critique of the concept's "newness." In our view, this is not a particularly legitimate basis for critique. If it were, it surely could apply to domestic violence laws in the 1970s, sexual harassment laws in the 1980s, and stalking laws in the 1990s.

The question raised by hate crime as a recently developed criminal category is not whether the concept is hopelessly ambiguous. Instead, we should ask, "What features of the social organization of various sectors of the criminal justice system influence variation in understandings and uses?" Thus, the vagueness of the concept must be analyzed longitudinally rather than concluded from a static impression gathered early in its life course. Similarly, comparison cases are extremely important to evaluating hate crime laws. There is heterogeneity in the interpretation of many kinds of laws. The question is not "Do understandings of hate crime vary across jurisdictions?" but rather "How does the variability in hate crime compare with that in other crimes?" To address this question, the comparison case should not be a crime like assault or burglary, whose meaning and associated investigative and prosecutorial practices have been institutionalized for centuries. Instead, hate crime should be compared with crime concepts that are comparatively new and yet have achieved a certain measure of acceptance, such as sexual harassment, stalking, and domestic abuse.

A similar response is appropriate to the critique of hate crime statistics. Because the statistics are contingent upon the part of the hate crime policy domain that is the least institutionalized—that is, policing—data collection remains problematic in the pursuit of evaluating the extent and character of hate crime in the United States. This should not, however, be the final judgment. In fact, given the efforts to improve the knowledge of law enforcement and to homogenize the data collection techniques currently under way by federal and some state law enforcement agencies, we expect data collection to become more systematic and reliable—and, incidentally, more useful for traditional criminological analyses, as well.

In the end, the development of the hate crime policy domain reflects a familiar pattern in policy making in the United States, especially crime control policy. The "career" of a policy concept follows a predictable pattern, stretching from social movement concept to law enforcement practice. Social problems are identified and rendered visible by social movements operating in a historical context that shapes the way the problem is conceptualized and which movements can claim authority over the issue. Policy makers, once their attention has been drawn to the problem, work to develop policy responses; in doing so, they negotiate and redefine the nature of the problem. Policy responses are attempted, and some subset of approaches emerges as the best available approach toward the problem. This is accomplished within a context of specific cultural and political opportunity structures, which shape the form and content of what emerges as the most desirable policy. As a result, those approaches diffuse across jurisdictions. Courts enter the picture to clarify and delimit (and occasionally expand) the range of application of the policy. Those interpretations then also diffuse across jurisdictions. Law enforcement develops protocols and organizational routines to apply the policy in concrete circumstances. Once again, the meaning of the policy concept is reworked. Each of these spheres is somewhat "decoupled" from the previous one; each poses new obstacles to the acceptance of the policy concept; and each influences the way the concept evolves over time. As with individual careers, evaluation must be made relative to other careers, relative to the stage of the career, and relative to institutional context.

═══ Notes ═══

Chapter 1

1. Capitalizing on this imagery, the first book on the subject is titled *Hate Crimes: The Rising Tide of Bigotry and Bloodshed* (Levin and McDevitt 1993).

2. Other terms have been used to describe much the same combination of cultural and organizational elements of political processes—for example, "policy areas" (Amenta and Carruthers 1988, 666), "sectors" (Scott and Meyer 1983, 137), "fields" (Grattet 1994, 15), and "programs" (Rose 1985, 9).

3. For a recent review of this approach to social problems, see Mauss and Jenness 2000.

4. Whether the definitional approach to social problems is equivalent to the study of social movements has been the topic of periodic debate. Ronald Troyer (1984, 1989), for example, has noted the similarities and differences between the definitional approach, the standard structural approach (Smelser 1963), and the more recent resource mobilization approach to social movements (Jenkins 1983; McCarthy and Zald 1973, 1977; Oberschall 1973). More recently, Bert Klandermans (1992, 77) has observed that "many situations that could be considered a social problem never become an issue, even though they may be no less troublesome than situations that do become a rallying point. Further, a social problem does not inevitably generate a social movement."

5. For descriptions of how the institutional perspective has developed within political science, see Powell and DiMaggio 1991 and Schneiberg and Clemens 1999.

Chapter 2

1. The younger sector of the contemporary women's movement in particular emerged from the civil rights and New Left movements (Ferree and Hess 1985; Goldberg 1991).

2. This ideology is based on the view that victimization is widespread, consequential, unambiguous, and yet unrecognized. Individuals must be taught to recognize others' and their own victimization. Thus, claims of victimization must be respected. Joel Best (1999, 117) demonstrates how this "set of beliefs makes it easy to label victims, and very difficult to dispute those labels." Moreover, the ideology of victimization has found support in a broad range of institutional sectors, including law, medicine, the "helping professions," education and academia, the mass media, religion, and government. Combined, these sectors produce a "victim industry—a set of social arrangements capable of labeling large numbers of people as victims" (Best 1999, 119).

3. Civil rights advocates, for the most part, have regarded victim's rights as a threat to hard-won social progress, particularly in the area of defendant's rights. The two movements have taken opposing positions on a number of issues, notably the death penalty, the "war on drugs," and federal sentencing guidelines (Maroney 1998, 577–58).

4. For a more thorough description of each of these organizations, see the works cited throughout the remainder of this section.

5. For a thorough review of the history and mission of the ADL, see Grusd 1966.

6. The nature of the ADL's model statute is discussed more fully in chapter 4.

7. This fact becomes relevant in the next chapter.

8. See Jenness and Broad 1997, appendix A, for a partial listing of these organizations.

9. In 1998 the National Victim Center was renamed the National Center for Victims.

10. As just one example, the National Center for Victims maintains a web page entitled "Statistics: Hate Crime." This site (www.ncvc.org/stats/hc.htm) provides a list of statistical data on hate crime. These data derive from many of the organizations identified and described in this chapter.

Chapter 3

1. For some of the exceptions, see Kingdon 1995 and Chock 1991, 1994, 1995.

2. As this book went to press, the Hate Crimes Prevention Act (HCPA) was being debated. The HCPA "amends the Federal criminal code to set penalties for persons who, whether or not acting under the color of law, willfully cause bodily injury to any person or, through the use of fire, firearm, or explosive device, attempt to cause such injury, because of the actual or perceived: (1) race, color, religion, or national origin of any person; and (2) religion, gender, sexual orientation, or disability of any

person, where in connection with the offense, the defendant or the victim travels in interstate or foreign commerce, uses a facility or instrumentality of interstate or foreign commerce, or engages in any activity affecting interstate or foreign commerce, or where the offense is in or affects interstate or foreign commerce" (S. 1529).

3. The act was declared unconstitutional by the U.S. Supreme Court in *Brzonkala v. Morrison* on the basis that the act was an impermissible extension of federal authority, which only allows regulation of criminal activities that impact interstate commerce. The majority opinion argued that "gender-motivated crimes of violence were not—in any sense of the phrase— economic activity." The hate crimes provision was subsequently left out of the renewal of the VAWA in 2000.

4. The Hate Crimes Prevention Act of 1998 (S. 1529) is excluded from this analysis because at the time of this writing it was currently being debated by federal lawmakers.

5. Discursive moments are a form of practice, a manifestation of the structure of social relations. According to Michel Foucault (1979) and, more recently, Kathy Ferguson (1984), administrative discourse expresses and reflects a particular structure of institutions and practices. As such, it both creates and represents the positions of persons and events. In this case, the administrative discourse is legislative, the positions are "hate crime victims," and the events are "hate crime."

6. During 1987, representatives of the ADL testified before the U.S. Commission on Civil Rights and served as a resource for a report prepared for the Justice Department's National Institute of Justice, entitled "The Response of the Criminal Justice System to Bias Crime: An Exploratory Review."

7. The Coalition on Hate Crimes included civil rights, religious, ethnic, and law enforcement groups as well as a diverse array of professional organizations, including the ADL, the American Bar Association, thirty state attorneys general, the National Institute Against Prejudice and Violence, the National Gay and Lesbian Task Force, the American Psychological Association, the American Psychiatric Association, the Center for Democratic Renewal, the American Civil Liberties Union, the American Jewish Congress, People for the American Way, the National Organization of Black Law Enforcement Executives, the U.S. Civil Rights Commission, the Police Executives Research Forum, the Criminal Justice Statistics Administration, the International Association of Police Chiefs, the National Council of Churches, the National Coalition of American Nuns, and the American Arab Anti-Discrimination Committee.

8. During the hearings on crimes against religious practices and property, Representative Robert Matsui (D-Calif.) remarked that "hate based on one's race, creed, color, or national origin have no place in America" (Congress 1985a, 17) but subsumed these provisions under the rubric of

the race, religion, and ethnicity provisions. Also during these hearings, Representative Raymond McGrath (R-N.Y.), who has worked with the handicapped and the elderly in New York, gave testimony but did not mention, much less introduce, age or handicap provisions.

9. For example, in his work on child abuse and threats to children as a social problem, Best examined the evolving definitions and characterizations of child abuse. He found that "by 1976, the issue encompassed a much broader array of conditions threatening children. The more general term 'child abuse' had replaced the earlier, narrower concept of the 'battered child,' and the even broader expression 'child abuse and neglect' had gained currency among professionals" (Best 1990, 67). At the same time, the law expanded the official domain of child abuse by requiring more categories of professionals to report suspected abuse while also adopting broader definitions of what constitutes abuse and neglect (Best 1990). Regardless of the empirical referent and the specific mechanism of employment, domain expansion ultimately involves rendering more and more conduct or social conditions "at issue."

10. The CUAV is the one of the larger and better-funded projects addressing violence against gays and lesbians in the United States; see Jenness and Broad (1997) for a more detailed description.

11. This is the case even in hearings devoted to a specific type of violence. Throughout the May 1988 hearings on racially motivated violence, for example, discussions of race-based violence were sprinkled with references to violence based on sexual orientation. Joan Weiss, the executive director of the National Institute Against Prejudice and Violence, noted that "we are talking about violence motivated by bigotry based on race, religion, ethnic background and sexual orientation" (Congress, 1988c, 18).

12. Although these changes swayed some legislators, others remained unconvinced. As Representative Gekas noted, "sexual orientation by any other names does not smell as sweet, and homosexuality is just a substitute for sexual orientation" (*Congressional Record* 1988, 11407). At the same time, others, like Senator Alan Cranston (D-Calif.), remained convinced that the amendment was inappropriate: "This amendment should be rejected because it sends the wrong message. This amendment suggests that hate crimes against gays and lesbians are not as reprehensible as crimes against racial, ethnic, or religious minorities. Clearly, this undermines the purpose of this legislation" (*Congressional Record* 1990, 1084).

13. Following the passage of the HCSA, Congress held hearings to determine its status (Congress 1992a; 1994) as well as a hearing on its reauthorization (Congress 1996a).

14. Since the passage of the HCSA, the HCSEA and the Hate Crimes Prevention Act have included a sexual orientation provision.

15. The "homosexuality or heterosexuality" provision remains in the HCSA, even after its reauthorization (Congress 1996a, 1996b). The term, "sexual orientation" has been included in the HCSEA, which became law in 1994.

16. Representative Gekas referenced gender along with a slew of other status provisions in an effort to exclude the sexual orientation provision in the HCSA but not in an effort to assert the legitimacy of gender as a provision in hate crime law. As he argued in 1988, "to add sexual orientation into this bill is to segregate . . . those who would come within that definition of sexual orientation away from and apart from, and separate them to a position higher than other people who are in perhaps worse circumstances objectively speaking than victims who are victims because of sexual orientation: namely, women themselves. . . . women who are not lesbians, women who do not come within the purview of heterosexuality or of sexual orientation, or homosexuality or sexual orientation, women who are the subject and victims of rape. It has been proved beyond a shadow of a doubt that women who are the victims of rape are victims of a hate crime, yet we choose, if we keep sexual orientation as one of the criteria in the main bill, to say that those who are victims of sexual orientation are in a more recognizable position than are women who are victims of rape. How about the handicapped? How about those who are octogenarians who are victims of hate crime? How about child abuse, infants who are the target of hate and who are victims beyond description sometimes of the hate of their parents or elders in the household? They are not included here. They are all protectable groups. [I] say to the Members that sexual orientation has no place in this bill, to be elevated to the status of religion and of race and of ethnicity as a criterion for mandating the Attorney General to look into the motivation of the people committing the crime." (*Congressional Record* 1988, 11394).

17. Although the name of the law implies otherwise, technically speaking the VAWA covers gender-based violence directed at both men and women. That is, men, too, can sue on the grounds that violence against them stemmed from gender bias. However, as Ann Noel (1995, 35) has pointed out, "A disparate-treatment analysis also potentially leaves male rape victims without remedy under the VAWA because men, unlike women, are not deprived of civil rights as a group because of rape and other forms of gender motivated violence."

18. Before the passage of the HCSA, the Coalition on Hate Crimes contemplated recommending the inclusion of gender as a protected status in the HCSA but eventually decided against it for a variety of reasons. First, some members of the coalition believed that the inclusion of gender would delay, if not completely impede, the timely passage of the HCSA. Second, some members of the coalition argued that the inclusion of gender in the HCSA would open the door to demands for age, disability, position in a labor dispute, party affiliation, and membership in the

armed forces provisions. Third, some believed that including gender would make the enactment of the HCSA too cumbersome, if not entirely impossible, given the pervasiveness of violent crimes against women. Fourth, others argued that not all acts of violence against women fit the definition of a hate crime. Fifth, some members of the coalition argued that expanding the categories of officially recognized hate crimes to include gender would not improve upon current efforts to collect official data on rape and domestic violence. Focusing on feasibility, opponents feared that adding gender as a victim category would simply overwhelm the data collection efforts of law enforcement agencies and human rights organizations that track hate crimes. The large number of crimes against women would overshadow statistics on hate crimes against members of other groups. The failure to include gender in the HCSA, as well as other key pieces of legislation and policy designed to address violence, did not go unrecognized (Jenness 1995a; Jenness and Broad 1994, 1997; Levin 1994).

19. Nonetheless, objections to the VAWA, especially Title III of the act, captured media attention disproportionate to the intensity with which they were expressed and debated in official federal testimony, hearings, and reports. Discussions about whether or not to incorporate gender into larger discussions of hate crime caught the attention of the national press; see, for example, "Florio Signs Anti-Bias Law," *New York Times*, June 11, 1993, 8; "In Crackdown on Bias, a New Tool," *New York Times*, June 12, 1993, 8; "A Million Mrs. Bobbits," *New York Times*, January 28, 1994, A26; "Crime and Punishment" 1992, 7; "Caught in the Act" 1993; "Rape and Denial" 1993, 14–15; "Rape Is Not an Act of Bias" 1990; "Radical Feminism in the Senate" 1993; Leo 1989; "Are All Men Rapists?" 1993; "Congressional Democrats," *Wall Street Journal*, January 15, 1993, A1; "High Court Ruling Expected to Increase Hate-Crime Sentences in More States," *Wall Street Journal*, June 14, 1993, B5; "The Sexist Violence Against Women Act," *Wall Street Journal*, March 23, 1994, A13; "Hate Crimes Hit Record High in 1992," *Los Angeles Times*, March 23, 1993, B1, B8; "Mere Talk Won't Make Life Any Safer for Women," *Los Angeles Times*, August 16, 1993, B7; "Beware Stiffer Sentences for Thought Crimes," *Washington Post,* June 19, 1993, A21; and "Gender Poisoning," *Washington Post*, January 16, 1994, C5.

20. A significant portion of one of the longest hearings on the VAWA was devoted to determining the constitutionality of its Title III (Congress 1992b). Before its passage, and in light of congressional testimony and debates, the wording of VAWA was altered in three ways. First, several findings were added to the bill to make clear the basis and purposes of the civil rights remedy. Second the term "overwhelming," as a way of defining the level of animus required to qualify as hate-motivated, was omitted as unnecessary and restrictive. Third, language enumerating various crimes was eliminated from the original definition of "gender-motivated" crime to eliminate the negative implication that only these

crimes would give rise to a cause of action under Title III. For a review of these changes, as well as the justifications that underlie them, see Congress 1991b.

21. Emphasis in the original.

22. Ramirez, Soysal, and Shanahan (1997) find that nations adopting women's rights later in the adoption period under study (1890 to 1990) were less influenced by protracted national struggles and the local social mobilization of women than those who did so earlier in the adoption period. They conclude that "by the 1930s the localized national movements and their organizational infrastructure were overshadowed by transnational influences that eventually dictated a particular model of citizenship in which women held the franchise" (1997, 736).

Chapter 4

1. These laws appeared as early as the late nineteenth century in response to a perceived escalation of Ku Klux Klan activity. They are distinct from the contemporary hate crime laws insofar as they are considerably older, do not contain a bias "intent standard" (Berk, Boyd, and Hamner 1992; Jenness and Grattet 1996), do not specify protected statuses, and most notably, were not introduced under the rubric of "hate crimes legislation" (Jenness 1995a).

2. Studies suggest that rates of offensive behavior generally constitute a weak predictor of escalating public concern and increased social control. See, for example, Edwin Sutherland's (1950) early work on the diffusion of sexual psychopathy laws, Mark Fishman's (1978) classic work on "crime waves as ideology," Joachim Savelsberg's (1987) assessment of the relation between the crime rate and the incarceration rate in Germany and the United States, and works by Erich Goode (1990), Craig Reinarman and Harry Levine (1989), and Katherine Beckett (1994) on the relation between the rate of drug use, public hysteria surrounding "the drug problem," and social control efforts designed to curb drug use.

3. We contacted each state's attorney general and requested an inventory of all hate crime statutes in their state. More than half of the attorney general's offices responded with the requested information.

4. Frederick Lawrence (1999, 29–30) has conceptualized "two analytically distinct, but somewhat overlapping [statutory] models of bias crimes." These models—the discriminatory selection model and the racial animus model—posit different criteria for assessing what constitutes a bias-motivated crime. The discriminatory selection model defines hate crime solely on the basis of the perpetrator's discriminatory selection of a victim, regardless of why such a selection was made; for example, like girls and women, people with disabilities may be targeted simply because they are perceived to be more vulnerable victims. In contrast, the racial animus model focuses attention on the reason for discriminatory selec-

tion of victims. This approach assumes that the motivation for the selection of a victim is more expressive than instrumental; perpetrators use the act of victimization to express animus toward the category of persons the victim represents (a person of color, a homosexual, a Jew, a disabled person). As such, the racial animus model follows the distinction between actuarial and symbolic crimes by defining the former as beyond and the latter as within the desirable domain of hate crime law.

5. As we discuss in the next chapter, most courts have not yet specifically distinguished between these wordings. Those that have addressed the distinctions have interpreted all statutes as meaning "because of"; see, for example, *State v. Stalder* (630 So. 2d 1072 [1994]), *Richards v. State*, (643 So. 2d 89 [1994]). Nonetheless, the struggle over the precise wording was crucial to the conceptualization of hate crime long before the judicial interpretation phase began.

6. Homogenization has been observed in local (Knoke 1982; Tolbert and Zucker 1983), interstate (Berry and Berry 1990; Gray 1973; McCammon 1995; Pavalko 1989; Walker 1969), and global political systems (Strang 1990; Thomas et al. 1987).

Chapter 5

1. Boyd, Berk, and Hamner (1996) employ Sudnow's framework to understand the routine practices law enforcement officers use to categorize hate crimes. They also address the implications of those practices for the production of official statistics about hate crime. We turn to this issue in the next chapter.

2. To investigate the judicial meaning assigned to hate crime law, we examine appellate-level judicial opinions published before March 1999 in which judges have ruled on the constitutionality of hate crime law. Cases involving summary judgments or case-specific challenges to the constitutionality of the law "as applied" were discarded because these decisions deal with issues that are relevant only to a particular case rather than to the law in general. The remaining thirty-eight cases, including two U.S. Supreme Court cases, deal with legislation in seventeen states and address the facial validity of hate crime.

    The Lexis on-line database used to compile the list of cases includes all published state and federal cases at the appellate level. Cases thought to have no precedential value are usually not published and are therefore not included. However, because they have precedential implications, it is unlikely that constitutional cases regarding hate crime laws would not be published. Moreover, given the process we are studying (the meaning making of legal concepts) it is relevant to examine only those cases that have been published since unpublished cases, because they are invisible to other courts (as well as to us), are unlikely to have an effect on the meaning making of subsequent courts. Thus, the list of cases analyzed is comprehensive.

3. Method and content are the two general dimensions along which state hate crime laws can be classified (see discussion in chapter 4). In the case of hate crime law, method refers to the way in which the criminal code is altered to add a hate crime law and the precise way criminal intent is worded and conceptualized in the statute. Content, on the other hand, refers to the kinds of intergroup conflict referenced in the law and the types of conduct that qualify as hate crime.

4. The compelling interest test involves determining the conditions under which government can regulate the content of expression. It consists of an evaluation of whether the interest of the government is related to the suppression of free speech (for example, curbing rising levels of intergroup violence), whether the potential gains of pursuing the interest outweigh a slight regulation of speech, and whether non-content-based alternatives exist ("Hate Is Not Speech" 1993).

5. We are not suggesting that hate crimes are actually increasing. Jacobs and Henry (1996) provide extensive criticism of the validity of such assertions. Rather, we are arguing that the notion that hate crimes are widespread or increasing (or both) reveals assumptions by judges about the common varieties of hate crime. Furthermore, what judges recognize as hate crime is, at least in part, a reflection of which social movements are involved in raising the visibility of the issue.

6. Several commentators have responded to logical flaws in Gellman's argument; see Grannis 1993 and Tribe 1993 for summaries of this work.

7. Other states have statutes that also emphasize the precise character of an offender's motive. For example, New Hampshire's statute mentions "hostility" toward the victim, Connecticut's and Pennsylvania's statutes require that "maliciousness" be present (see table 4.2); see Grannis 1993 and Dillof 1997, as well as chapter 4 of this book, for discussions of the implications of different ways of wording the motivational parts of hate crime statutes.

8. Utah and Texas both have laws that do not list status provisions; however, those laws do not target expressive conduct in the way the St. Paul ordinance did.

9. This position contains two arguments. The first part presumes that the harms that hate crime law are designed to remedy are not as clearly "identifiable" as those protected under antidiscrimination laws. This is possible only if one takes an extremely narrow view of what antidiscrimination laws are designed to remedy. The basic remedies of antidiscrimination laws involve individual and class compensation and state-mandated organizational and procedural changes. It is a reductionist inference to conclude that this means that the harms of discrimination are limited to material outcomes of individuals and members of a "class." If you consider that these remedies are not just about compensation but are ultimately a means of removing or reducing social practices

that socially and economically marginalize some groups of people on the basis of race, religion, color, and national origin, then they appear to have much in common with the harms addressed in hate crime laws. Moreover, "identifiability," which is useful for translating the "loss" involved in discrimination into a material quantity, is not a standard upon which criminal law is based. By that logic the theft of an item worth a hundred dollars should be equal to a robbery and burglary of the same amount. The identifiability of the harms in that situation would not be a basis for differentiating punishments. The second part of argument put forth by Jacobs and Potter (1998), as well as others, suggests that the preexistence of a legal remedy in hate crime cases undermines the discrimination parallel. It is true that in the absence of the antidiscrimination laws discrimination would go unpunished and in the absence of hate crime laws bias crime is still punishable.

Chapter 6

1. For a review of these problems, see Martin 1995, 317–21; see also U.S. Department of Justice 1999.

2. After eight appellate decisions affirming the state's hate crime laws, California appeals courts have not accepted a facial validity challenge since 1995. Thus, uncertainty about the legitimacy of the laws has apparently lessened.

Chapter 7

1. For more than two decades social problems theorists commonly used the term putative condition, originally suggested by Malcolm Spector and John Kitsuse (1977), to refer to the social conditions that get defined as a social problem. More recently, however, Peter Ibarra and Kitsuse (1993, 26) have proposed replacing the term "putative condition" with "condition-category" as a way to move beyond epistemological debates addressing the degree to which theorists engage in "ontological gerrymandering" (Woolgar and Pawluch 1985) whereby analysts themselves imbue the problem with meaning (for a review, see Mauss and Jenness 2000).

2. Consistent with Ibarra and Kitsuse's proposal to replace "putative condition" with "condition-category," Donileen Loseke (1993) proposes using the term "people-categories" to refer to the "putative people" that inhabit those categories.

3. Obviously, the stages and underlying processes summarized in table 7.1 overlap considerably. Although we have enumerated them sequentially for the purpose of clarity, like most social processes, they do not necessarily occur in a linear procession. Moreover, they are not mutually exclusive from processes identified in other approaches to understanding social movements, social problems, legal reform, or the process of insti-

tutionalization. Finally, this formulation of a model is tentative and certainly incomplete; the stages are, no doubt, in need of further empirical testing and subsequent qualification. Indeed, we invite empirical research that more clearly articulates and accounts for variation in the timing, form, and content of the processes identified in the second column of table 7.1.

4. The American Civil Liberties Union (ACLU) endorsed specific statutory forms but opposed others. Most notably, the ACLU opposed the St. Paul ordinance contested in *R.A.V. v. St. Paul* (see chapter 5). Similarly, several Christian and conservative groups opposed hate crime legislation when sexual orientation was included.

5. Although one aspect of the campaign for hate crime laws has focused on creating civil remedies, it always has been secondary to the strategy of winning greater criminal penalties.

6. The conditions vary considerably across states. For example, in Alaska an offender's sentence can be increased if he or she "knowingly directed the conduct constituting the offense at an active officer of the court or at an active or former judicial officer, prosecuting attorney, law enforcement officer, correctional employee, fire fighter, emergency medical technician, paramedic, ambulance attendant, or other emergency responder during or because of the exercise of official duties" (Alaska, *Statutes*, sec. 12.55.155 [13]). In New Jersey, extended terms of imprisonment may be given to a "professional" criminal, defined as "a person who committed a crime as part of a continuing criminal activity in concert with two or more persons, and the circumstances of the crime show he has knowingly devoted himself to criminal activity as a major source of livelihood" (New Jersey, *Statutes*, sec. 2C44-3).

7. For a more developed argument along these lines, see Grattet, Jenness, and Curry 1998.

═ References ═

Adam, Barry. 1987. *The Rise of a Gay and Lesbian Movement*. Boston: Twayne Publishers.

Alaska. *Statutes*. (1982) 12.55.155.

Albert, Edward. 1986. "Illness and/or Deviance: The Response of the Press to Acquired Immunodeficiency Syndrome." In *The Social Dimensions of AIDS: Method and Theory*, edited by Douglas A. Feldman and Tom Johnson. New York: Praeger Publishers.

———. 1989. "AIDS and the Press: The Creation and Transformation of a Social Problem." In *Images of Issues: Typifying Contemporary Social Problems*, edited by Joel Best. Hawthorne, N.Y.: Aldine de Gruyter.

Albonetti, Celesta. 1987. "Prosecutorial Discretion: The Effects of Uncertainty." *Law & Society Review* 21(2): 291–313.

Altman, Dennis. 1971. *Homosexual Oppression and Liberation*. New York: Outerbridge and Dienstfrey.

———. 1982. *The Homosexualization of America*. New York: St. Martin's Press.

Amenta, Edwin, and Bruce Carruthers. 1988. "The Formative Years of U.S. Social Spending Policies." *American Sociological Review* 53(5): 661–78.

Anti-Defamation League (ADL). 1990. *1989 Audit of Anti-Semitic Incidents*. New York: Anti-Defamation League of B'nai B'rith.

———. 1997. *Hate Crimes Laws: A Comprehensive Guide*. New York: Anti-Defamation League of B'nai B'rith.

"Are All Men Rapists? The New Violence Against Women Act Is Sexual Politics with a Vengeance." 1993. *National Review*, August 23, 44–47.

Aronoff, Marilyn, and Valerie Gunter. 1992. "Defining Disaster: Local Constructions for Recovery in the Aftermath of Chemical Contamination." *Social Problems* 39(4): 345–65.

Arthur, W. Brian. 1988. "Urban Systems and Historical Path Dependence." In *Cities and Their Vital Systems: Infrastructure Past, Present, and Future*. Washington, D.C.: National Academy Press.

Bader, Hans F. 1994. "Penalty Enhancement for Bias-Based Crimes." *Harvard Journal of Law and Public Policy* 17(1): 253–62.

Baird, Robert M., and Stuart E. Rosenbaum. 1992. *Bigotry, Prejudice, and Hatred: Definitions, Causes, and Solutions*. Buffalo, N.Y.: Prometheus Books.

Barnes, Larry, and Paul H. Ephross. 1994. "The Impact of Hate Violence on

Victims: Emotional and Behavioral Responses to Attacks." *Social Work* 39:247–51.

Bash, Harry. 1995. *Social Problems and Social Movements: An Exploration into the Sociological Construction of Alternative Realities*. Atlantic Highlands, N.J.: Humanities Press.

Baumgartner, M. P. 1992. "The Myth of Discretion." In *The Uses of Discretion*, edited by Keith Hawkins. New York: Oxford University Press.

Beckett, Katherine. 1994. "Setting the Public Agenda: 'Street Crime' and Drug Use in American Politics." *Social Problems* 41(3): 425–47.

Benford, Robert. 1997. "An Insider's Critique of the Social Movement Framing Perspective." *Sociological Inquiry* 67(4): 409–30.

Bensinger, Gad. 1992. "Hate Crimes: A New/Old Problem." *International Journal of Comparative and Applied Criminal Justice* 16(1): 115–23.

Ben-Yehuda, Nachman. 1992. "Criminalization and Deviantization as Properties of the Social Order." *Sociological Review* 40(1): 73–108.

Berger, Ronald, Patricia Searles, and W. Lawrence Neuman. 1988. "The Dimensions of Rape Reform Legislation." *Law & Society Review* 22(2): 329–57.

Berk, Richard, Elizabeth A. Boyd, and Karl M. Hamner. 1992. "Thinking More Clearly About Hate-Motivated Crimes." In *Hate Crimes: Confronting Violence Against Lesbians and Gay Men*, edited by Gregory Herek and Kevin Berrill. Newbury Park, Calif.: Sage Publications.

Berry, Frances Stokes, and William D. Berry. 1990. "State Lottery Adoptions as Policy Innovations: An Event History Analysis." *American Political Science Review* 84(2): 395–415.

Best, Joel. 1987. "Rhetoric in Claims-Making: Constructing the Missing Children Problem." *Social Problems* 34(2): 101–21.

———. 1990. *Threatened Children: Rhetoric and Concern About Child Victims*. Chicago: University of Chicago Press.

———. 1999. *Random Violence: How We Talk About New Crimes and New Victims*. Berkeley: University of California Press.

Black, Donald. 1980. *The Manners and Customs of the Police*. New York: Academic Press.

Bloom, Jack M. 1987. *Class, Race, and The Civil Rights Movement*. Bloomington: Indiana University Press.

Blumberg, Abraham. 1967. *Criminal Justice*. Chicago: Quadrangle Books.

Boyd, Elizabeth, Richard Berk, and Karl Hamner. 1996. "Motivated by Hatred or Prejudice: Categorization of Hate-Motivated Crimes in Two Police Divisions." *Law & Society Review* 30(4): 819–50.

Broad, Kendal, and Valerie Jenness. 1996. "The Institutionalizing Work of Contemporary Anti-Violence Against Women Campaigns in the U.S.: Meso-level Social Movement Activism and the Production of Cultural Forms." *Research in Social Movements, Conflicts, and Change* 19: 75–123.

Brooks, Thomas D. 1994. "First Amendment Penalty Enhancement for Hate Crimes: Content Regulation, Questionable State Interests, and Non-Traditional Sentencing." *Journal of Criminal Law and Criminology* 84(4): 703–42.

Brownworth, Victoria. 1993. *Too Queer: Essays from a Radical Life*. Ithaca, N.Y.: Firebrand Books.

Buechler, Steven M. 1990. *Women's Movements in the United States.* New Brunswick: Rutgers University Press.

Burstein, Paul. 1991. "Policy Domains: Organization, Culture, and Policy Outcomes." *Annual Review of Sociology* 17: 327–50.

———. [1985] 1998. *Discrimination, Jobs, and Politics: The Struggle for Equal Employment Opportunity in the United States Since the New Deal.* Chicago: University of Chicago Press.

California. *Penal Code.* 422.6 (1984).

California. Peace Officer Standards and Training. 1995. *Guidelines for Law Enforcement's Design of Hate Crimes Policy and Training.* Sacramento.

Call, Jack E., David Nice, and Susette M. Talarico. 1991. "An Analysis of State Rape Shield Laws." *Social Science Quarterly* 72(4): 774–88.

Caputi, Jane. 1992. "To Acknowledge and Heal: 20 Years of Feminist Thought and Activism on Sexual Violence." In *The Knowledge Explosion: Generations of Feminist Scholarship,* edited by Cheris Kramarae and Dale Spender. New York: Teachers College Press.

Carter, Lief H. 1974. *The Limits of Order.* Lexington, Mass.: Lexington Books.

Caufield, Susan, and Nancy Wonders. 1993. "Personal and Political Violence Against Women and the Role of the State." In *Political Crime in Contemporary America,* edited by Kenneth D. Tunnell. New York: Garland Publishing.

"Caught in the Act." 1993. *New Republic,* July 12, 13–16.

Center for Democratic Renewal (CDR). 1991. "Hate Crimes Laws: How Are They Doing?" 1991. *Monitor,* December 15–18.

———. 1992. *When Hate Groups Come to Town: A Handbook of Effective Community Responses.* Montgomery, Ala.: Black Belt Press.

Chambliss, William, and Robert Seidman. 1982. *Law, Order, and Power.* Reading, Mass.: Addison-Wesley.

Chambliss, William J., and Marjorie S. Zatz. 1993. *Making Law: The State, The Law, and Structural Contradictions.* Bloomington: Indiana University Press.

Chandler, Amanda. 1996. "The Changing Definition and Image of Hackers in Popular Discourse." *International Journal of the Sociology of Law* 24(2): 229–51.

Chauncey, Robert. 1980. "New Careers for Moral Entrepreneurs: Teenage Drinking." *Journal of Drug Issues* 10(2): 45–70.

Chilton, Paul. 1987. "Metaphor, Euphemism, and the Militarization of Language." *Current Research on Peace and Violence* 10(1): 7–19.

Chock, Phyllis Pease. 1991. "Illegal Aliens and Opportunity: Myth-Making in Congressional Testimony." *American Ethnologist* 18(2): 279–94.

———. 1994. "Remaking and Unmaking 'Citizen' in Policy-Making Talk About Immigration." *PoLAR: Political and Legal Anthropology Review* 17(2): 45–55.

———. 1995. "Ambiguity in Policy Discourse: Congressional Talk About Immigration." *Policy Sciences* 28(2): 165–84.

Cicourel, Aaron. 1969. *The Social Organization of Juvenile Justice.* New York: John Wiley and Sons.

Coltrane, Scott, and Neal Hickman. 1992. "The Rhetoric of Rights and Needs: Moral Discourse in the Reform of Child Custody and Child Support Laws." *Social Problems* 39(4): 400–20.

Congressional Record. July 22, 1985. 131 Cong Rec H 5988, vol. 131 no. 98. Hate Crimes Statistics Act. 99th Congress, 1st session.

———. May 18, 1988. 134 Cong Rec H 3373, vol. 134 no. 70. Hate Crimes Statistics Act. 100th Congress, 2nd session.

———. June 27, 1989. 135 Cong Rec H 3179, vol. 135, no. 87. Hate Crimes Statistics Act. 101st Congress, 1st session.

———. February 8, 1990 (legislative day of January 23, 1990). 136 Cong Rec S 1067, vol. 136, no. 11. Hate Crimes Statistics Act. 101st Congress, 2nd session.

———. April 3, 1990. 136 Cong Rec H 1423, vol. 136, no. 39. Hate Crimes Statistics Act. 101st Congress, 2nd session.

Conrad, Peter. 1975. "The Discovery of Hyperkinesis: Notes on the Medicalization of Deviant Behavior." *Social Problems* 23(1): 12–21.

"Crime and Punishment." 1992. *New Republic,* October 12, 7.

Daniels, Arlene Kaplan. 1970. "The Social Construction of Psychiatric Diagnosis." In *New Sociology,* vol. 2, edited by H. P. Dreitzel. New York: Macmillan.

Davies, Miranda, ed. 1994. *Women and Violence.* Atlantic Highlands, N.J.: Zed Books.

D'Emilio, John. 1983. *Sexual Politics, Sexual Communities: The Making of a Homosexual Minority in the United States, 1940–1970.* Chicago: University of Chicago Press.

D'Emilio, John, and Estelle B. Freedman. 1988. *Intimate Matters: A History of Sexuality in America.* New York: Harper and Row.

DiChiara, Albert, and John F. Galliher. 1994. "Dissonance and Contradiction in the Origin of Marijuana Decriminalization." *Law & Society Review* 28(1): 41–77.

Dillof, Anthony M. 1997. "Punishing Bias: An Examination of the Theoretical Foundations of Bias Crime Statutes." *Northwestern University Law Review* 91(3): 1015–81.

Dobash, R. Emerson, and Russell P. Dobash. 1981. "Community Responses to Violence Against Wives: Charivari, Abstract Justice, and Patriarchy." *Social Problems* 28(5): 563–81.

———. 1992. *Women, Violence, and Social Change.* New York: Routledge.

Dobbin, Frank. 1994. *Forging Industrial Policy: The United States, Britain, and France in the Railway Age.* New York: Cambridge University Press.

Ehrlich, Howard J. 1989. "Studying Workplace Ethnoviolence." *International Journal of Group Tensions* 19(1): 69–80.

Ewick, Patricia. 1992. "'Postcards from the Edge': Cutting-Edge Issues in Socio-legal Research." Plenary address to the graduate student workshop, Law and Society Association. Philadelphia (May 31).

Farr, Kathyrn. 1995. "Fetal Abuse and Criminalization of Behavior During Pregnancy." *Crime and Delinquency* 41(2): 235–45.

Feeley, Malcolm. 1973. "Two Models of the Criminal Justice System." *Law & Society Review* 7(3): 407–25.

Feldman, Martha. 1992. "Social Limits to Discretion: An Organizational Perspective." In *The Uses of Discretion,* edited by Keith Hawkins. New York: Oxford University Press.

Ferguson, Kathy. 1984. *The Feminist Case Against Bureaucracy*. Philadelphia: Temple University Press.

Fernandez, Joseph. 1991. "Bringing Hate Crimes into Focus." *Harvard Civil Rights–Civil Liberties Law Review* 26(1): 261–92.

Ferree, Myra Marx, and Beth B. Hess. 1985. *Controversy and Coalition: The New Feminist Movement*. Boston: Twayne Publishers.

Fishman, Mark. 1978. "Crime Waves as Ideology." *Social Problems* 25(5): 531–43.

Florida. *Florida Statutes, Annotated*. 775.085.

Foucault, Michel. 1979. *Discipline and Punish: The Birth of the Prison*. New York: Vintage Books.

Freeman, G. P. 1985. "National Styles and Policy Sectors: Explaining Structured Variation." *Journal of Public Policy* 5(4): 467–96.

Friedman, Lawrence M. 1967. "Legal Rules and the Process of Social Change." *Stanford Law Review* 19(4): 786–840.

———. 1985. *Total Justice*. New York: Russell Sage Foundation.

Frohmann, Lisa. 1997. "Convictability and Discordant Locales: Reproducing Race, Class, and Gender Ideologies in Prosecutorial Decision-Making." *Law & Society Review* 31(3): 531–55.

Galliher, John F., and Linda Basilick. 1979. "Utah's Liberal Drug Laws: Structural Foundations and Triggering Events." *Social Problems* 26(3): 284–97.

Galliher, John F., and John R. Cross. 1983. *Morals Legislation Without Morality: The Case of Nevada*. New Brunswick: Rutgers University Press.

Gamson, William. 1992a. "The Social Psychology of Collective Action." In *Frontiers in Social Movement Theory*, edited by Aldon C. Morris and Carol McClurg Mueller. New Haven: Yale University Press.

———. 1992b. *Talking Politics*. New York: Cambridge University Press.

Gamson, William A., and David S. Meyer. 1996. "Framing Political Opportunity." In *Comparative Perspectives on Social Movements: Political Opportunities, Mobilizing Structures, and Cultural Framings*, edited by Doug McAdam, John D. McCarthy, and Mayer N. Zald. New York: Cambridge University Press.

Gaumer, Craig Peyton. 1994. "Punishment for Prejudice: A Commentary on the Constitutionality and Utility of State Statutory Responses to the Problem of Hate Crimes." *South Dakota Law Review* 39(1): 1–48.

Gellman, Susan. 1991. "Sticks and Stones Can Put You in Jail, But Words Can Increase Your Sentence? Constitutional and Policy Dilemmas of Ethnic Intimidation Laws." *UCLA Law Review* 39(2): 333–96.

Gerhards, Jürgen, and Dieter Rucht. 1992. "Mesomobilization: Organizing and Framing in Two Protest Campaigns in West Germany." *American Journal of Sociology* 98(3): 555–95.

Goldberg, Robert A. 1991. *Grassroots Resistance: Social Movements in the Twentieth Century*. Belmont, Calif.: Wadsworth Publishing.

Goode, Erich. 1990. "The American Drug Panic of the 1980s: Social Construction or Objective Threat?" *International Journal of Addictions* 25(9): 1083–98.

Goode, Erich, and Nachman Ben-Yehuda. 1994. "Moral Panics: Culture, Politics, and Social Construction." *Annual Review of Sociology* 20: 149–71.

Goode, Erich, and Richard Troiden, eds. 1974. *Sexual Deviance and Sexual Deviants: The Social Side of Sex, Pornography, Prostitution, Male Homosexuality, Lesbianism, Rape, and Kinky Sex*. New York: William Morrow.

Grannis, Eric J. 1993. "Fighting Words and Fighting Freestyle: The Constitutionality of Penalty Enhancement for Bias Crimes." *Columbia Law Review* 93(1): 178–230.

Grattet, Ryken. 1994. "At Play in the Field of the Law: Professionals and the Transformation of Industrial Accident Law." Ph.D. diss., University of California, Santa Barbara.

———. 1998. "Substantiating a Worker Right to Compensation." In *Public Rights/Public Rules: Constituting Citizenship in the World Polity and National Policy*, edited by Connie McNeely. New York: Garland.

Grattet, Ryken, Valerie Jenness, and Theodore Curry. 1998. "The Homogenization and Differentiation of Hate Crime Law in the United States, 1978–1995: Innovation and Diffusion in the Criminalization of Bigotry." *American Sociological Review* 63(2): 286–307.

Gray, Virginia. 1973. "Innovation in the States: A Diffusion Study." *American Political Science Review* 67(4): 1174–85.

Green, Donald, and Andrew Rich. 1998. "White Supremacist Activity and Crossburnings in North Carolina." *Journal of Quantitative Criminology* 14(3): 263–82.

Green, Donald, Dara Z. Strolovitch, and Janelle S. Wong. 1998. "Defended Neighborhoods, Integration, and Racially-Motivated Crime." *American Journal of Sociology* 104(2): 372–403.

Grusd, Edward. 1966. *B'nai B'rith: The Story of a Covenant*. New York: Appleton-Century.

Gunnlaugsson, Helgi, and John F. Galliher. 1986. "Prohibition of Beer in Iceland: An International Test of Symbolic Politics." *Law & Society Review* 20(3): 334–53.

Gusfield, Joseph R. 1963. *Symbolic Crusade*. Urbana: University of Illinois Press.

———. 1967. "Moral Passage: The Symbolic Process in Public Designations of Deviance." *Social Problems* 15(2): 175–88.

———. 1975. "Categories of Ownership and Responsibility in Social Issues: Alcohol Abuse and Automobile Use." *Journal of Drug Issues* 5(1): 285–303.

———. 1976. "The Literary Rhetoric of Science: Comedy and Pathos in Drinking Driver Research." *American Sociological Review* 41(1): 16–34.

———. 1981. *The Culture of Public Problems: Drinking, Driving, and the Symbolic Order*. Chicago: University of Chicago Press.

Hagan, John. 1980. "The Legislation of Crime and Delinquency: A Review of Theory, Method, and Research." *Law & Society Review* 14(3): 603–28.

Haider-Markel, Donald P. 1998. "The Politics of Social Regulatory Policy: State and Federal Hate Crime Policy and Implementation Effort." *Political Research Quarterly* 51(1): 69–88.

———. 1999. "Redistributing Values in Congress: Interest Group Influence Under Suboptimal Conditions." *Political Research Quarterly* 52(1): 113–44.

"Hate Crimes." 1993. *Congressional Quarterly Researcher* 3(1): 1–24.

Hate Crimes Prevention Act of 1999 (S.622). Vol. 18.

"Hate Is Not Speech: A Constitutional Defense of Penalty Enhancement for Hate Crimes." 1993. *Harvard Law Review* 106(4): 1314–31.

"Hate Violence and White Supremacy: A Decade Review, 1980–1990." 1989. *Klanwatch Intelligence Report* 47. Montgomery, Ala.: Southern Poverty Law Center.

Haynie, Stacia, and Earnest Dover. 1994. "Prosecutorial Discretion and Press Coverage." *American Politics Quarterly* 22(3): 370–81.

Herek, Gregory M., and Kevin T. Berrill. 1990. "Documenting the Victimization of Lesbians and Gay Men: Methodological Issues." *Journal of Interpersonal Violence* 5(3): 301–15.

———. 1992. *Hate Crimes: Confronting Violence Against Lesbians and Gay Men.* Newbury Park, Calif.: Sage Publications.

Heritage, John. 1984. *Garfinkel and Ethnomethodology.* Cambridge: Polity Press.

Hilgartner, Stephen, and Charles L. Bosk. 1988. "The Rise and Fall of Social Problems: A Public Arenas Model." *American Journal of Sociology* 94(1): 53–78.

Hollinger, Richard C., and Lonn Lanza-Kaduce. 1988. "The Process of Criminalization: The Case of Computer Crime Laws." *Criminology* 26(1): 108–26.

Holmes, Oliver Wendell. 1897. "The Path of Law." *Harvard Law Review* 10: 457–78.

Holstein, James A., and Gale Miller. 1989. "On the Sociology of Social Problems." In *Perspectives on Social Problems*, edited by James A. Holstein and Gale Miller. Greenwich, Conn.: JAI Press.

———. 1990. "Rethinking Victimization: An Interactional Approach to Victimology." *Symbolic Interaction* 13(1): 103–22.

Humphries, Drew, and David F. Greenberg. 1981. "The Dialectics of Crime Control." In *Crime and Capitalism*, edited by David F. Greenberg. Palo Alto, Calif.: Mayfield Publishing.

Ibarra, Peter R., and John I. Kitsuse. 1993. "Vernacular Constituents of Moral Discourse: An Interactionist Proposal for the Study of Social Problems." In *Constructionist Controversies: Issues in Social Problems Theory*, edited by Gale Miller and James A. Holstein. Hawthorne, N.Y.: Aldine de Gruyter.

Idaho. *Idaho Code* (1983). §18–7902.

Illinois. *Illinois Compiled Statutes* (1982). §720ILCS 5/12–7.1.

Iowa. *Iowa Code, Annotated* (West) (1990). §712.9.

Jacobs, James B. 1998. "The Emergence and Implications of American Hate Crime Jurisprudence." In *Hate Crime: The Global Politics of Polarization*, edited by Robert Kelly and Jess Maghan. Carbondale: Southern Illinois University Press.

Jacobs, James B., and Jessica S. Henry. 1996. "The Social Construction of a Hate Crime Epidemic." *Journal of Criminal Law and Criminology* 86(2): 366–91.

Jacobs, James, and Kimberly Potter. 1998. *Hate Crimes: Criminal Law and Identity Politics.* New York: Oxford University Press.

Jacobs, Herbert. 1988. *Silent Revolution: The Transformation of Divorce Law in the United States.* Chicago: University of Chicago Press.

Jayyusi, Lena. 1984. *Categorization and the Moral Order*. Boston: Routledge and Kegan Paul.

Jenkins, J. Craig. 1983. "Resource Mobilization Theory and the Study of Social Movements." *Annual Review of Sociology* 9: 527–53.

Jenness, Valerie. 1990. "From Sex as Sin to Sex as Work: COYOTE and the Reorganization of Prostitution as a Social Problem." *Social Problems* 37(3): 403–20.

———. 1993. *Making It Work: The Prostitutes' Rights Movement in Perspective*. Hawthorne, N.Y.: Aldine de Gruyter.

———. 1995a. "Hate Crimes in the United States: The Transformation of Injured Persons into Victims and the Extension of Victim Status to Multiple Constituencies." In *Images and Issues: Typifying Contemporary Social Problems*, edited by Joel Best. Hawthorne, N.Y.: Aldine de Gruyter.

———. 1995b. "Social Movement Growth, Domain Expansion, and Framing Processes: The Gay/Lesbian Movement and Violence Against Gays and Lesbians as a Social Problem." *Social Problems* 42(1): 145–70, 701–26.

———. 1996. "Prostitutes, Rights, and Contemporary Feminism: Multiple Discourses and a Difficult Dilemma." In *Individuality and Social Control: Essays in Honor of Tamotsu Shibutani*, edited by Margareta Bertilsson and Kian M. Kwan. Greenwich, Conn.: JAI Press.

———. 1999. "Managing Differences and Making Legislation: Social Movements and the Racialization, Sexualization, and Gendering of Federal Hate Crime Law in the U.S., 1985–1998." *Social Problems* 46(4): 548–71.

Jenness, Valerie, and Kendal Broad. 1994. "Anti-Violence Activism and the (In)visibility of Gender in the Gay/Lesbian and the Women's Movement." *Gender & Society* 8(3): 402–23.

———. 1997. *Hate Crimes: New Social Movements and the Politics of Violence*. Hawthorne, N.Y.: Aldine de Gruyter.

Jenness, Valerie, and Ryken Grattet. 1996. "The Criminalization of Hate: A Comparison of Structural and Polity Influences on the Passage of 'Bias-Crime' Legislation in the United States." *Sociological Perspectives* 39(1): 129–54.

Johnson, David. 1998. "The Organization of Prosecution and the Possibility of Order." *Law & Society Review* 32(2): 247–308.

Johnson, John M. 1989. "Horror Stories and the Construction of Child Abuse." In *Images of Issues*, edited by Joel Best. Hawthorne, N.Y.: Aldine de Gruyter.

Johnston, Hank. 1995. "A Methodology for Frame Analysis: From Discourse to Cognitive Schemata." In *Social Movements and Culture*, edited by Hank Johnston and Bert Klandermans. Minneapolis: University of Minnesota Press.

Johnston, Hank, and Bert Klandermans. 1995. *Social Movements and Culture*. Minneapolis: University of Minnesota Press.

Jones, Brian, Bernard Gallagher, and Joseph A. McFalls. 1988. *Social Problems: Issues, Opinions, and Solutions*. New York: McGraw-Hill.

Justice, J. Steven. 1993. "Ethnic Intimidation Statutes Post-*R.A.V*: Will They Withstand Constitutional Scrutiny?" *University of Cincinnati Law Review* 62(1): 11–171.

Kagan, Elena. 1992. "The Changing Faces of First Amendment Neutrality:

R.A.V. v. St. Paul, Rust v. Sullivan, and the Problem of Content-Based Under-inclusion." *Supreme Court Review.* 2: 29–77.

Katz, Jack. 1976. *Gay American History: Lesbians and Gay Men in the U.S.A.* New York: Thomas Y. Crowell.

Kelly, Andrea Ines, and Elisa Long. 1992. "Violence Against Women: Proposed Legislation." *Texas Journal of Women and the Law* 1(1): 285–90.

Kelly, Robert J., ed. 1993. *Bias Crime: American Law Enforcement and Legal Responses.* Chicago: Office of International Criminal Justice and the University of Illinois at Chicago.

Kingdon, John. W. 1995. *Agendas, Alternatives, and Public Policies.* New York: HarperCollins.

Klandermans, Bert. 1992. "The Social Construction of Protest and Multi-organizational Fields." In *Frontiers in Social Movement Theory,* edited by Aldon D. Morris and Carol McClurg Mueller. New Haven: Yale University Press.

Knoke, David. 1982. "The Spread of Municipal Reform: Temporal, Spatial, and Social Dynamics." *American Journal of Sociology* 87(6): 1314–39.

Kressel, Neil K. 1996. *Mass Hate: The Global Rise of Genocide and Terror.* New York: Plenum Press.

Labi, Nadyi. 1998. "The Hunter and the Choirboy." *Time,* April 6, 28–39.

Lawrence, Frederick M. 1993. "Resolving the Hate Crimes/Hate Speech Paradox: Punishing Bias Crimes and Protecting Racist Speech." *Notre Dame Law School* 68(3): 673–721.

———. 1994. "The Punishment of Hate: Towards a Normative Theory of Bias-Motivated Crimes." *Michigan Law Review* 93(2): 320–81.

———. 1999. *Punishing Hate: Bias Crimes Under American Law.* Cambridge, Mass.: Harvard University Press.

Leo, John. 1989. "The Politics of Hate." *U.S. News and World Report,* October 9, 24.

Leonard, Arthur S. 1992. "Gay/Lesbian Rights: Report from the Legal Front." In *Race, Class, and Gender in the United States: An Integrated Study,* edited by Paula S. Rothenberg. New York: St. Martin's Press.

Levin, Brian. 1994. "Violence Against Women: Is It a Hate Crime?" *Klanwatch Intelligence Report* (June): 4–7.

Levin, Jack, and Jack McDevitt. 1993. *Hate Crimes: The Rising Tide of Bigotry and Bloodshed.* New York: Plenum Press.

Loseke, Donileen R. 1993. "Constructing Conditions, People, Morality, and Emotion: Expanding the Agenda of Constructionism." In *Constructionist Controversies,* edited by Gale Miller and James A. Holstein. Hawthorne, N.Y.: Aldine de Gruyter.

Lowney, Kathleen S., and Joel Best. 1995. "Stalking Strangers and Lovers: Changing Media Typifications of a New Crime Problem." In *Images of Issues*: Typifying Contemporary Social Problems, edited by Joel Best. Hawthorne, N.Y.: Aldine de Gruyter.

Markle, Gerald E., and Ronald Troyer. 1979. "Smoke Gets in Your Eyes: Cigarette Smoking as Deviant Behavior." *Social Problems* 26(5): 611–25.

Maroney, Terry A. 1998. "The Struggle Against Hate Crime: Movement at a Crossroads." *New York University Law Review* 73(2): 564–620.

Marotta, Toby. 1981. *The Politics of Homosexuality*. Boston: Houghton Mifflin.

Martin, Susan. 1995. "A Cross-Burning Is Not Just an Arson: Police Social Construction of Hate in Baltimore County." *Criminology* 33(3): 303–26.

———. 1996. "Investigating Hate Crimes: Case Characteristics and Law Enforcement Responses." *Justice Quarterly* 13(3): 455–80.

Marx, Gary T., and Douglas McAdam. 1994. *Collective Behavior and Social Movements: Processes and Structure*. Englewood Cliffs, N.J.: Prentice-Hall.

Mauss, Armand. 1975. *Social Problems as Social Movements*. New York: J. B. Lippincott.

———. 1989. "Beyond the Illusion of Social Problems Theory." In *Perspectives on Social Problems*, edited by James A. Holstein and Gale Miller. Greenwich, Conn.: JAI Press.

Mauss, Armand, and Valerie Jenness. 2000. "Social Problems." In *The Encyclopedia of Sociology*, edited by Edgar Borgatta and Rhonda J.V. Montgomery. New York: Macmillan.

McAdam, Doug. 1982. *Political Process and the Development of Black Insurgency*. Chicago: University of Chicago Press.

———. 1994. "Culture and Social Movements." In *Ideology and Identity in Contemporary Social Movements*, edited by Joseph R. Gusfield, Hank Johnston, and Enrique Larana. Philadelphia: Temple University Press.

———. 1996. "Conceptual Origins, Current Problems, Future Directions." In *Comparative Perspectives on Social Movements: Political Opportunities, Mobilizing Structures, and Cultural Framings*, edited by Doug McAdam, John D. McCarthy, and Mayer N. Zald. New York: Cambridge University Press.

McCammon, Holly. 1995. "The Politics of Protection: State Minimum Wage and Maximum Hours Laws for Women in the United States, 1870–1930." *Sociological Quarterly* 36(2): 217–49.

McCann, Michael. 1991. "Legal Mobilization and Social Reform Movements: Notes on Theory and Its Application." *Studies in Law, Politics, and Society* 11: 225–54.

McCarthy, John D., and Mayer N. Zald. 1973. *The Trend in Social Movements in America: Professionalization and Resource Mobilization*. Morristown, N.J.: General Learning Press.

———. 1977. "Resource Mobilization and Social Movements: A Partial Theory." *American Journal of Sociology* 82(6): 1212–41.

McCleary, Richard. 1977. "How Parole Officers Use Records." *Social Problems* 24(5): 576–89.

McCormick, John. 1998. "The Schoolyard Killers." *Newsweek*, April 6, 21–27.

McDonagh, E. L. 1989. "Issues and Constituencies in the Progressive Era: House Roll Call Voting on the Nineteenth Amendment, 1913–1919." *Journal of Politics* 51(1): 119–36.

McGarrell, Edmund, and Thomas C. Castellano. 1991. "An Integrative Conflict Model of the Criminal Law Formation Process." *Journal of Research in Crime and Delinquency* 28: 174–96.

———. 1993. "Social Structure, Crime, and Politics: A Conflict Model of the Criminal Law Formation Process." In *Making Law: The State, The Law, and*

Structural Contradictions, edited by William J. Chambliss and Marjorie S. Zatz. Bloomington: Indiana University Press.

McLaughlin, Karen A., Kelly Brilliant, and Cynthia Lang. [1995] 1997. *National Bias Crimes Training for Law Enforcement and Victim Assistance Professionals: A Guide for Training Instructors.* Washington: U.S. Department of Justice, Office of Justice Programs.

Merry, Sally Engle. 1995. "Resistance and the Cultural Power of Law." *Law & Society Review* 29(1): 11–26.

Meyer, John W., and Brian Rowan. 1977. "Institutionalized Organizations: Formal Structure as Myth and Ceremony." *American Journal of Sociology* 83(2): 340–63.

Miller, Berkeley, and William Canak. 1988. "The Passage of Public Sector Collective Bargaining Laws: Unions, Business, and Political Competition in the American States." *Political Power and Social Theory* 7: 249–92.

Miller, Gale, and James A. Holstein, ed. 1993. "Constructing Social Problems: Context and Legacy." In *Constructionist Controversies: Issues in Social Problems Theory,* edited by Gale Miller and James A. Hostein. Hawthorne, N.Y.: Aldine de Gruyter.

Minkoff, Debra C. 1995. *Organizing for Equality: The Evolution of Women's and Racial-Ethnic Organizations in America, 1955–1985.* New Brunswick: Rutgers University Press.

Minow, Martha. 1990. *Making All the Difference: Inclusion, Exclusion, and American Law.* Ithaca, N.Y.: Cornell University Press.

Mitchell, Timothy. 1990. "Everyday Metaphors of Power." *Theory and Society* 19(5): 545–77.

Montana. *Montana Code, Annotated* (1989). 45–5–221.

Morris, Aldon D. 1984. *The Origins of the Civil Rights Movement: Black Communities Organizing for Change.* New York: Free Press.

Morris, Aldon D., and Carol McClurg Mueller, eds. 1992. *Frontiers in Social Movement Theory.* New Haven: Yale University Press.

Morsch, James. 1992. "The Problem of Motive in Hate Crimes: The Argument Against Presumptions of Racial Motivation." *Journal of Criminal Law and Criminology* 82(3): 659–89.

Mueller, Abby. 1993. "Can Motive Matter? A Constitutional and Criminal Law Analysis of Motive in Hate Crime Legislation." *University of Missouri-Kansas City Law Review* 61(3): 619–33.

National Coalition of Anti-Violence Projects. 1999. *Anti-Lesbian, Gay, Bisexual, and Transgender Violence in 1998.* New York: New York City Gay and Lesbian Anti-Violence Project.

National Gay and Lesbian Task Force (NGLTF). 1987. *Anti-Gay/Lesbian Violence, Victimization, and Defamation in 1987.* Washington, D.C.: National Gay and Lesbian Task Force Policy Institute.

———. 1991. *Anti-Gay/Lesbian Violence, Victimization, and Defamation in 1990.* Washington, D.C.: National Gay and Lesbian Task Force Policy Institute.

National Institute Against Prejudice and Violence (NIAPV). 1991. *Striking Back at Bigotry: Remedies Under Federal and State Law for Violence Motivated by*

Racial, Religious, or Ethnic Prejudice. National Institute Against Prejudice and Violence. Baltimore, Maryland.

National Victim Center. 1993. *Annual Report.* New York: National Victim Center.

Neuman, W. Lawrence. 1998. "Negotiated Meanings and State Transformation: The Trust Issue in the Progressive Era." *Social Problems* 45(3): 315–35.

New Jersey. *New Jersey Statutes, Annotated* (1998). §2C: 44–3.

Newton, Michael, and Judy Ann Newton. 1991. *Racial and Religious Violence in America: A Chronology.* New York: Garland.

Noel, Ann. 1995. "Federal Case." *Los Angeles Lawyer,* March, 32–37.

Oberschall, Anthony. 1973. *Social Conflict and Social Movements.* Englewood Cliffs, N.J.: Prentice-Hall.

Ohlin, Lloyd. 1993. "Surveying Discretion by Criminal Justice Decisionmakers." In *Discretion in Criminal Justice: The Tensions Between Individualization and Uniformity,* edited by Lloyd Ohlin and Frank J. Remington. Albany: State University of New York Press.

Orcutt, James, and J. Blake Turner. 1993. "Shocking Numbers and Graphic Accounts: Quantified Images of Drug Problems in the Print Media." *Social Problems* 40(2): 190–206.

Pavalko, Eliza. 1989. "State Timing of Policy Adoption: Workmen's Compensation in the United States, 1909–1929." *American Journal of Sociology* 95(3): 592–615.

Petrosino, Carylyn. 1999. "Connecting the Past to the Future: Hate Crime in America." *Journal of Contemporary Criminal Justice* 15(1): 22–47.

Pfohl, Stephen J. 1977. "The Discovery of Child Abuse." *Social Problems* 24: 310–23.

Phillips, Scott, and Ryken Grattet. 2000. "Judicial Rhetoric, Meaning-Making, and the Institutionalization of Hate Crime Law." *Law & Society Review* 34(3): 567–602.

Pinderhughes, Howard. 1993. "The Anatomy of Racially Motivated Violence in New York: A Case Study of Youth in Southern Brooklyn." *Social Problems* 40(4): 478–92.

Piven, Frances Fox, and Richard Cloward. 1977. *Poor People's Movements.* New York: Pantheon.

Powell, Walter W., and Paul J. DiMaggio, eds. 1991. *The New Institutionalism in Organizational Analysis.* Chicago: University of Chicago Press.

Radford, Jill, and Diana E. H. Russell, eds. 1992. *Femicide: The Politics of Woman Killing.* New York: Twayne Publishers.

"Radical Feminism in the Senate." 1993. *U.S. World and News Report,* July 29, 19.

Rafter, Nicole H. 1990. "The Social Construction of Crime and Crime Control." *Journal of Research in Crime and Delinquency* 27(4): 376–89.

Ramirez, Francisco, Yasemin Soysal, and Suzanne Shanahan. 1997. "The Changing Logic of Political Citizenship: Cross-national Acquisition of Women's Suffrage Rights, 1890 to 1990." *American Sociological Review* 62(5): 735–45.

"Rape and Denial." 1993. *New Republic,* November 22, 14–15.

"Rape Is Not an Act of Bias." 1990. *U.S. News and World Report*, October 8, 25.

Reinarman, Craig, and Harry G. Levine. 1989. "The Crack Attack: Politics and the Media in America's Latest Drug Scare." In *Images of Issues: Typifying Contemporary Social Problems*, edited by Joel Best. Hawthorne, N.Y.: Aldine de Gruyter.

Reno, Janet. 1999. *FY 2000 Summary Performance Plan*, sec. 3.1.1: *Hate Crimes*. U.S. Department of Justice, Office of Attorney General (March). Accessed on February 9, 2001 at *www.usdoj.gov/ag/summary/part1.htm*.

Richardson, James T., Joel Best, and David Bromley. 1991. "Satanism as a Social Problem." In *The Satanism Scare*, edited by James T. Richardson, Joel Best, and David Bromley. Hawthorne, N.Y.: Aldine de Gruyter.

Rittenhouse, C. Amanda. 1992. "The Emergence of Premenstrual Syndrome as a Social Problem." *Social Problems* 38(3): 412–25.

Rose, Richard. 1985. "The Programme Approach to the Growth of Government." *British Journal of Political Science* 15(1): 1–28.

Rose, Vicki McNickle. 1977. "Rape as a Social Problem: A By-product of the Feminist Movement." *Social Problems* 25(1): 75–89.

Rovella, David E. 1994. "Attack on Hate Crime Is Enhanced." *National Law Journal* 16(52): A1.

Rubin, Herbert. 1984. "The Meshing Organization as a Catalyst for Municipal Coordination." *Administration and Society* 16(1): 215–38.

Savelsberg, Joachim J. 1987. "The Making of Criminal Law Norms in Welfare States: Economic Crime in West Germany." *Law & Society Review* 21(4): 529–61.

———. 1994. "Knowledge, Domination, and Criminal Punishment." *American Journal of Sociology* 99(4): 911–43.

Schneiberg, Marc, and Elisabeth S. Clemens. 1999. "The Typical Tools for the Job: Research Strategies in Institutional Analysis." In *Bending the Bars of the Iron Cage*, edited by Walter W. Powell and Dan L. Jones. Chicago: University of Chicago Press.

Schneider, Joseph. 1985. "Social Problems Theory: The Constructionist View." *Annual Review of Sociology* 11: 209–29.

Schultz, Vicki. 1998. "Reconceptualizing Sexual Harassment." *Yale Law Review* 107(6): 1755–1878.

Scott, W. Richard, and John W. Meyer. 1983. "The Organization of Societal Sectors." In *Organizational Environments*, edited by John W. Meyer and W. Richard Scott, with the assistance of Brian Rowan and Terrance E. Deal. Beverly Hills, Calif.: Sage Publications.

Scott, Wilbur J., and Sandra Carson Stanley, eds. 1994. *Gays and Lesbians in the Military: Issues, Concerns, and Contrasts*. Hawthorne, N.Y.: Aldine de Gruyter.

Shapiro, Joseph P. 1993. *No Pity: People with Disabilities Forging a New Civil Rights Movement*. New York: Random House.

Sheffield, Carole J. 1987. "Sexual Terrorism and the Social Control of Women." In *Analyzing Gender: A Handbook of Social Science Research*, edited by Beth B. Hess and Myra Marx Ferree. Newbury Park, Calif.: Sage Publications.

———. 1992. "Hate Violence." In *Race, Class, and Gender in the United States*, edited by Paula Rothenberg. New York: St. Martin's Press.

Skocpol, Theda, and Edwin Amenta. 1986. "States and Social Policies." *Annual Review of Sociology* 12: 131–57.

Smelser, Neil. 1963. *Theory of Collective Behavior*. New York: Free Press.

Snitow, Ann, Christine Stansell, and Sharon Thompson. 1983. *Powers of Desire: The Politics of Sexuality*. New York: Monthly Review Press.

Snow, David A., and Robert D. Benford. 1988. "Ideology, Frame Resonance, and Participant Mobilization." *International Social Movements Research* 1(1): 197–217.

———. 1992. "Master Frames and Cycles of Protest." In *Frontiers in Social Movement Theory*, edited by Aldon C. Morris and Carol McClurg Mueller. New Haven: Yale University Press.

Snow, David A., E. Burke Rochford Jr., Steven K. Worden, and Robert Benford. 1986. "Frame Alignment Processes, Micromobilization, and Movement Participation." *American Sociological Review* 51(4): 464–81.

Soule, Sarah, and Jennifer Earl. 1999. "'All Men Are Created Equal': The Differential Protection of Minority Groups in Hate Crime Legislation." Paper presented at the annual meeting of the American Sociological Association, Chicago, August 9, 1999.

Spector, Malcolm. 1977. "Legitimizing Homosexuality." *Society* 14(1): 20–24.

Spector, Malcolm, and John Kitsuse. 1977. *Constructing Social Problems*. Menlo Park, Calif.: Benjamin-Cummings.

Stanko, Elizabeth Anne. 1981. "Prosecutors Screening Decisions: The Case of the New York County District Attorney's Office." *Law & Society Review* 16(2): 225–39.

Steury, Ellen Hochstedler. 1991. "Specifying the 'Criminalization' of the Mentally Disordered Misdemeanant." *Journal of Criminal Law and Criminology* 82(2): 334–59.

Stinchcombe, Arthur. 1965. "Social Structure and Organizations." In *Handbook of Organizations*, edited by James G. March. Chicago: Rand McNally.

Stivison, David. 1982. "Homosexuals and the Constitution." In *Homosexuality*, edited by William Paul, James D. Weinrich, John C. Gonsiorek, and Mary Hotvedt. Beverly Hills, Calif.: Sage Publications.

Strang, David. 1990. "From Dependency to Sovereignty: An Event History Analysis of Decolonization, 1870–1987." *American Sociological Review* 55(6): 846–60.

Strang, David, and John W. Meyer. 1993. "Institutional Conditions for Diffusion." *Theory and Society* 22(4): 487–512.

Strossen, Nadine. 1993. "Yes: Discriminatory Crimes." *ABA Journal* 79: 44.

Sudnow, David. 1965. "Normal Crimes: Sociological Features of the Penal Code in a Public Defender Office." *Social Problems* 12(3): 255–76.

Sullivan, Andrew. 1999. "What's So Bad About Hate?" *New York Times Magazine*, September 26, 50–113.

Sutherland, Edwin H. 1950. "The Diffusion of Sexual Psychopath Laws." *American Journal of Sociology* 56(2): 142–48.

Sykes, Charles J. 1992. *A Nation of Victims: The Decay of American Culture*. New York: St Martin's Press.

Texas. *Penal Code. Texas Codes, Annotated* (1993). §12.47.

Thomas, George M., John Meyer, Francisco Ramirez, and John Boli. 1987. *Institutional Structure: Constituting State, Society, and the Individual.* Newbury Park, Calif.: Sage Publications.

Tolbert, Pamela, and Lynne G. Zucker. 1983. "Institutional Sources of Change in the Formal Structure of Organizations: The Diffusion of Civil Service Reform, 1880–1935." *Administrative Science Quarterly* 28(1): 22–39.

Tribe, Laurence. 1993. "The Mystery of Motive, Private and Public: Some Notes Inspired by the Problems of Hate Crime and Animal Sacrifice." *Supreme Court Review* Annual 1: 1–36.

Troyer, Ronald J. 1984. "Better Read than Dead: Notes on Using Archival Material in Social Problems and Deviance Research." In *Studies in the Sociology of Social Problems*, edited by Joseph W. Schneider and John I. Kitsuse. Norwood, New Jersey: Ablex.

———. 1989. "Are Social Problems and Social Movements the Same Thing?" In *Perspectives on Social Problems*, edited by James A. Holstein and Gale Miller. Greenwich, Conn.: JAI Press.

U.S. Congress. House. 1985a. "Crimes Against Religious Practices and Property." Hearings before the subcommittee on criminal justice of the Committee on the Judiciary. 99th Cong. 1st sess. 16 May and 19 June. Serial 134. Washington: U.S. Government Printing Office.

———. House. 1985b. "Hate Crimes Statistics Act." Hearings before the subcommittee on criminal justice of the Committee on the Judiciary. 99th Cong. 1st sess. 21 March. Serial 137. Washington: U.S. Government Printing Office.

———. House. 1986a. "Anti-Gay Violence." Hearings before the subcommittee on criminal justice of the Committee on the Judiciary. 99th Cong. 2d sess. 9 October. Serial 132. Washington: U.S. Government Printing Office.

———. House. 1986b. "Ethnically-Motivated Violence Against Arab Americans." Hearings before the subcommittee on criminal justice of the Committee on the Judiciary. 99th Cong. 2d sess. 16 July. Serial 135. Washington: U.S. Government Printing Office.

———. House. 1987. "Anti-Asian Violence." Oversight hearing before the subcommittee on civil and constitutional rights of the Committee on the Judiciary. 100th Cong. 1st sess. 10 November. Serial 116. Washington: U.S. Government Printing Office.

———. House. 1988a. "Hate Crimes Statistics Act." Report from the Committee on the Judiciary. 100th Cong. 2d sess. 20 April. Washington: U.S. Government Printing Office.

———. Senate. 1988b. "Hate Crimes Statistics Act of 1988." Report from the Committee on the Judiciary. 100th Cong., 2d sess. 15 September (legislative day, 7 September). Washington: U.S. Government Printing Office.

———. House. 1988c. "Racially Motivated Violence." Hearings before the subcommittee on criminal justice of the Committee on the Judiciary. 100th Cong., 2d sess. 11 May and 12 July. Serial 144. Washington: U.S. Government Printing Office.

———. 1989. "Hate Crimes Statistics Act." Washington: U.S. Government Printing Office.

———. Senate. 1990a. "The Violence Against Women Act of 1990." Report from the Committee on the Judiciary. 101st Cong., 2^d sess. 10 October (legislative day, 2 October). Washington: U.S. Government Printing Office.

———. Senate. 1990b. "Women and Violence, Part 1." Hearing before the Committee on the Judiciary. 101st Cong., 2^d sess. 20 June. Serial J-101-80. Washington: U.S. Government Printing Office.

———. Senate. 1990c. "Women and Violence, Part 2." Hearings before the Committee on the Judiciary. 101st Cong., 2^d sess. 29 August and 11 December. Serial J-101-80. Washington: U.S. Government Printing Office.

———. Senate. 1991a. "The Violence Against Women Act of 1991." 102^d Cong., 1st sess. 29 October. Washington: U.S. Government Printing Office.

———. Senate. 1991b. "Violence Against Women: Victims of the System." Hearing before the Committee on the Judiciary. 102^d Cong., 1st sess. 9 April. Serial J-102-10. Washington: U.S. Government Printing Office.

———. Senate. 1992a. "Hate Crimes Statistics Act." Hearing before the subcommittee on the Constitution of the Committee on the Judiciary. 102^d Cong., 2^d sess. 5 August. Serial J-102-79. Washington: U.S. Government Printing Office.

———. House. 1992b. "Violence Against Women: Victims of the System." Hearing before the subcommittee on crime and criminal justice of the Committee on the Judiciary. 102^d Cong., 2^d sess. 6 Feb. Serial 42. Washington: U.S. Government Printing Office.

———. 1992c. "Hate Crimes Sentencing Enhancement Act of 1992." Washington: U.S. Government Printing Office.

———. House. 1993a. "Crimes of Violence Motivated by Gender." Hearing before the subcommittee on civil and constitutional rights of the Committee on the Judiciary. 103rd Cong., 1st sess. 16 Nov. Serial 51. Washington: U.S. Government Printing Office.

———. Senate. 1993b. "Violence Against Women: Fighting the Fear." Hearing before the Committee on the Judiciary. 103rd Cong., 1st sess. 12 November. Serial J-103-36. Washington: U.S. Government Printing Office.

———. Senate. 1993c. "The Violence Against Women Act of 1993." Report from the Committee on the Judiciary. 103rd Cong., 1st sess. 10 September (legislative day, 7 September). Washington: U.S. Government Printing Office.

———. Senate. 1993d. "Violent Crimes Against Women." Hearing before the Committee on the Judiciary. 103rd Cong., 1st sess. 13 April. Serial J-103-11. Washington: U.S. Government Printing Office.

———. Senate. 1994. "Hate Crimes Statistics Act." Hearing before the committee on the Constitution of the Committee on the Judiciary. 103rd Cong., 2nd sess. 28 June. Serial J-103-63. Washington: U.S. Government Printing Office.

———. Senate. 1996a. "Reauthorization of the Hate Crimes Statistics Act." Hearing before the Committee on the Judiciary. 104th Cong., 2^d sess. 19 March. Serial J-104-71. Washington: U.S. Government Printing Office.

———. Senate. 1996b. "To Reauthorize the Hate Crimes Statistics Act." Report from the Committee on the Judiciary. 104th Cong., 2nd sess. 13 May. Washington: U.S. Government Printing Office.

————. Senate. 1999. *Uniform Crime Reports.* Washington: U.S. Government Printing Office.

————. Senate. *Hate Crimes Sentencing Act.* (1994) 28 USC 994.

————. Senate. *Hate Crimes Statistics Act.* (1990) 25 USC 534.

U.S. Department of Justice. 1998. *Hate Crimes Training and Curriculum.* 4 volumes. Rockville, Md.: Bureau of Justice Assistance, Office of Justice Programs.

————. Bureau of Justice Statistics. 1992. *Law Enforcement Management and Administrative Statistics, 1990: Data for Individual State and Local Agencies with One Hundred or More Officers.* Washington: U.S. Government Printing Office.

————. 1999. *Law Enforcement Management and Administrative Statistics, 1997: Data for Individual State and Local Agencies with One Hundred or More Officers.* Washington: U.S. Government Printing Office.

Vaid, Urvashi. 1995. *Virtual Equality: The Mainstreaming of Gay and Lesbian Liberation.* New York: Anchor Books.

Vermont. *Vermont Statutes, Annotated.* (1989) § 1455.

Virginia. *Code of Virginia, Annotated.* (1994) § 18.2-56.2.

Walker, Jack L. 1969. "The Diffusion of Innovations Among the American States." *American Political Science Review* 63(3): 880–97.

Walker, Samuel, and Charles M. Katz. 1995. "Less than Meets the Eye: Police Department Bias-Crime Units." *American Journal of Police* 14(1): 29–48.

Waxman, Barbara Faye. 1991. "Hatred: The Unacknowledged Dimensions in Violence Against Disabled People." *Sexuality and Disability* 9(1): 185–99.

Weed, Frank. 1995. *Certainty of Justice: Reform in the Crime Victim Movement.* Hawthorne, N.Y.: Aldine de Gruyter.

Weeks, Jeffrey. 1985. *Sexuality and Its Discontents: Meanings, Myths, and Modern Sexualities.* Boston: Routledge and Kegan Paul.

Wexler, Chuck, and Gary T. Marx. 1986. "When Law and Order Works: Boston's Innovative Approach to the Problem of Racial Violence." *Crime and Delinquency* 32(2): 205–23.

Wilson, James Q. 1973. *Varieties of Police Behavior: The Management of Law and Order in Eight Communities.* New York: Atheneum.

Winer, Anthony S. 1994. "Hate Crimes, Homosexuals, and the Constitution." *Harvard Civil Rights–Civil Liberties Law Review* 29(2): 387–438.

Wisconsin. *West's Wisconsin Statutes, Annotated.* (1987) 939.645.

Woolgar, Steve, and Dorothy Pawluch. 1985. "Ontological Gerrymandering. *Social Problems* 32(3): 214–27.

Young, Iris Marion. 1990. *Justice and the Politics of Difference.* Princeton: Princeton University Press.

Zucker, Lynne. 1987. "Institutional Theories of Organizations." *Annual Review of Sociology* 13: 443–64.

= Index =

Boldface numbers refer to figures and tables.

Abourezk, James, 45–46
ADL. *See* Anti-Defamation League of B'nai B'rith
Alaska, 93, 193*n*6
Albonetti, Celesta, 148
Americans with Disabilities Act, 161
Anti-Defamation League of B'nai B'rith (ADL), 22, 33, 48, 53, 77, 171
anti-hate-crime movements: civil rights movements and, 20–21, 26–27, 30–32; and the emergence of hate crime, 17–18, 157–58; epidemic of violence, discovering and publicizing, 39–41; kinds of, 27; organizations, 32–39
Anti-Violence Project, 36–37
Arkansas, 5

Bash, Harry, 11
Beckett, Katherine, 169
Berk, Richard, 78, 117, 129–30, 132–37, 190*n*1
Berman, Howard, 56
Berrill, Kevin, 54–55, 61
Best, Joel, 30, 60, 184*n*2, 186*n*9
Biaggi, Mario, 2–3, 53
bias crime as statutory motivational standard, 87, 116
Biden, Joseph Jr., 63, 65–67
Bloom, Jack, 21
Blumberg, Abraham, 148
Boyd, Elizabeth, 78, 117, 129–30, 132–37, 190*n*1

Broad, Kendal, 21
Bryant, John, 61
Brzonkala v. Morrison, 185*n*3
Burstein, Paul, 6, 13, 43, 158, 177
Bush, George, 2, 44
Byrd, James Jr., 4

California: court cases, 111, 118; law enforcement, 128; legislation, 80, 91–93; police training, 142–46; prosecution, 149–51
Carter, Lief, 147–48
CDR. *See* Center for Democratic Renewal
Center for Democratic Renewal (CDR), 22, 35, 77
Chin, Vincent, 91
Christianson, Diana, 55
civil rights movements, 21–23, 33–36, 184*n*3
Clinton, William, 2, 140
Coalition on Hate Crimes, 53, 159, 185*n*7, 187–88*n*18
coattailing statutes, 81–82
Coble, Howard, 58
compelling interest argument, 112–14, 122, 191*n*4
Connecticut, 191*n*7
construction of social problems: epidemic of violence, discovery and publicizing of, 39–41; theoretical perspective, 8–10, 158
Conyers, John, 3, 42, 48, 56, 60, 158

213